Reading the Signs
and other itinerant essays

Also By Stephen Benz

Topographies
Americana Motel
Green Dreams
Guatemalan Journey

In his progress from "the place we called home" to "remote and little visited," Stephen Benz meets a lot of out-of-the-ordinary people: Dale the tobacco-spitting harvest field-crew hand; Mr. Johnson, the gruff Bible-reading grounds crew boss; Carolyn Terry, the curator of the world's only apron museum; an unnamed Elko, Nevada waitress who bets all her tip money; his own suddenly-appearing but finally-disappearing Uncle Joe; Daniel the Romanian partisan. He also sees a lot of out-of-the-way places: the Palouse; Iuka, Mississippi; Quanah, Texas; the Parting-of-the-Ways; Transnistria; Camaguey. Benz journeys from the bones to the stars, and along the way he makes himself into Everyperson: *Reading the Signs* offers up the stories of the Listener, the memories of the Watcher.

—H. L. Hix, *Demonstrategy*

Stephen Benz's essays are simultaneously personal and universal in the way they tap into human experience. From family stories to travels of great distance, Benz takes readers on a compelling journey. Rich in sense of place, these essays deftly challenge physical and spiritual divides while exploring various crossroads near and far.   —Diane Thiel

Benz's essays hold the reader all the way, section after section. This is a book for anyone who has a traveling heart.

—William Heyen, *Nature: Selected & New Poems 1970-2020*

Benz's fascinating new book teaches us to read the land through his experience, whether driving a truck, cruising battle sites or Indian and Latin American culture. By the end, he helps us understand what it means to find one's place in history.

—David King Dunaway, *The Ballad of Pete Seeger*

Reading the Signs
and other itinerant essays

Stephen Benz

Etruscan Press

Etruscan Press
Wilkes University
84 West South Street
Wilkes-Barre, PA 18766
(570) 408-4546

www.etruscanpress.org

Published 2022 by Etruscan Press
Printed in the United States of America
Cover design by Logan Rock
Interior design and typesetting by Aaron Petrovich
The text of this book is set in Mrs Eaves

First Edition

17 18 19 20 5 4 3 2 1

Library of Congress Cataloguing-in-Publication Data

Library of Congress Control Number: 2021906702

Please turn to the back of this book for a list of the sustaining funders of
Etruscan Press.

This book is printed on recycled, acid-free paper

For my children, Rachel, Nathan, and Steve
whose inspiration is everywhere in these pages

Table of Contents

Reading the Signs
and other itinerant essays

Acknowledgments

Grateful acknowledgment is made to the following publications where some of these essays first appeared.

Boulevard	En Route: Iuka, Mississippi; En Route: Quanah, Texas; En Route: Bingham Canyon, Utah
Cardinal Sins	Siboney
Creative Nonfiction	The Grounds Crew
Essay Daily	"Strange and Beautiful": Ambrose Bierce at Shiloh
Front Range Review	House and Home
Map Literary	En Route: Elko, Nevada
Miami Herald	On Jury Duty, Talkin' 'Bout My Generation, Father Knows Nothing, Small World, An Immigrant's Story
New England Review	Overlooking Guantánamo
Pinyon	Harvest on the Palouse
Shadowgraph	Horse Slaughter Camp
Soundings Review	Cottonwood Campground
Sun–Sentinel	The Partisan
TriQuarterly	Soviet Bloc Rock

Prelude:

Horse Slaughter Camp

When I was a boy, my friends and I often rode our bicycles along the old river road out past city limits and across the valley where, near the state line, we rested on the riverbank. Our turnaround point was a monument placed by "the County Pioneer Society and Loyal Citizens of the State." The granite pillar told a story, a story we learned by heart and pondered as we probed the tall grass and dirt mounds in search of old bones.

In September 1858, following the Battle of Four Lakes, Colonel George Wright marched across the Spokane Plains, burning Native American storehouses and lodges. On the eighth, his command came upon horses belonging to the Palouse. Wright's dragoons wrangled in eight hundred and nine mounts, an exact count taken to satisfy the army's penchant for recordkeeping.

Wright convened a board of officers to decide the horses' fate. Official policy discouraged horse slaughter. But this was war, and all was fair, the colonel reasoned. Keeping the beasts would invite raids, and they were far too wild to herd east with the command. Slaughter was a chance, he said, to strike a blow the savages would never forget.

The board agreed with Wright: horses gave the enemy their best means of resistance. "Without horses, redskins are powerless," the board declared in recommending slaughter. The record does not say whether anyone dissented or spoke in the horses' favor.

Troops were detailed to build a corral. The quartermaster chose the horses one by one and sent them down to a river bar, where the soldiers first shot the older horses then crushed the skulls of colts, causing the brood mares kept waiting to neigh long into the night. That sound, carrying far in the darkness, left its imprint on one soldier, a corporal, who years later would weep whenever he heard horses neigh at night.

"A cruel sight," the corporal wrote his wife, "to see so many noble creatures shot down; even now I hear their forlorn appeal for our mercy. It was not granted."

The killing went on all night while Donati's comet crossed the cold sky. The Palouse warriors, held in chains, saw the falling stars as souls, the souls of horses running free.

At dawn, with hundreds yet to kill, the officer in charge ordered two companies to line the riverbank and fire volleys into the corral. A contest was held to see who could kill the greatest number. Spirits were high—a sign, the corporal's letter said, of man's ferocious character.

Years after the troops had gone, the corral remained a midden, the mounds of horsehair and bleached bones called by newly arrived pioneers "Wright's Boneyard."

Wright himself, in his log and on the map he made to accompany his report, settled on a blunter name for the place. "This happened," he wrote, "at Horse Slaughter Camp."

We never found any skeletal remains at the site. But we carried away the bones of the story, which stayed in our memory and changed the way we understood the history of the place we called home.

I

Home Ground

> How can you value other places if you do not have
> one of your own? If you are not yourself placed,
> then you wander the world like a sightseer, a col-
> lector of sensations, with no gauge for measuring
> what you see. Local knowledge is the grounding
> for global knowledge.

> —Scott Russell Sanders

Harvest on the Palouse

Each day during the wheat harvest of 1976, I spent many hours behind the wheel of an old International Harvester truck, sometimes driving the truck, mostly just sitting in the cab, stuck in the middle of a field, surrounded by wheat or wheat stubble. I passed the hours reading or daydreaming, now and then looking up to check the progress of the combine as it worked its way around the field. I waited for the signal—flashing headlights—that meant the combine's bin had filled. Then I drove over the already harvested portion of the field—stubble crunching under the tires—and positioned the truck beneath the combine's chute. The harvested grain shot with a whoosh into the truck's hopper. When the combine had emptied its load, it started around the field again, and I went back to reading, waiting for the next full bin and the next transfer of grain from combine to truck. When the truck's hopper had filled, I drove out of the field, bouncing over furrows, and then followed the two-lane highway up and down hills into the tiny town of Fairfield to deposit the load at the grain elevator. I then headed back out to the field where the combine was still at it.

So it went, morning, noon, and evening, around fifteen hours a day for the two weeks of harvest. During that time, I read a lot of Kurt Vonnegut, I listened to a lot of country and western music, and I ate a lot of bologna sandwiches. I had very few interactions with other people.

All this took place in the Palouse, a wheat-growing region of rolling hills in eastern Washington State, one of the great landscapes of North America. Traveling around it, I frequently crested a hill to find a vast panorama spread before me—miles and miles of undulating wheat fields with great cloud shadows drifting across the golden hillscapes. Reaching the crest and looking out over those hills, I felt that the vehicle might become some kind of aircraft, a glider maybe, about to soar into the wide-open sky.

But gawking at the view was dangerous in a ten-ton truck, especially for me, a novice truck driver. It took all of my concentration to control the cumbersome vehicle as it started the descent. I had to double-clutch then find the lower gear that would keep speed in check and prevent a runaway. This was not as easy as it sounds, as the gear box on the old truck was stubborn, and I had a hard time getting the stick shift to slip into gear. If I had too much trouble, the truck would coast in neutral, gaining speed rapidly because of its weight, and the brakes would strain to slow the vehicle. If the descent was long, the brakes would smoke. During my drives around the region, back and forth from the fields to the grain elevator, I was too apprehensive—sweating profusely in the cab, which had no air conditioning—to truly enjoy the magnificent views of the Palouse.

During the harvest, I lived in what was called "the bunkhouse," though it was nothing like the structures so designated in Western films or television shows. This bunkhouse was a single-wide mobile home sitting on concrete blocks in a weed-infested lot on the outskirts of Fairfield: one main room, one small bedroom, one closet-sized bathroom. The kitchen facilities occupied one end of the main room: a sink, a token cabinet, a hot plate (microwave ovens were not yet common in those days), and a small refrigerator. I don't remember much about the bunkhouse because I spent only a few hours there each day, and during those hours I was either asleep or barely awake, exhausted from the long, hot day in the fields and on the road. I don't remember anything about curtains, rugs, or furnishings other than the four cots in the main room, the fold-up bed in the small bedroom, and some broken chairs outside where farmhands liked to sit around a fire ring and drink, the bunkhouse being too hot and stuffy for comfort.

I do remember the contents of the refrigerator: packets of bologna, a jar of mayonnaise, a jar of mustard, and quite a few cans of Rainier Beer. The top of the refrigerator was stacked with bags of Wonder Bread and hamburger buns. Each morning I made several bologna sandwiches for me and Dale, the bunkhouse's only other occupant that summer. These sandwiches were our breakfast, lunch, and dinner for the working day, each meal unceremoniously consumed in the truck cab, washed down with water from the jugs we carried, occasionally supplemented with a cold Coke or some milk bought in town if we had time after a run to the grain elevator.

Some summers there were as many as five farmhands in the bunkhouse. Most of the harvest workers—high school kids like me—came from the immediate area and lived at home in or around Fairfield. If a farmhand came from farther off—as I did— he stayed at the bunkhouse in order to be closer to the action, which each day began before dawn.

As the senior member of the crew, Dale got the fold-up bed in the small bedroom, while I slept on one of the cots. Dale had been working the harvest year in, year out for quite some time. I guessed he was about forty years old, but he was only a truck driver like me (combine drivers being the big wheels of the crew). Most of the year he lived in a trailer park up in Spokane, where he worked as a journeyman janitor or construction worker or took whatever job he could find. Summers, he hired out down on the Palouse driving truck, "bringing in the cut," as folks in Fairfield referred to the harvest.

Dale had a crew cut and he didn't like "sissy boys" or "hippie-dippies" with long hair (it was the 1970s and I was a teenager so, of course, I had long hair). He chewed tobacco and spit a lot. Many of his utterances began with three words—*what the hell*—spoken in a variety of tones that indicated anything from bemusement to anger, annoyance, or good-old-boy humor. *What the hell is that, what the hell you talking about, what the hell's that mean, what the hell for.* And so on. If he was particularly riled, he might say *what the fuck.*

I met Dale before starting on the job. Since I, too, lived in Spokane, the farm arranged for Dale to give me a ride. On the day before the harvest was expected to begin, we rode down to Fairfield in Dale's pickup truck.

That first evening at the bunkhouse, I took some books out of my suitcase and stacked them next to my cot. Beer in hand, Dale said, "What the hell are those?"

"Books."

"Books? What the hell for?"

"Just something to read, pass the time. I was told there's a lot of sitting around in the trucks and you have to entertain yourself."

"Sure, you do. Why the hell can't you just sleep or play with your pecker like a normal dude? Books. For Christ's sake." He looked over the stack. "Got any comic books or dirty books there?"

"No."

"Well, shit."

For the next two weeks, the workday began at 4:30 with the alarm clock's buzz and some choice words from Dale. With only a few hours of sleep after a long day, I groggily went through the motions, pulling on my jeans and boots, making sandwiches, filling water jugs, while Dale stumbled into the john and loudly pissed for what seemed like five minutes. We ate the first bologna sandwich of the day on the drive to the John Deere dealership, where our harvest trucks were parked each night.

Mr. Hayner—or "the old cuss," as Dale referred to him—was the field boss, the crew's head honcho. Out in the fields, his word was first and last. Because of his long experience, he had particular notions about how things ought to be done, and he snapped and growled at anyone not following proper procedure. Harvest was a time of stress for all involved. It was especially stressful for Mr. Hayner because he was responsible for the success of the operation—and a lot could go wrong. That was why proper procedure mattered so much. In hindsight, I can understand why he was so ornery about it all and about me in particular. At the time, though, I thought Mr. Hayner was just being a hard ass for no good reason. Later, I came to recognize that there were, in fact, good reasons—damn good reasons—for his particularity. I should have taken the cue from the other teenage boys on the crew. They were goof-offs in many ways, but not when it came to the actual work. Growing up in a farming region, they understood that harvest time meant getting serious, working hard, busting your ass, and doing things the right way. Livelihoods were at stake.

This "right way" of doing things began, every day, with proper care of the equipment. First thing in the morning, before daybreak, we prepared our machines for the day's hot, hard work. Truck drivers serviced their trucks, while combine drivers meticulously checked over their combines, which were incredibly sophisticated pieces of machinery. So much could go wrong. Breakdowns cost time and money. Dirty machinery could lead to malfunction, overheating, and possibly fires that could consume an entire field and endanger lives.

During the first few days, Dale tried to get me up to speed, instructing me on the daily maintenance of the truck—checking belts, spark plugs, tires, oil, radiator, gear box. Such things did not come naturally for me, but I kept at it and asked questions when I didn't know (persisting even when my question elicited, as it often did, yet another look of incredulity). I don't know that I ever did the job all that well, but at least the truck didn't break down during the time I operated it.

It took me a while to get used to driving the truck, to figure out how to smoothly double clutch, work the dump mechanism, make competent (or at least somewhat less clumsy) turns. It must have been irritating to observe the city boy's ineptitude, but the rest of the crew was more or less good-natured about it. Anyway, it would be tedious to review all the mistakes I made, all the ways in which I was sorely lacking and made for a poor farmhand. There were incidents at the grain elevator, incidents on the streets of Fairfield, incidents on the many hills of Palouse country (I found it very difficult to get the balky truck into lower gears when it was slowing down on an incline). I was honked at numerous times, laughed at, sworn at. Two or three times a day, Mr. Hayner had to climb down from the combine to yell at me and call me a jackass.

From the get-go, I succeeded in astonishing Mr. Hayner, astonishing him so much that as the fortnight wore on, his habitual wrath at all manner of stupidity and tomfoolery subsided in the face of my incompetence. Mute incomprehension replaced blind fury, and something like bewilderment and maybe even pity emerged, Mr. Hayner finally coming to regard me the way he might regard the runt of the hound dog litter—a poor little feller who wasn't ever going to figure out how to pick up the scent and give chase, not the way the real hounds could. "You ain't got a lick of sense," he often said to me, but with time his tone changed from condemnation to wonderment.

Before my summer of farm work, I had been somewhat familiar with the landscape of the Palouse, or so I thought, having crossed it many times on field trips from Spokane to Pullman, the university town, where numerous events for regional high schools were held: debate tournaments, Model UN, basketball games, and the like. Since these were school events, most of the trips took place in winter when strips and pockets of snow mixed with the brown, tilled earth and the beige-brown wheat stubble. We traveled on a school bus down Route 195, the main highway, at a good clip, fifty or sixty miles per hour, rolling past the seemingly undifferentiated landscape. These trips were a bit dull to teenagers, and we either slept or passed the time playing word games like "hangman." I paid little attention to the scenery, which appeared monotonous. Endless fields. A whole lot of nothing. The occasional small town, such as Spangle, Rosalia, or Colfax, along with isolated farmhouses. The Palouse was not in the least impressive to anyone just passing through.

The one notable landmark on the drive down Route 195 was Steptoe Butte, a quartz protrusion jutting a thousand feet above the surrounding terrain. Since the rock that formed the butte is millions of years older than the Palouse bedrock, Steptoe Butte holds geological interest, but at the time I knew only that the butte was a state park and that a road led to the top where you could take in the panorama of Palouse country.

From my Pacific Northwest History class, I had learned that the butte was named for a Colonel Steptoe, who was ignobly routed by American Indians in a battle that took place somewhere nearby. This battle, which occurred in 1858, was part of the Yakima Wars, specifically the Coeur d'Alene phase of the long-running campaign against the native peoples of the interior Northwest. Though these wars were brutal and eventually led to the total transformation of the region from grasslands to farm country, we didn't learn many details about them in class. Our textbook—as history textbooks tend to do—merely summarized the events, content to report on the obvious outcome. What we got out of it was the gist of the story: white settlers encroached on American Indian lands, which resulted in conflicts (some of them grisly, as in the Whitman massacre, which occurred near Walla Walla, at the southern edge of Palouse country). The US Army then came to the rescue of the settlers, drove the American Indians from their lands and corralled them on reservations. With the land "pacified," as the textbook put it, Washington became a state in 1889.

Along with removal of the American Indians, "pacification" meant that farming could begin in earnest. A land rush of sorts occurred in the Palouse, such that by 1890 (the year that Frederick Jackson Turner famously identified as the end of the frontier experience in American history) almost all of the Palouse grasslands had been plowed under and converted to wheat farms.

At first, it was tough going for the farmers. The soil—windblown loess sediment—was rich and fertile enough, but the contours of the hilly land forced farmers in the Palouse to use antiquated, labor-intensive techniques (horse- and human-powered) long after mechanization and technology had made farming much more efficient in the flatlands. Eventually, innovations in tractor and combine harvester design, particularly the use of hydraulics, enabled farmers to plow and harvest the steep slopes. In the 1940s, "hillside leveling" technology was introduced, allowing combines to adjust to the contours of the land. These "hilltoppers" were the machines I watched from the truck as they made their way over and along the golden Palouse hills.

To this day, Palouse farmland is amazingly productive, supposedly the best in the United States, with more grain harvested per acre than any other region. Farmers in the Palouse have long practiced "dryland farming," which is entirely dependent on natural rainfall—no irrigation—a somewhat risky proposition since eastern Washington lies in the rain shadow of the Cascade

Mountains and usually receives fewer than twenty inches of rain a year. Some of the farms also practice "contour strip farming," meaning that strips of land are left fallow each year. As a consequence, many hillsides have a banded appearance— alternating brown, green, and gold bands, depending on the time of year. Such was the land I gazed at and drove over during my time as a farmhand.

In 1976, Fairfield was a very small town, population five hundred or thereabouts. In layout it was what Westerners call a "T-town," with the railroad line and the principal road forming a capital T. In Fairfield, Main Street ran perpendicular to the tracks, and it was there, in a two-block stretch, that you'd find the commercial district, such as it was. Bank, drug store, post office, a couple of churches. After a few blocks, Main Street converted to a country road that wound its way across farmland for several miles to the Idaho border. The main road in and out of Fairfield was Highway 27, which within Fairfield proper—which is to say for about a half a mile—became First Street. Just about every other road in town dead-ended at a farmhouse or a wheat field.

On the outskirts of town, where Highway 27 entered Fairfield, you'd encounter the town's only other enterprises: a fertilizer warehouse, a hardware store, a lot crowded with farming implements and equipment for rent, a tire store. By any measure it was a no-account town, but I was always glad to head into Fairfield; it was a relief to enter town after the somewhat nerve-wracking test of getting the ten-ton truck from the field to the grain elevator. Fairfield also had trees, making it a small, somewhat shady oasis in the middle of the nearly treeless Palouse. Sometimes after delivering the load, I would stop at the town's tiny park to stretch my legs a bit and enjoy a brief respite in the shade.

My main purpose in town, though, was to deliver the wheat to the elevator, which was located alongside the railroad tracks just off Main Street. Operated by a co-op, the grain elevator was, to me, another of the little mysteries in farm country, the wonders of its inner workings made all the more intriguing because of the familiarity of such structures across the American landscape. Throughout my life, on sundry drives I had seen many grain elevators and silos without ever having any idea what went on inside them. During my stint as a farmhand, I made around fifty trips to the grain elevator, and in the process came to understand—albeit sketchily—how the elevator worked. Most of what happened, happened out of sight. The process began when the wheat truck entered the elevator and dumped the grain onto a grate in the floor that covered what was called the pit. The grain vanished through the grate and into the pit, sucked down like a whirlpool. But that was all I saw of the process. What happened next was a mystery to me. After a few trips I began to wonder why I was dumping grain into a hole in the ground when the silos where the grain was stored stood seventy or so feet tall. How did the grain get up into the silos? Curiosity led me to talk to the co-op workers, especially Ray, a talkative Vietnam War veteran who worked the floor of the elevator. From Ray I learned that the grain in the pit was scooped up in buckets attached to a long belt that carried the grain to the top of the silo. This contraption was called the leg, and it did the elevating work that gave the whole structure its name. From the top, the grain was sent down chutes into one or another of the silos.

One of the big concerns at the grain elevator was quality control. The grain was immediately tested for dryness and cleanness. At some point it was also tested for starchiness and protein content. In the first days of harvest, as the initial crop came in, everyone was eager to find out the "test weights." They were hoping for "high numbers" indicating good starchiness, which translated to higher quality. I remember Ray reaching his hand into the stream of grain pouring from my truck and catching a handful. He studied it then pronounced, "Looking good. Clean and fat. Gonna be a good harvest this year, I bet."

I heard some other things from Ray as well. He had grown up in the Palouse, near the town of Colfax. He had intended to go to Washington State University, but he drew a high draft number and ended up in the army. He spent just over a year in Vietnam.

I asked him what it was like.

"Boring, to be honest," he said. "Nonstop boredom. Nothing to do but smoke dope and wait for Charlie to do something, anything. Attack, retreat, whatever, but nothing ever happened, not where I was anyway."

I said that Vietnam sounded like a pretty scary place to me.

"Yeah, sure, it was intense sometimes," Ray said. "Mostly because you're waiting for something to happen. Something bad. You know it's coming and there's nothing you can do. And every day it's the same damn thing—waiting for the shit to hit the fan, day after day, until it was just so damn boring. It was like just get it over with already, just kill me now, know what I mean?"

I didn't know what he meant. I said that sitting in a truck out in the middle of a wheat field was all that I knew about boredom.

"Yeah, well that's nothing," Ray told me. "That's pure pleasure compared to the boredom I'm talking about."

Thinking about Ray's stories as I drove back to the fields, I was grateful for the thousandth time in 1976—the year I came of draft age—that the war had ended before I could be drafted and sent over there.

I necessarily learned a little bit about wheat—the smell of wheat dust, the glare a field of ripened wheat gives off in bright sunlight, the sound of a wheat field in wind and in rain, the feel of wheat stubble under your boots. Before I worked on the farm, wheat had no particularity to it in my mind. It was just wheat. After listening to Ray and the crew, I learned that there were different varieties of wheat. I learned the difference between spring wheat and winter wheat. I learned that there were different classes—not only "soft white," which is what we were bringing in, but also hard white and hard red winter and hard red spring. I learned that each class had different qualities that made it suitable for different end-uses. Soft white, the type most commonly grown in the Palouse at the time, was best for non-yeast products, such as cookies, crackers, cakes, pastries, and cereal. I never heard anyone mention an Asian market in 1976, but in the years to come most of the wheat grown in the Palouse would be shipped to Japan and Korea for processing into noodles.

A few times I left the cab and wandered into the stalks, touched the wheat, pulled up a plant, studied it, tasted it (bland, dry, maybe a little nutty). I had known very little about wheat before I found myself sitting in the middle of a half-harvested field of it. My attitude would have been: What's to know? Vast fields of it extending to the horizon, the sameness of it making it both impressive and uninteresting. But on the job, looking closely, I could see something of a wheat stalk's fascinating complexity: the beard, the glumes, the kernels.

For those two weeks of my life, wheat was everywhere, its chaff and dust wafting in the air, coating everything, including the truck, my clothes, my hair. I was itchy with it, dirty with it, hot with it. It drifted inside the cab, inside the bunkhouse, all over town. It gave the sunset a reddish-orange glow, turned the sky hazy, smeared windows and sunglasses. I sneezed often. My eyes watered. I wondered why nobody on the crew wore a bandanna. The chaff blew onto the road and swirled around when vehicles passed. Wheat was everything, and everything was wheat.

When I was driving and unable to read, the radio became my source of entertainment. The truck radio could only receive AM stations, and because of a broken antenna only a few Spokane stations came in well without static. I could choose between a Top 40 station and a country music station. I went with the country station, trying to get into the spirit of the work I was doing and the place where I was doing it. Besides, I really, really did not like Top 40 at the time. In 1976, country radio was dominated by trucker songs, especially those that involved CB radio talk in some way or another ("Convoy," "The White Knight"). During the summer, the big hit was Red Sovine's "Teddy Bear," an incredibly maudlin song—actually a spoken-word piece set to music—which told the story of truckers coming to the aid of a crippled boy—the lyrics actually used the word "crippled"—who had lost his trucker father. Apparently, the listening audience couldn't get enough of the over-the-top sentimentality; the radio station played the song hourly.

Otherwise, there were numerous male-female duets on the radio at that time: George Jones and Tammy Wynette, of course; and Jim Ed Brown with Helen Cornelius; and a cheesy act called Dave and Sugar. I found myself liking some songs I might not otherwise have heard, in particular Don Williams's "Till the Rivers All Run Dry," Marty Robbins's "El Paso City," and Tom T. Hall's "Faster Horses." And the so-called "outlaw country" artists—Waylon Jennings, Merle Haggard, Willie Nelson, David Allen Coe—made for perfect listening on back roads and two-lane highways. I also came to appreciate classic country music, namely the songs of Hank Williams, Patsy Cline, Kitty Wells, and Lefty Frizzell.

But by far the discovery of the summer for me—and what would become a lifelong love—was the voice of Emmylou Harris. That summer was the first time I heard her sing. Her radio hit at the time was a Buck Owens cover, "Together Again," and when I first heard it, I was stunned by the purity of her voice. Even over a tinny AM radio in a truck cab with the windows down, engine growling, road noise and all, she sounded absolutely heavenly, and I listened in a kind of rapture, completely in love. It's a wonder I didn't drive off the road into a ditch. When the song ended the first time I heard it, and the disc jockey said the name of artist and song, I pulled over to the edge of the road and wrote it down, underlining her name and vowing to buy the record as soon as I got back to Spokane. It was one of those moments when you instantly know that everything will be different because of something you've just experienced for the first time—a poem read, a dish tasted, a face seen, a song heard. To this day, hearing Emmylou sing, I can smell the wheat dust, see the heat rising from the highway, feel the spine-tingling frisson pass over me.

At the top of the hour, the country station gave five minutes to news and weather. The two weeks I was in the Palouse featured deadly floods in Colorado, a sniper rampage in Wichita, Viking 1's orbit of Mars, two hundred thousand dead in a Chinese earthquake, and Legionnaires mysteriously coming down ill at a convention in Philadelphia. And above all, at least in terms of news coverage, there was the intrigue at the Republican National Convention as Ronald Reagan challenged President Ford for the nomination. All of these dramatic events seemed strange and impossible from the perspective of my truck cab, as if the seemingly endless and perfectly lonely landscape of the Palouse somehow invalidated catastrophe, murder, disease, and political intrigue.

At noon, following the news, Paul Harvey came on with his conservative, folksy take on these unreal current affairs. This was a syndicated show called *The Rest of the Story*, which was heard across America and was especially popular in rural areas. Harvey's unique delivery included extended pauses for dramatic effect as he spun some heart-warming tale or reviewed the latest example of moral decay in America. Fiscal irresponsibility or plain lack of common sense were evident from sea to shining sea in Harvey's worldview; this malfeasance and stupidity was occasionally thwarted and redeemed by the honest acts of decent common folk and upstanding American citizens. Harvey had a way of sounding at the same time patriotic and deeply pessimistic about the country—odd to hear in that summer of bicentennial celebrations.

Bradshaw, Truax, Prairie View, Rattler Run, Marsh, Darknell: these were some of the roads I drove on to get to the fields. Some were paved; many were dirt. Wherever they went, these roads passed, bypassed, or cut across wheat fields. Only in a few places did the landscape vary. One such place was the confluence of Rattler Run Creek and Hangman Creek. Here, the road— Kentuck Trail Road—descended from tableland (planted in wheat, of course) to the river bottoms, a marshy place thick with cattails. As it descended, the road passed through a forested belt, stands of pine trees casting shadows across the road. The change from open and treeless fields to shadowy woodlands was abrupt enough to give the place an enchanted, possibly eldritch, feel. I had recently read *The Hobbit,* and there was something about this brief stretch that reminded me of the book's setting. There was, anyway, a fairy tale quality that sharply contrasted with the wide-open landscape of the Palouse.

I drove along this section of the road three or four times, noticing as I passed a sign that read "Historical Marker." An arrow pointed off road into the woods. I was curious: what historical event could have occurred in such a remote and seemingly gloomy spot? One day, I decided to turn in. A short and narrow dirt lane led into the woods and up to a stone pillar, on which a brief text explained that in 1858, a "sub-chief" named Qualchew and six other Indians were hanged at the spot. Nothing else by way of information—no mention of the Indians' tribal affiliation, no identification of those responsible for the hangings, no indication of the reason for the executions. Later,

I would learn more of the story. For the moment, however, I could infer that the event must have given the nearby creek its name, a creek I was familiar with because it flowed north across the Palouse and skirted Spokane near my family's house before joining the Spokane River just west of city limits. I had passed over Hangman Creek numerous times in my life without ever thinking about its name.

The rest of the story, as Paul Harvey would say, was this: the "sub-chief" (actually named Qualchan, not Qualchew, as the marker had it), was a Yakama Indian who had been harassing settlers and the US Army for several years, conducting raids and attacks on those who had encroached on the Yakama's ancestral lands. The army considered him a fugitive and sought his capture. For unknown reasons, in September 1858, Qualchan appeared at the camp of Colonel George Wright near a ford on what was then called Latah Creek. Neither Fairfield nor any other nearby community existed at that time, and Fort Spokane was but a small frontier outpost. Some accounts speculate that Wright was holding Qualchan's father captive. Other versions suggest Qualchan believed that Wright wanted to parley. But no one knows for sure why Qualchan suddenly appeared in Wright's camp. Only one truncated record of the event exists—two terse sentences in Colonel Wright's log: "Qualchan came to see me at nine o'clock. At nine-fifteen he was hung." Wright provided no other details to justify this act of summary justice.

The colonel's name was well known to me, as it appeared in various places in Spokane, most notably as Fort George Wright, a residential section of the city where an army post had once been located. But the reasons for Wright's fame, the reasons that had supposedly made him worthy of commemoration, had largely escaped me before I happened upon the historical marker and later followed up on the story. This, too, became part of my education that summer.

* * *

About day ten of my stint in the Palouse, an incident occurred that changed—fleetingly and ever so slightly—my relationship with Mr. Hayner, whom I had taken to thinking of, per Dale, as "the old cuss." Actually, there were one or two incidents every day between Mr. Hayner and me, but they all tended to confirm or solidify Mr. Hayner's opinion, namely that I was "the sorriest excuse for a farmhand" that he had ever had the misfortune to deal with in all his fifty goddamned years of farm work.

My lack of knowledge was irksome enough, but what really set Mr. Hayner off was my inattentiveness. There was a signal—flashing headlights—that meant I was supposed to bring the truck over to the combine. Usually, the signal came when the combine had filled its bin with cut grain and was ready to disgorge the grain into the truck's hopper. This occurred more or less regularly, so I had a good idea when to look up from my book and pay closer attention to the combine's meanderings. But there were a few occasions when the combine signaled unexpectedly for a reason other than a full bin. Absorbed with reading, I failed to apprehend the signal in good time, and when I finally responded I had to confront an infuriated Mr. Hayner. It irked him no end that I would be reading books when I should be paying attention to the job at hand. It was on these occasions that Mr. Hayner would snarl his habitual put-down: "You ain't got a lick of sense for all your book reading." He made it known, in no uncertain terms, that he thought my penchant for reading was detrimental to the performance of honest work and the foremost cause of bringing in the cut. What can I say? He was right. In one instance, a blade on the combine's header had broken and he needed me to take him back to the John Deere shop to get some part or tool necessary to effect the repair. My slow response to the signal had meant a loss of invaluable time—and one of the curious, almost paradoxical lessons about harvest work was that no matter how slow, monotonous, and repetitive things appeared, time was of the essence and time was money. We were always desperately pressed for time, even though during the working day time seemed to pass ever so slowly.

On another occasion, Mr. Hayner again signaled sooner than expected and once again I missed it. I really should have known better this time. During the last dispensing of grain from combine to truck, Mr. Hayner had emerged from the cab, which he almost never did, and stood on the platform staring to the west where thunderheads had developed. He picked up some stubble and tossed it in the air, gauging the direction of the wind, much as I had done as a high school outfielder. He shook his head, a grim look on his face. I should have been able to read the signs. I should have known—and actually did know, having heard throughout the harvest fortnight plenty of conversation fretting over the prospects of rain—that an impending storm required heightened awareness and concern from the work crew. The combines could not cut damp wheat. An excessively wet field ran the risk of sprouting, thereby ruining the crop, hundreds of thousands of dollars lost. So, Mr. Hayner, hoping that the thunderstorm would stay in the offing, continued with the cut, no doubt keeping a close eye on the distant storm, alert to any change in the conditions. Which I, too, should have been doing. Instead, I resumed my reading, got caught up in developing events on Vonnegut's planet Trafalmadore, and missed the shift in the wind. At which point, Mr. Hayner signaled—and was signaling frantically by the time the gathering gloom caught my attention. I rushed the truck over to where Mr. Hayner was waiting. He yanked open the driver's side door, yelled "move over," climbed in, and drove us at breakneck speed toward town. All that harvested wheat—open to the elements in the truck hopper—would be worthless if it got wet. We reached the grain elevator as the first splattering drops hit. While we were inside the elevator dumping the load, the deluge opened up. I can still hear Mr. Hayner yelling over the rain and thunder, "For Chrissakes, son, what're you waiting for—lightning to strike your thick head? What's it take for you to recognize a goddamned thunderstorm?"

The incident that momentarily, infinitesimally changed our relationship also involved a signal from the combine. This time I was a little more prompt in responding. Instead of reading, I was eating my lunch and watching the combine. I thought I saw the headlight flicker once, but I wasn't sure, the sunlight being so bright. The combine, however, appeared to have come to a halt—not always easy to tell from a distance since the lumbering machine normally traveled at about two miles per hour. Having messed up before, I decided it was better to respond needlessly to nothing rather than react too slowly to a matter of urgency. So I drove over to meet the combine and find out what the old cuss needed this time.

I positioned the truck underneath the chute and waited, but nothing happened. I got out of the truck. A hot wind blew, dust and stubble clouding the air, and I suddenly felt uneasy. The combine stood stock-still—silence instead of the usual rattle and hum. Just then, Mr. Hayner opened the door to the cab and stumbled onto the platform, grabbing on to the railing, noticeably unsteady.

"C'mon over here and help me down the ladder."

"Are you all right?"

"Bit shaky is all. Lightheaded. Musta forgot the medicine this morning."

Mr. Hayner wanted me to drive him to his house in Fairfield so that he could get the necessary pills. As we bounced along over the field and onto the highway, Mr. Hayner groaned a few times. "Take her easy, son," he said. "No need to rush. I ain't gonna die." The usual irritation was gone from his voice, and he actually smiled, the first time I had seen him do so, as he said, "Not yet, no how."

I helped him up the steps to his house just as Mrs. Hayner opened the door. "Oh, Floyd," she said, "Did you go and forget the medication again?"

We stayed at the house for about an hour. Mrs. Hayner made Mr. Hayner rest in his favorite chair and collect himself, as she put it. Meanwhile, she served me pie and milk in the kitchen and gabbed on and on—all about how forgetful Floyd was of late and how happy she would be when all the stress of harvest was behind them, but thank the good Lord the weather had cooperated so far. She brought out a photo album and told me all about the people in the photos, people I did not know, except for Mr. Hayner, who appeared in the pictures as a much younger man in military uniform. And all the while, Mrs. Hayner kept up a running commentary ("Oh, he had a terrible time of it in the Pacific, never talks about it, you won't get a word out of him on the subject, but I just know it was something awful") while popping up now and then to attend to her canning project on the stove before returning to the photo album. She asked me a few questions about my family and seemed to be unduly pleased that we were Presbyterians.

Finally, Mr. Hayner appeared in the doorway.

"All right, enough with the chitchat. Time to get back to work. That wheat ain't gonna cut itself."

"Are you sure you'll be all right, dear?"

"Sure as sure can be."

She made me promise to look after him, to which Mr. Hayner growled, "He's got enough trouble looking after himself."

"Such a nice young man," Mrs. Hayner said, patting my arm and giving me two jars of jam to take back to my good Presbyterian family.

In the truck on the way back to the fields, Mr. Hayner was silent. It was noteworthy that he had not insisted on doing the driving himself. At one point, I fumbled with a gear change, grinding the gears badly. But when I quickly apologized, Mr. Hayner merely grunted and said, "It's all right, son. You got a lot to learn. Just takes some practice, that's all. Keep at it and you'll be all right."

It was a nice little moment, and I could tell from his tone of voice that he was sincere. But somehow I also understood that this small instance of encouragement would in no way exempt me from a tongue-lashing should I mess up in the future. Mr. Hayner could allow for rookie mistakes, but he was of the firm belief that the best way to teach a rookie to avoid repeating the mistake was to blast him with the wrath of God.

When the two weeks were up and the harvest work done, Dale and I had our own little party in the bunkhouse.

"What the hell," Dale said, "no sense letting the rest of this case go to waste." He cracked open a Rainier and handed me a can. We settled ourselves in the broken chairs around the outdoor fire ring and over the next few hours drank off the rest of the case. Luckily for me, it was 3.2 beer—"just piss water," as Dale called it.

We talked about this and that, and then Dale asked, "Hey, how many of them books did you read?"

"All of them," I said.

"What the hell—*all* of them? Jesus Christ."

"Some of them twice."

"Man, that's messed up. You got to leave off them books or you'll turn into an egghead. Better get yourself a gal to poke. Better use of time."

A few minutes passed in silence. Then Dale said, "Naw, I take that back. You go on reading, go on studying. Get your diploma, go to college. You don't want to end up like me. Nothing but ass-busting jobs. Shit for pay. Bone-tired and half-dead. Just another dumbass. So yeah, keep studying, keep reading all them books. I bet you go to college, top of the class."

Overhead, wheat dust lingering in the air hazed the moon, giving it a muted orange glow that was strangely beautiful.

The next day, I rode in Dale's pickup truck back to Spokane. For the first time in my life, I had an actual physical sensation to associate with the word "hangover." Dale must not have been feeling all that great, either. He killed the radio and we traveled in silence. Everything there was to say had been said the night before anyway. The miles passed, gorgeously austere Palouse miles. Most of the wheat had now been harvested, but at one point we drove alongside a field of ripe, uncut wheat—no sign of harvest activity. I wondered why not. Shouldn't the wheat have been cut already?

Dale pointed to the field and said, "What the hell's going on there—that wheat's as ripe as it's going to get and not a combine in sight."

That I saw the same thing Dale saw—and recognized the aberration before he pointed it out—indicated that my perception had changed. After two weeks of hard work, I was seeing the land differently. The long hours on the job had definitely taught me something.

There were other invaluable lessons that summer, though at the time I couldn't yet understand or appreciate them. Farm work was my first real experience with blue-collar labor—and my first lesson in just how involved and sophisticated such work could be. The job taught me that so-called manual labor was much more mentally challenging than I had presumed. After two weeks I had to acknowledge that "book learning" wasn't the only way to be smart; in many ways, Mr. Hayner, Dale, and everybody else I worked with were all much smarter than I was. It was a lesson that would be reinforced in years to come when I worked alongside mechanics, plumbers, carpenters, and electricians. Problems would arise, machines would break down, systems would fail, and these people had the wherewithal, the intelligence, the insight to analyze the problem and devise a solution while I watched, hapless and clueless. They possessed a kind of logic and perceptivity that I was unable to summon.

It wasn't just that these people had a set of knowledge or tools that I lacked. They had a way of looking at and understanding the world that was different from my own. They had insight where I had none. They had powers of perception while I remained in darkness. They could solve problems that I couldn't even identify. For an apprentice writer, this was a great gift: on these jobs, I had the chance to learn from those who saw the world differently. I had the chance to learn other ways of thinking. You can't write characters, I would one day discover, unless you can get outside yourself and think the way someone else does. You cannot, for that matter, even write about yourself without being able to recognize, allow for, and adopt different outlooks, different mindsets, different cognitive powers. My experience on the farm gave concrete meaning to Thoreau's well-known words on the great miracle of seeing through another's eyes for an instant.

It was a significant lesson that would eventually sink in as the years passed. But for me there was another, even greater lesson: down on the farm I learned, or started to learn, that no matter where you are, no matter how dull and monotonous your circumstances appear to be, there is always something worthy of attention. Through heightened awareness, you can always attend and discover. Indeed, the least promising circumstances might well offer the greatest opportunities for discovery. Spend hour after hour alone in a truck cab in the middle of a wheat field, and you might begin to perceive hitherto unrecognized wonders in the world and the miracle of your part in it. Sitting still, with nothing to do, you must necessarily open up to observation. If you do, you will experience difference and depth rather than monotony and flatness. This is the message of the transcendentalists—Emerson, Thoreau—and great poets such as Whitman, Dickinson, Frost, and Bishop. Observe carefully. Put down the book, turn off the radio, roll down the window, and take in everything that you can in this moment. Easier said than done, to be sure. And I certainly struggled to make the most of the time I was stuck in the truck cab. But sometimes you need to spend an hour or two or ten in utter boredom before you can perceive the dazzle that lies beyond boredom. What you thought was nothingness turns out to be something after all—a vast, teeming, complex world. Pay closer attention, and brilliance starts to emerge—from everywhere and everything, until it all glows like the rays of the setting sun seen through air thick with wheat dust. And then—suddenly, unexpectedly—you are given to understand, with Emerson, that "beauty breaks in everywhere."

The Grounds Crew

1. First Day

Two weeks into my freshman year at college, I came out of the financial aid office carrying paperwork that approved me for an on-campus job. The choice jobs—in the library or the computer lab or the sports center—went to experienced upper-classmen. They had first pick. Freshmen had to settle for the jobs no one else wanted. I was sent to Maintenance.

The maintenance building—a long, concrete bunker—was on the backside of the campus down a hill behind the sports center. In the musty administrative office, a secretary handed me yet another form, a survey on which I was supposed to circle my skills. I read the list: *painting, plumbing, electrical, locksmith*. Nothing I knew how to do. Most of my work experience had involved mowing lawns, pulling weeds, doing odd jobs for the neighbors. Simple labor that didn't require training or skills. At the bottom of the list, I checked "Other" and wrote in "Odd Jobs."

The secretary looked at the paper, sighed, and said to the typist behind her, "Hey, Darlene, here's another one who can't do anything."

"So send him to Grounds," Darlene said. Her intonation suggested that "Grounds" was the bottom of the barrel, the only resort for those who were unskilled and incompetent.

The secretary shrugged. "Grounds it is."

I was sent to the end of the building, past all other offices, to the very last door. A battered pick-up truck stood out front.

A sign read GR UN S OF ICE. The warped, weathered door was halfway open.

I pushed my way into a cluttered, ill-lit workshop. Two men were inside. One, a huge Black man, sat at a desk near the door. Farther back in the shadows, the other man occupied a scruffy armchair, an oversized yellow hard hat cocked on his head. He flicked a jackknife at a section of green hose that curled snake-like over the dusty floorboards. The knife stuck the hose and the man in the hard hat giggled. A derelict table filled the middle of the shed, the tabletop piled with hardware I couldn't even begin to identify.

There was a split second when I had the chance to back out, to mumble *sorry, excuse me*, and make my escape. The moment passed. The man in the hard hat snatched up the knife. "Howdy," he sang out. "What can we do you for?"

"Mr. Johnson?" I said.

He jerked his thumb at the other man. "That'd be the big guy."

Squeezed into an office chair that should have been tossed out decades ago, a coal-black linebacker of a man with snow white hair stared at me, a hard penetrating stare made all the more menacing by the fact that we were almost eye to eye even though he was sitting and I was standing. His yellow, bloodshot eyes hinted of viciousness.

Timidly, I handed him the work authorization and said I had been assigned to the grounds crew.

"This here's the place all right," the hard-hatted man said as he flung the knife into the hose again. "So you're the lucky one gets to be student assistant?"

Mr. Johnson studied the paper then glared at me again.

"Stephens," he barked.

"Yes," I said. Then added, "Sir," almost as an involuntary reflex.

He tapped an open book, a Bible, on his desk. "You know what this is, Stephens?"

I nodded.

He handed me the book. "Then read."

I hesitated, longing for the chance to bolt. But I didn't move, spellbound by an authority I hadn't expected.

"Well, go on, then" he said. "Devil got your tongue? Read out loud. Start here."

With no way out, I did as told, my voice trembling in the stillness of the shop. It was Job he wanted read, the King James Version. Man overturned mountains, it said, cut out channels, bound up streams, brought hidden things to light. But where would wisdom be found? Man did not know the way to it.

Mr. Johnson grunted and hummed while I read. Finally, he said, "You understand that, Stephens?"

"Yes, sir."

"Tell me."

I stared at him, then at the dusty, splintering floorboards.

"Tell me."

He grunted and hummed some more as I stumbled through a summary of the text.

"Listen to me, Stephens," he interrupted. "You better learn that lesson like old Job. Man do not—repeat, do not—know the way to wisdom." He growled and laughed like there was some private joke involved. "Simple as that. Man do not know. Only wisdom there is come from God. If you can remember that, you can work for me. All right now, don't just stand there—get yourself a sack and get on out there with Max. He's going to show you how to pick up trash. All these students learning what all but can't think to use the garbage can."

Relieved to escape the suffocating grease-gas-dust smell of the shop and get back into the warm September breeze, I carried a burlap sack and trailed Max up to the quad, the center of the campus. Out in the light of day, removed from the shadows of the shop, Max looked like he belonged in a clown act, one of those circus interludes where the clowns impersonate firemen or construction workers and amuse the crowd by bollixing the job. Max was short and stumpy, not much bigger than a dwarf. His head was out of proportion to his body, made the larger by his silly yellow hard hat. Then the thick glasses, the toothpick in his mouth, the oversized flannel shirt, the baggy dime store jeans, and the clomping rubber boots—I had never seen anyone so bizarre, so freakish. Stuck in my late-teenager way of thinking, I wondered how anyone could invite ridicule by going out in public looking like that.

That first hour on the job I felt miserable. We walked around picking up paper and plastic cups and aluminum cans and candy wrappers (if nothing else, Mr. Johnson was right: the students were slobs). Everywhere we went, the campus hummed with activity—stereos blasted from dorm windows, Frisbee games were in full swing, girls sunned themselves on towels and blankets. I felt humbled and humiliated: all for lack of spending money I was reduced to picking up trash with a freak for a partner. I fervently hoped I wouldn't run into anyone I knew. I agonized over each slowly passing minute as I dragged around that ridiculous, increasingly conspicuous trash sack, emblem of my embarrassment. And yet, it seemed that no one noticed us. Professors, students, deans—they all passed us by without a second glance. I thought for sure that Max's appearance would elicit giggles—maybe even little yelps of fright—from some of the students. But no. No one paid the least attention; it was as though we were invisible. Two or three people even dropped trash onto the grass not ten yards from us. But Max seemed not the least bit conscious of either his outlandish appearance or his lowly status. He nodded at people and said, "Afternoon." He babbled about movies I had never heard of and told stupid jokes, so excited that spittle trickled on his lips when he giggled over the punch lines. I decided he was an utter fool. Before my sack was half full, I resolved to quit at the end of the day.

But when I went back to the maintenance office, the secretary shook her head. "You got no trade skills, honey," she said. "We can't use you anywhere else. Take it or leave it."

2. Shoptalk

I dreaded going to work, dreaded it more than my required calculus class or the tedium of the language lab. Three times a week that long fall semester, I trudged down to the grounds shop to report for work. More than anything else about the job, I hated the shop. To me, it was an alien, somewhat sinister place—a place of dust, grease, and cobwebs. A suffocating place of grime, clutter, and the odor of old oil. I couldn't wait to get out of there, and yet I was invariably forced to spend an excruciating fifteen minutes, twenty minutes, half an hour, trapped in the dim, airless shop while Max and Mr. Johnson tinkered and talked. Before entering the shop and abandoning all hope, I had to take a deep breath and steel myself.

Just past the threshold, Mr. Johnson sat at his desk, squinting at the small print of his Bible. Over his head, a single fluorescent tube provided harsh light to the front part of the shop. On the desk, pipe joints held down stacks of yellowed requisition forms, timesheets, memos. An ape head carved from a coconut rocked on the gritty desktop, the ape's astonished eyes fixed on the doorway, greeting whoever entered. Mr. Johnson's yellow eyes glanced up, already set in a scowl.

"Sit down, Stephens, while we sort out this mess."

"Have a seat, take a load off," Max said, pointing his jackknife at a castoff, grease-stained executive chair missing one caster.

I moved to the back of the shop, where flickering fluorescence surrendered to shadow, and the pervasive smell of oil mixed with the stink of fertilizers and poisons. I sat in what became my appointed spot, behind the worktable that took up the middle of the shop. Clutter surrounded me. The table was piled with assorted pipes, pipe wrenches, sprinkler heads, hoses, lawnmower blades, spark plugs, and pieces of broken tools—hoe heads, shovel shafts, saw blades. Slanted shelves along the walls gave tentative support to boxes of nails, paper cups of washers, and canisters of bleeding chemicals.

"Have a look at this new parts calendar," Max said. "You seen knockers like that before?"

"Max, quit your clowning," Mr. Johnson said.

"You're just jealous 'cause you never seen knockers like these."

"Max, when a man's in the army twenty-seven years he sees plenty. More than he wants to."

"I bet Steve here sees plenty over in Taylor Hall."

"Quit it, Max. Young man don't need no more foolish thoughts than he already got."

So the shoptalk went, Max and Mr. Johnson bantering away their quarter-hour break and then some, while I awaited my assignment, pining to escape. From scattered comments I learned bits and pieces about their lives. During a career of twenty-seven years, Mr. Johnson had advanced only to sergeant, apparently the most a Black man without a formal education could expect from the army. Max was an epileptic—that explained why he wore the hard hat everywhere and rode a bicycle to work.

But other than superficial details, I avoided taking much interest in Max and Mr. Johnson. I wouldn't have admitted it at the time but part of my discomfort in the shop came from having to spend time around them. Subconsciously, I shied away. They represented difference I didn't know how to deal with. As a consequence, I remained aloof and afraid, as if their "conditions"—blackness and epilepsy—and their blue-collar status—might somehow rub off on me. In my sheltered life, I had never before worked closely with a Black person. For all I knew, epilepsy was no different than leprosy. It was as though they had contagious diseases—though surely the dis-ease was entirely my own.

Early in the semester, I received a writing assignment to interview someone interesting. It never crossed my mind to interview Max or Mr. Johnson.

3. Trash and Leaves

Whenever Mr. Johnson decided the shoptalk had gone on long enough, he took out his Bible. Max, in turn, picked up anything close at hand—a broken sprinkler head, a malfunctioning nozzle—and began to tinker, trying to appear occupied.

Mr. Johnson didn't really read the Bible. He improvised, taking as prompts whatever words his curtailed elementary education and years of church attendance allowed him to recognize. In a robust baritone, he intoned our daily lesson: "And in those days the prophet Jose, he forgot the Lord God and he betook hisself to consort the prostitutes of Old Babylon. And the Lord God got good and angry and sent an angel saying, Behold Jose, you lost the favor of your Lord God and yea the wages of your sins is death."

Then, putting down the Bible, Mr. Johnson turned to me and said, "Young Stephens, you listen up. I want you to read up on the Book of Jose and tell me about it tomorrow. For now, get yourself a rake and get on over to Taylor Hall and rake up all them leaves. That old buck maple been dropping its leaves like nobody's business. And you think about Jose now, and his troubles with those ladies of the night. Max, you going to fool with that old pipe all the day? Come on now, we got to get on over to the ministration and see to some problem with the flowerbed that got Miss Dean upset."

I spent most of the fall semester raking leaves and picking up trash. From the first, I loathed the work. The physical labor didn't bother me. I didn't mind going out in the sharp, cool autumnal air, a fresh change from long hours in the stuffy labs and lecture halls. What I couldn't tolerate was the sense of humiliation I felt doing such lowly work in public. I tended to loiter on the job, raking desultorily, occasionally stopping to pick up trash if no students were around to see me. I tried to act with aplomb, as if it were only by some quirk of fate that I was outside with a rake or a trash bag. To me, this sense of humiliation was the worst part of the job. I wondered how the maintenance regulars could tolerate doing such menial work every day of their lives. I was relieved to know that, in the long run, I would escape such a fate.

I didn't do a very good job and I didn't really care what anybody thought about it. And for the first two months, Mr. Johnson didn't say a word about my work, or lack of it. Then, on a cold drizzly day in November, Mr. Johnson came around in his truck. He rolled down the window and said, "Let's go, Stephens. Too cold and wet. We're calling it a day."

I climbed into the cab, and for a long minute we just sat there while Mr. Johnson contemplated the courtyard I was supposed to have been raking and the small mound of leaves I had managed to rake, the woeful result of two hours' work. The silence became uncomfortable. Then he said, "Thought you be finished by now." It was a matter-of-fact comment, no tone of reproach.

"It's a big yard," I said.

He put the truck in gear and drove off. He didn't answer until we were almost back to the shop.

"Yes, sir, that's a big yard, big yard with a lot of leaves. But don't worry, Stephens. Some day you'll be man enough for the job. That's right, you still growing. You still a boy."

Still his voice suggested no reproach, but Mr. Johnson saw my annoyance. "Don't like that, eh? Huh. Stephens don't like being called boy. No, young Stephens don't want to be called boy. Thinks he's a man. Make his blood boil when he's called boy. Believe me, I know, I know. Been called boy too goldarn much not to know. And let me tell you this: boy don't become a man less he learns to put in a day's work, a honest day's work. Remember that, boy."

Such was the first of many hard lessons Mr. Johnson would administer during the next few years.

The next lesson came during homecoming week. Mr. Johnson told me to meet Max and him at the football field on Sunday morning. He needed an extra hand to clean the football stadium the day after the big game. On Sunday I dragged myself from bed and went to the stadium. Max and Mr. Johnson were already busy when I arrived in the gray half-light of that cold November morning. Flurries—the first of the year—eddied in the wind currents. The goal posts shivered whenever the wind gusted. Max and Mr. Johnson were climbing the concrete rows of the stands, stooping to pick up trash the crowd had left behind for them. With each cold blast, hot dog wrappers and Styrofoam cups scuttled across the steps. I had come unprepared, and after twenty minutes my hands were red and raw. I was wearing tennis shoes and soon my feet were numb. Mr. Johnson made me sit in the truck with the heater on until I warmed up. Then he gave me his gloves to wear.

We spent another two hours picking up trash until the bed of the truck was full of black polyethylene sacks. I was about to leave when Mr. Johnson called me over. "Don't really like doing this work, do you?" he said.

I said nothing.

The flurrying snow caught in Mr. Johnson's white curly hair and melted into droplets. His yellow, watery eyes glistened. "Let me tell you something," he said. "I druther be someplace else, too. That's the way it is with work. Always somewhere else better'n what you got to do. I been in all kinds of nice places. I been in brothels with sweet-as-sin gals. I been in mansions, servant to a rich lady. I been in dance halls with the trumpet blowing glory halleluiah. I go to the best place there is, the House of the Lord, often as I can. Sometimes you think anywhere is better than right where you at."

He fell silent and looked up into the gray sky, the swirls of snow whipping around and above us like a Biblical pestilence. Mr. Johnson looked out over the empty and now clean stadium.

Then he grabbed my shoulder and held it tight. "But you know there's worse things, too. I been in plenty worse places. I been in jail kicked and punched by the Mon-roe County sheriff. I've gone into swamps and jungles all because of some lieutenant's fool ideas. I've seen enough to know here ain't so bad. I'll take honest hard work any day. Now you listen to me. I don't want you to come back until you think you're ready and willing. Man's got to be in the right frame of mind to do a good job."

Then he walked over to the truck, and I watched as he and Max drove off to the dump. Only later, as I was walking back to the dorms, did I realize I had just been fired.

4. Snow Day

The night before the winter term begins, a blizzard hits, burying the campus under a foot of snow. Well before dawn, I hear in my sleep a steady scraping sound beginning far off and drawing closer. I look out the window and see Max pushing a shovel along the sidewalk outside the dark dormitory. Wet snow glistens off his hard hat. Mr. Johnson's truck is in the parking lot, loaded with sand and fitted in front with a plow. I lie down again on my bed, glad I'm not out there. Two months have passed since Mr. Johnson dismissed me from the job, and I haven't missed it in the least. Or so I tell myself.

I try to fall back asleep, but the sound of the shovel and the churning of the plow keep me awake. Before long, I feel sorry for Max and Mr. Johnson out there working before dawn in a snowstorm so that the college can follow its normal schedule. During my brief stint on grounds, I learned just how much the college depends on its anonymous crew of blue-collar workers. I learned, too, just how little those people are acknowledged. People who have families and warm houses and who sure as hell don't want to get up for work on a cold snowy morning, but who do it anyway. Even now, at this moment, the dining hall workers, having driven through snow-filled streets, are mixing batter and heating grills for the students' breakfast. And Max, who can't drive because of the epilepsy, must have walked to campus, hours before his regular starting time, just to clean snow from campus sidewalks.

Lying in bed, thinking about these people, I get a strange feeling—a combination of guilt, regret, and curiosity. I would prefer to stay in the warm bed. Instead, I get up, put on several layers of my warmest clothes, and go out to join the grounds crew. Max, his ears bright red, laughs when he sees me all bundled up. "You ain't cold, are you? C'mon and join the picnic." I find Mr. Johnson behind the truck, shoveling sand onto the road. He glances at me, then turns away, keeps shoveling. He throws down three shovels-full of dirt before he speaks.

"Stephens, that's your shovel there. You get on over with Max and start cleaning. Double-time. We're going to be busy as the devil today."

"Yes, sir."

Max and I start on the walkways around the student union building. As soon as one walk is done, Mr. Johnson is honking and pointing us somewhere else. We shovel out the administration building, the science building, the library, the dining hall. It's damn hard work, backbreaking, but I discover rewards, too: seeing fresh snow heavy on pine branches, hearing drift-deadened sounds, experiencing the eerie blue light of a winter morning without sunrise. I remember what Mr. Johnson told me back in the football stadium: Here's not so bad. That's what work's all about.

We're still at it when the snow starts falling harder, big flakes now, a new layer forming on the paths we've already shoveled, all our work wasted.

Mr. Johnson appears in the truck and waves us over. "That's it for now," he says. "Let's go down, get warm, see what this snow's going to do."

I could leave. Here's my chance to go back to my room, change, head over for a hot breakfast in a dining hall warm with hearty smells and the hum of college talk, the windows steamed so that you can't even see the falling snow. That's where I want to be, but Max is telling me to come on down to the shop for donuts and hot chocolate. He moves over to make room for me on the truck's bench seat.

The shop is steamy, the radiator crackling and whistling. We strip to our long johns and hang up the wet clothes by the radiator. Max pulls out old, stained blankets that smell of oil and gasoline, and we toss them over the derelict chairs and burrow in like wet dogs. Mr. Johnson passes around a box of day-old donuts and Max boils water in a beat-up electric pot. Outside, the snow is falling, piling up, all our hard work obliterated. Inside, powdered sugar crumbs fall on our clothes. Our skin itches and tingles as it warms up.

Mr. Johnson leans back in his chair, gives me his stern sergeant's glare. "Max," he says. "We got a college boy with us today."

"That's right," Max says.

"Yep. Smart boy. Maybe he can tell us what this word means." Mr. Johnson leans over his Bible and spells out a word.

"Retribution?" I say. "It's like revenge, pay-back. Giving what somebody's got coming."

"That right? Stephens, you a smart boy. Yep, real smart boy. Getting good grades? Good. Good. Well, then, maybe you can tell me something. Why is it dogs go round sniffing each other's asses? See that, Max. He don't know. All his studying and he don't know the first thing about nature. Well, Stephens, let me tell you."

He then launches into a long, involved story about Bulldog, the boss of all other dogs, who saw to it that there was order and harmony and justice in Dogland. But one disgruntled mutt talked the other dogs into rebellion, until finally Bulldog had to show the rebels their place. Bulldog whupped all the other dogs, whupped their asses off, so that afterwards they had to grab whatever hind end they could. And that was why to this day, dogs go around sniffing each other—looking for their proper hinny.

Mr. Johnson eyes me severely. "So you see, Stephens, smart man's got to know who's who and what's what in this world, or watch out—someone always ready to whup your ass. That's retribution."

I listen, spellbound by the storytelling and the quasi-Chaucerian tale. An entire class period has slipped by. It's the best lecture I've heard all term.

The snow is still coming down, hard as ever. Mr. Johnson says, "Okay, we're going to give it another couple hours, and if this snow don't quit we have to clear off what's cumulated." He dismisses me to my studies but gets me to promise I'll come back in the afternoon.

"You're on call, now. You know what that means?"

"Yes, sir," I say.

"All right, then. What's it mean?"

"It means I've got to come when I'm called."

Once again, he gives me the sergeant's glare with his yellow, watery eyes. "It means, Stephens, somebody needs you. It means your services are indispensable. I need me a good man to do this job." He jabbed my chest. "You that man."

5. Summers

I spent the better part of the next three years on the grounds crew. More desirable jobs opened up in the library and in the labs, but I turned them down to stay with Max and Mr. Johnson. Each summer, I worked full time, eight to five, learning the different tasks, such as lawn mowing, sprinkler–setting, and weed–pulling. But mostly I helped Max and Mr. Johnson fix pipes. The water lines on campus had been laid before World War II, and by the time I worked on grounds the pipes had turned rusty and weak. Rather than replace the whole system, the administration found it cheaper to keep Max and Mr. Johnson busy with the Sisyphean task of replacing corroded sections of pipe wherever leaks sprang. Seemingly every few days a new leak was discovered, and we would dig a hole or trench down to the pipe, then figure out how to patch it.

Max was the expert. He liked solving problems, and he liked explaining the finer points of his solutions to a tyro like me. Kneeling in the dirt, he would take pipe wrenches, hacksaws, clamps, and other tools, all the while describing his procedures in exact detail. There was always a hint in the description that he was taking some maverick approach to pipe repair that so-called experts would disapprove of. "Now most folks'd tell you a T–joint's best here, but you ask me an elbow's the best way to go. How come? Let me tell you." And then Max would expound his theory on elbow pipe joints or on clamp replacement, as carefully as any professor in the classroom would. In fact, Max took his role as teacher seriously, and he always tested the lesson by having me do some of the work while he observed and instructed. "A little tighter there," he would say. "You don't want to cut it too close now, reason being you won't have room for the clamp."

Max's dissertations on pipe work formed only a small part of a daylong discourse. Each morning before we could set out for our worksites, Mr. Johnson had me read from the Old Testament. Then he gave another of what Max called "the big guy's sermons," which were in fact exegeses on the text I had just read. Mr. Johnson would lean back in his beat-up office chair, brow knit in concentration, an occasional grunt issuing from his throat. If he held up his hand and said, "What's that, Stephens, what's that?" I had to read the passage again, slowly, while he nodded and approved.

"Now it seems old David got himself in a bind," he might say when I finished. "He thought he could do it all on his own, but he forgot he needs God. That was his first mistake. Got a mind all his own, and that's what lead him into trouble, un-huh. Well, all right now, let's go do our job."

But that wasn't the end of it. Driving the truck, Mr. Johnson would comment on the passage a little more. And still more while we were digging holes or eating lunch. He kept the text in his head all day. Sometimes he might talk about other things—roadrunner cartoons, Duke Ellington, army life, Jackie Robinson, Amos and Andy, and a soldier he called dumb old Butch. But always he would be turning the Biblical story over in his head until he had thought it through and had his say. David was his particular favorite, but it wasn't until the second summer, when I learned that Mr. Johnson's given name was David, that I started to hear the double edge to his commentaries: "David got a hard head, all right." "David thinks he knows all the answers." "David can make a pretty psalm but sometimes he forget why he's singing." Mr. Johnson told and re-told Biblical stories in a Miltonic manner, elaborating the story line as he went along and commenting like an epic narrator. Unlike Milton, he had no one to write it all down.

He was full of stories. On any given day, I heard about segregation in the army, Georgia in the 1920s, jazzmen, comedy classics, and football before helmets. His running commentary favored occasional moments of triumph and a seemingly endless series of exempla on the theme of humility. To be humble was, for this giant man, life's ultimate lesson.

"That coyote, he been kilt must be about a thousand times. Why? 'Cause he's careless. He always forget what he done and why he done it."

"I'm telling you, son, when Duke's band is blowing the A train from the station there's no finer sound in this world. Repeat, in *this* world. 'Cause when Gabriel blows the judgment horn even the Duke gonna fall to his knees and bow to the glory of the Lord."

"Now dumb old Butch thought he got clean away with one, but the Sarge done watched the whole thing and kicked that poor boy assbackwards."

As the long, hot summers wore on, I even grew to like the work well enough. At least I came to understand that even the most menial task had an art to it, a perfect execution to strive for. This was a lesson I learned the day Mr. Johnson left me alone to dig a hole. When he returned, he criticized my hurried, lazy work, and explained to me why the shape of a hole mattered. These were things I had never before considered. When I first started on the grounds crew, I had hated the work. I hated it in part because it seemed silly and pointless, hardly worth the effort. And I hated it, too, because I assumed that I was smarter than the blue-collar workers whose directions I was supposed to follow. Now I knew better.

Other students came to work on grounds. On breaks, they would say things like, "Man, this is the pits" and "Those two guys are real freaks" and "Does the big guy ever shut up?" They wondered how I could put up with it. After a week or two, they disappeared.

6. The Boneyard

Behind the maintenance building, down a dirt slope, was the place that Max and Mr. Johnson called the boneyard. It was chockablock with long pipes, stacks of broken bricks, toilets, sinks, odd chunks of marble and granite, rolled-up cyclone fencing, bales of barbed wire, rusted truck parts, even an old H-shaped goalpost painted in faded school colors. Maybe once a month we had to go down to the boneyard, usually to hunt for a long section of pipe for a major repair job.

Mr. Johnson picked and hunted through the debris of the boneyard, now and then tossing some serendipity into the truck bed.

"This is the boneyard, Stephens," he would say. "This is the junk pile. What-all nobody got use for, except us. We use the junk. That's what we do: we take everybody's junk and we put it to use."

But Max wouldn't go down to the boneyard. He waited up by the shop, tinkering with a sprinkler head or sharpening lawn mower blades while we went down to fetch some pipe. Once, Max had had a seizure while he was alone in the boneyard. Now he wouldn't go back down to the place, and he didn't like to work anywhere on campus alone. That's why Max wanted me to go along with him to fix the sprinklers. That's why he taught me how to repair pipes. That's why he taught me what to do if he had another seizure: how to lay his head, how to keep him from biting his tongue, whom to call.

Whenever I went to the boneyard with Mr. Johnson, I would look up at the pine tree tops against the blue summer sky, and I would imagine Max feeling the aura come on, the tingling in his hands rising to his head, then the shrill cry, the tonic spasm, the clonic contraction of the muscles, his face purple and gray with cyanosis. I saw him lying there alone, those same shimmering trees fading out on him, the wind in the pine trees making a sound like the ocean heard from a distance, and I would try to imagine the terror that Max must have felt in those helpless moments.

7. The Flood

Just before dawn, unseen on the empty campus, water begins bubbling up through the grass of the quad, the beautiful central section of the college. All Saturday morning the waters spread, until the inundation has turned the quad into a small lake.

The president of the college, out jogging on his campus, discovers the disaster. Red-faced, dripping with sweat, he splashes along a sidewalk mulling over a fiscal problem until his drenched feet recall him to the moment and he sees that something is not right. He scans the lawn. The lake has expanded now to overtake the flowerbeds near the administration building. Grass juts above the shimmering surface like reeds in a pond. It's an unmitigated disaster: tomorrow is commencement. Several receptions, not to mention the commencement ceremony itself, are scheduled to be held right here on the quad, the centerpiece of the campus. Featured in viewbooks and on catalogue covers, the quad is "a real selling point" in the president's estimation. Often, he has pointed out to trustees the importance of the campus's appearance in students' decisions to attend the college. That appearance also contributes to the satisfaction of the parents, who are, after all, paying the bills. With water lapping at his jogging shoes, the president is devastated. Soggy grass, flooded flowerbeds. Commencement could be ruined.

From his office, the president calls the provost with the news. The provost gets right on the situation and calls the head of maintenance. The head of maintenance calls the grounds supervisor, Mr. Johnson, who is cleaning the garage for his wife. Mr. Johnson calls his assistant, Max, and tells him that they are to head over to the campus right away.

Max was just about to go on a picnic with his wife to their favorite place, an abandoned drive-in theater out where the state highway intersects with University Boulevard. They like to spread a blanket on the cracked, weed-split concrete between the poles that once held the metal box speakers you would hang in your car window. The big concrete wall that once served as a screen is still there, its white paint peeling off in strips. Max and Ida eat liver sausage sandwiches and pickles and big Macintosh apples from their own tree. They look up at the screen and remember movies they've seen, hundreds of movies since they were teenagers and met at Epilepsy Foundation outings and fell in love, sharing something they had in common with no one else at the high school. They remember thrillers and comedies, shaggy dogs and darn cats, and Jerry Lewis being nutty. Great escapes and dirty dozens and all those Edgar Allen Poe stories, rated M for Mature. Now they see the same shows on television, Saturday afternoons or late night, and they hear the words for the first time. Back then, in the drive-in days, they had to watch from alongside the highway, sitting on their bicycles. Epileptics were not allowed to drive.

One look when he hangs up the phone tells Ida that there will be no picnic at the drive-in this afternoon. She takes the blanket and bottles of sodas and the lunch buckets from the side baskets on Max's bicycle and puts in his tool kit, his rubber boots. Max changes into overalls, puts on his yellow hard hat and rides over to the college.

Mr. Johnson is already there, standing in the middle of the new pond and staring at the bubbling water that indicates a break in the line, a burst pipe somewhere down in the ground. Max rides up whistling. "It's a doozy all right," he shouts. He puts on his waders and sloshes out to Mr. Johnson, grinning as he splashes. He's like a kid, can't help himself. He loves this sort of thing—there's a problem, something to tinker with, and by God he gets to do the tinkering. By the time he reaches the old man, Max is all whistles and smiles.

"Oh, come on now, Max, quit your clowning," Mr. Johnson says, in his severest voice, just like he's said a dozen times a day for the last six years and will no doubt have to say again and again in the years ahead.

Max ignores him. "She's a big one, all right," he says, "just like I like 'em."

Mr. Johnson grunts. "Just get on over there and turn off that main."

Max strolls over to the old truck that Mr. Johnson has parked on the sidewalk by the administration building. He takes a long rod from the truck bed—the "key" that opens and shuts the water main. Behind a bush outside the Dean of Students office, Max slides a metal plate aside and drops the key into the hole until he finds the valve. A few turns of the rod and the water is shut off.

Normally, they would wait for the water to recede before beginning work, but this is an emergency—tomorrow, commencement is to be held on these very lawns. Moreover, this is the water main to the administration building, nerve center of the campus; they can't just leave the venerable brick building without water. So, Max and Mr. Johnson start in with the shovels, thrusting into the watery muck. Each shovelful produces a sharp sucking sound from the earth.

The hot June sun bears down on them—good for drying out the lawn, bad for men digging holes. Max's overalls turn a dark wet blue as he digs. Sweat drips from Mr. Johnson's brow. Every few shovelfuls, the old man straightens, places a gloved hand on his lower back, arches his spine.

Max tells him to take it easy and rest, let him finish the hole. "Better not aggravate your condition," he says.

Finally, Max finds the pipe. They can hear the gurgling of the pipe's wound, but water from the lawn keeps pouring back into the hole making it impossible for Max to clear the mud away so they can have a look at the break.

"Hold on, Max. No sense wasting our time. Let's go get some sandbags to hold back this water."

An hour later, they have the sandbags in place, a circle of them around the hole.

And then Ida rides up on her bicycle with the picnic lunch they had planned to take to the old drive-in. The three of them sit in the pick-up bed eating the liver sausage sandwiches and drinking sodas.

By the time they get back to the hole, the water has drained away some, and they can examine the pipe, assess the problem, determine what they'll need to fix it. This is what Max loves. Pipes. Their wounds. Healing them. He takes off his gloves, wipes dirt from the break, fingers the split pipe.

"We'll give her a band aid," he says. "That's three-inch pipe and we'll cut back oh, 'bout yea far."

Mr. Johnson always yields to Max's authority on these matters, but he is gruff in his yielding. "All right, then, Max, let's get on with it. We got a lot more to do than just sit around all day."

Repairing the pipe involves sawing out the broken section, going down to the shop, finding two nipples for three-inch pipe, fitting these two nipples into a section of replacement pipe that will match what has been cut out, driving back to the repair site, and working the replacement pipe into place. This last procedure is the most delicate because they must lift up ever so slightly on the pipe in order to have enough leeway to get the precisely cut, nipple-extended replacement piece inside the original pipe. Too much lift and they'll crack the pipe somewhere else. Sweating madly—for now the afternoon sun is at its most intense—they groan and sweet-talk the pipe while they twist, nudge, wrench the replacement piece into place.

"Christ almighty, we got her in," Max says.

Mr. Johnson, breathing hard, warns Max not to take the Lord's name in vain.

Max is applying two clamps—he calls them band-aids—to the pipe, tightening down the metal clamps so that there will be no leaks. Again, his fingers must be ginger—too much tightening might crack the pipe.

Now they test their work. Max returns to the bush where the key still stands in the buried iron box that encases the main line's valve. He opens the valve. Mr. Johnson sits on a sandbag looking down at the repaired pipe. Water gurgles, rushes through the pipe.

"A little drip," he calls.

Max slogs back across the wet lawn, plops himself down in the hole. "No problem," he says, taking out a wrench and tightening the clamps a turn or two. The drip slows then stops altogether.

"All done," Max sings.

It is past six, dusk approaching, when they get the hole covered and the wet sandbags—so heavy it takes both men to move one—lifted into the truck.

The lawn is still soaked, a wide sheet of standing water. Mr. Johnson and Max take up the shovels again and dig channels across the lawn to the road where there is a drain. In two places they have to sledgehammer through a cement curb. Slowly, surely, the excess water begins to follow the channels and splatter into the drain. Mr. Johnson watches the water, holds his aching back with his hand.

"Take an hour for dinner," he says, "and meet me back here. We got some prettying up to do."

"Prettying up" means this: in the dark of the night, with the moon and the campus street lamps and sometimes the truck headlamps providing light, Max and Mr. Johnson gently rake the heavy mud over the wet grass until it is distributed evenly across the lawn. Then they break up the clods as best they can, water the lawn to settle the mud, rake it again, water it again, and rake it once more until the evidence of the flood has disappeared. Next, they mix concrete in a wheelbarrow and repair the curb that they have broken. A little after three in the morning, the campus deathly still except for the prowling of a security guard who periodically returns to watch their work, Max and Mr. Johnson drive the truck down to the greenhouse and by flashlight choose several dozen violets, pansies, and tulips. They return to the damaged flowerbeds, uproot the ruined flowers, dig holes for the new flowers, and plant them in neat rows along the administration building and the road that enters the campus. Then they return to the maintenance complex where, on a back lot, they load a pile of bark into the truck, haul it up to the flowerbeds, and shovel it all off the truck. At dawn, Mr. Johnson leaves Max working on the bark and drives over to a nursery to purchase, out of his own pocket—for there is no time to put in the requisition forms and wait for Purchasing's approval—enough sod to cover the scars left on the lawn after all their digging and channeling.

A few cars begin arriving on campus while Mr. Johnson lays down the sod, cutting it with a spade so that the pieces of turf fit snugly. This huge man—at least six foot six—is bending over, sore back and all, pressing the edges of sod into place, studying the seams carefully, frowning if they're too obvious. When he stands up, he takes the spade handle, holds it across his spine with the crook of his elbows, arches his back and winces.

The sod in place, Mr. Johnson crosses over to the flowerbeds. Max has dug a row of holes and is planting the new flowers. Mr. Johnson follows behind him, spreading bark with his cracked and callused hands. Meanwhile, a crew from the dining hall arrives with tables to set up on the still soggy lawn. Five people prepare the coffee service, the orange juice, the plates of donuts for the morning's reception. The aroma of coffee blows on the breeze. The parking lots begin to fill up.

"Here come the big boys," Max says.

"Max," Mr. Johnson says, "it's almost eight o'clock. Get on your bicycle, ride on down and punch us in."

A hundred yards away, I see Max riding his bicycle. I'm on my way to the hotel where my parents are staying. It's my graduation day, and my family is in town for the big event. As I walk toward the hotel, I see Mr. Johnson at work with the sod. I see the evidence, the telltale signs of what has happened, and instantly I know what Mr. Johnson and Max must have been doing for the last twenty hours, how the job played out. During my three years of work on the grounds crew I have learned how these things go.

Two hours later, a crowd of graduating students and their parents stands around on the quad chewing donuts and drinking coffee. Slants of light from the warm spring sun filter through the pine trees. The campanile chimes the hour. The college president circulates among the crowd, shaking hands, extending his warmest congratulations to the graduates. He approaches one family group, introduces himself, shakes hands all around—even the little girl's, calling her a future alumna. They all laugh, then the president asks the graduate what he intends to do next, nods approvingly at the young man's answer. The president assures the mother that it has been a pleasure having her son at the college. Then he points out the newly dedicated student dining hall, the health center, built with funds he has raised.

"Well, I must say," the mother tells him, "the campus is gorgeous."

The president agrees, beaming. "Yes, it is indeed a lovely place. Bucolic, if I may say so."

In the background, a giant Black man in soiled, soaked overalls and a dwarfish man in a yellow hard hat haul off plastic sacks full of the reception's trash.

8. Commencement

On the day I graduate from college, I attend a long series of social events, starting with a breakfast for graduating English majors and their families. A student poet reads a poem full of roads and seas and other allegorical images. The department chair quotes Aristotle, Pascal, and Mark Twain. The ceremonies continue at the baccalaureate service, where the campus chaplain speaks about trials in life and the ways in which God guides us.

During commencement, the president of the college reiterates his pride in the graduates and expresses his confidence that, as we climb our individual ladders of success in life, we will feel the support and training and love our alma mater has provided for us during these four years and which will continue to guide us in our long, prosperous futures. Then he advises us to take the opportunity one last time to thank the teachers who have taught us, worked with us, and brought us to where we are today.

It's a warm day in spring, the trees full of buds and green leaves, the grass soft and lush and perfect beneath our chairs. In between bagpipe anthems, cicadas sing softly in the treetops. The members of the stage party fan themselves with their mortarboard caps, and we graduates squirm in our seats, eager to celebrate. But first a US congressman takes the stage to urge us to remember five main points he has learned in his life. Each point seems to boil down to some version of the formula, "Love God, Neighbor, and Country." When he is finished, we assent and applaud.

Commencement ends with tossed caps, shouts, squeals, photographs. At a reception, the graduates introduce their parents to favorite faculty members, say their goodbyes, hug, kiss, and weep. I say goodbye to the English faculty, repeating several times my rather vague plans for the near future. These professors have lectured me on Chaucer, Milton, Shakespeare, Austen, Eliot, and O'Connor. They have listened to my semi-coherent comments in class, nodding, mulling, and sometimes refuting before proceeding with the lecture. They have marked my writing with long, illegible marginalia full of question marks and arrows. Now they say they'll miss me. They tell me to write letters and let them know what is going on in my life. But already

I can see they are looking over my shoulder at the students arriving to take my place in what for the faculty is an endlessly repeated four-year cycle. My face is already transforming into the composite face of students they have taught over the years. In turn, they are already blending in my mind into an amorphous, androgynous being—the English professor—who insisted a poem said something I couldn't hear, who assured me the poem did not say what I thought it said.

And so, rite of passage concluded, I go back to my dorm room to finish last-minute packing. I feel disappointed, but I don't know why. It's inevitable, I assume, to feel that the commencement ceremony is anti-climactic, to experience some sort of letdown. But I also feel that it has been incomplete, that I am about to leave the college without a sense of closure.

Then, sitting on the mattress of the stripped bed, looking out the window at the budding trees and the green lawn where a sprinkler shoots its spray in a wide prismatic arc across the grass, I realize what I have left undone. The president invited us to seek out and thank those who had taught us during our time at the college. Dutifully, I thanked the professors who had introduced me to books and ideas. But there are other teachers I have yet to thank.

I find them out on the quad, at the site of the ceremony. The stage is now abandoned, stripped of symbols, the flags, the insignia, the emblems, and the flowers all gone. Max is working his way between the folding chairs set up on the grass, picking up the ceremonial waste—programs, tissues, film canisters. Mr. Johnson is folding chairs and hauling them to the truck. They hear my call and come over to me, laughing, congratulating. We say our good-byes. "Don't be a stranger," Max says, his eyes suddenly red and wet. Then he pats my back, extends a plastic sack, and says "Hey, how about picking up some trash on your way out?"

Mr. Johnson throws a big arm around me, squeezes tight, and says, "Oh, shut your big mouth, Max. Stephens don't need to pick up trash—he's an educated man now."

Talkin' 'Bout My Generation

Tonight, I'm taking a van full of noisy boys to the junior high event of the season: the alternative rock band Smashing Pumpkins in concert. My wife and my forty-something friends wonder why I'm doing this. Why would I subject myself to something that will be at best boring and at worst a physical torture? It's hard to explain, but driving downtown with the boys—who are charged with excitement and enthusiasm—I get the feeling that I'm doing this in part because it's something my dad never did.

My father grew up before rock and roll. Bill Haley and the Comets didn't rock around the clock until after he had finished high school, and the new music always remained something alien and incomprehensible to him. Now and then a particular singer or band might interest him, but he never could bring himself to embrace the movement. Nor did I expect him to. We were, in those days when I was a teenager and he was a younger man than I am now, in the throes of the much-discussed "generation gap," or what was perceived to be a rather sharp and intrinsic difference in thought and appearance between those under a certain age—usually set somewhat arbitrarily at thirty—and those over. One of the defining differences between these two groups was the ability to understand rock and roll and to speak its idiom fluently. People my father's age—thirty-something in the late 1960s—were like people who start to learn a language too late in life. They could repeat some phrases, pick out a word here and there, but the nuances of the language remained and would forever remain inherently alien to them. We, the young, raised on rock and roll, were fluent, and our fluency made us impatient with those who couldn't understand, those who were not "with it." Their lack of fluency made them irremediably different from us in a fundamental way.

When I was thirteen, I suddenly, briefly, became intrigued by not just the language of rock and roll but the whole culture of it. Overnight, I went from collecting baseball cards and reading books about Hank Aaron and Willie Mays to collecting record albums and reading *Rolling Stone* articles about Jimi Hendrix and Led Zeppelin. The sudden change must have been disturbing to my baseball-loving father; in retrospect I can only imagine his dismay when the sports-hero posters came down from my bedroom wall, and up went posters of a scruffier, weirder, and less wholesome lot. Alice Cooper was not exactly the role model one would prefer for one's teenage son. Surely my father must have wondered what was happening to me.

What was happening, of course, was that I had passed into the age of teenage rebellion—that riled, roiled swirl of emotions that everyone seems to go through. It was, in fact, the universality of this phase that helped give birth to rock and roll, the raucous sound providing the perfect soundtrack for adolescent angst.

For some people this phase is quite profound, involving a near total revolt against parents specifically and authority more generally. For others it is shallower and manifests itself in a much less severe manner—the occasional moody day, a tendency to grunt and roll one's eyes a lot, a belief that almost everything associated with one's parents is a little bit silly and decidedly unstylish.

My phase of angst and rebellion was of the shallow variety. I liked the idea of outrageous, bizarre clothing, but I didn't actually wear it. I didn't sport an unusual hair style or look in any way different from anyone else my age. We didn't go through "scenes" at home—no angry displays, no shouting (well, there was one ugly scene when my mother tried to get me to wear a corduroy sport coat). Mostly, I had a tendency to be sullen at home, told my parents as little as possible about my life, and, of course, carefully concealed from them any hint of my emotions. It must amuse them no end to see me now, as a middle-aged writer, willingly committing my every random thought to the page for public display.

The one tangible manifestation of my "rebellion"—such as it was—was this sudden interest in rock, especially rock of the most extreme kind, which evolved when I was fourteen into an inexplicable fascination with an emerging genre called "glam rock." Today I am at a loss to explain why the likes of Alice Cooper and Elton John with their outlandish, androgynous appearance (glittery clothes, make-up, platform shoes) ever appealed to me. I probably don't want to know the psychological interpretation. I wore rather plain and boring clothes, leery of calling attention to myself. I thought make-up was unnatural on girls, let alone on boys. But for whatever reason, there was something in the histrionics of glam rock, something about its showiness and decadence, that captivated my imagination.

I can remember staying up late one night to watch a televised concert featuring Alice Cooper. I can remember the particular thrill of seeing androgynous Alice (whose real name was Vincent Furnier) writhe around the stage, heavily made-up, boa constrictor wrapped around his shoulders as he screamed, "I'm eighteen, don't know what I want, gotta get out of this place ...". The words, I am now somewhat chagrined to say, actually spoke to me back then. I had the song memorized.

When the glam rock acts came through my city, I naturally wanted very badly to go to the concerts. But at fourteen I was too young to go alone or even with a group of friends—rock concerts were, after all, notorious scenes, thick with smoke, open sexuality, and probably violence. Nor was my father likely to take me. It wasn't that he refused. It simply never occurred to me—and this is the key point—to ask him. The idea of my father at an Alice Cooper concert was beyond absurd. He would find the whole thing ridiculous and uncultured. He would say what he always said when "my music" played on the car radio: "That's not music, that's just noise." And, of course, his presence would ruin the show for me. I would be aware the whole time of his disapproval.

My father was certain to disapprove because my music was so drastically different from the classical music that he cherished. Whenever we drove anywhere, he tuned in the classical station, hummed the melody of every piece, and had a habit of turning up the volume and saying something like, "Listen to this adagio, here it comes, listen to that oboe! Incredible." He also had a habit of calling on me to identify different symphonies—a ludicrous game, since I could hardly distinguish Beethoven from Mahler, let alone Beethoven's Third from his Seventh. And yet my father always insisted I knew—or should know—whatever symphony was playing on the radio.

Actually, my father did take me to concerts. Not Led Zeppelin, not Alice Cooper, not David Bowie, of course, but the outdoor concerts of the philharmonic orchestra. The whole family went to these concerts in the park, where we would spread a blanket and sit under the stars. I remember being wildly bored—except perhaps during the cannon fire at the end of Tchaikovsky's *1812 Overture*—and falling asleep on the grass halfway through the performances.

So, it is because I never got to go to an Alice Cooper show that I now find myself with a van full of kids heading to the arena for the Smashing Pumpkins concert. Everyone's excited, filled with that nearly uncontainable energy that makes junior high at once the most enjoyable and the most difficult age. My son is bouncing on the back seat, talking loudly about the "awesome" evening that lies ahead. Some of that excitement rubs off on me, too, and I find myself looking forward to the show. The Smashing Pumpkins have received good reviews in the newspapers and in *Rolling Stone*. They're supposed to be musically innovative and somewhat introspective and thoughtful in their lyrics. Some critics have called them visionary. Their artistic ambition— putting out a double CD set—recalls the bands popular in my youth, bands like The Who and Pink Floyd, who put out long concept albums that made listeners think. From what I've heard, the Pumpkins sound like the kind of band I would be interested in if I still paid attention to trends in rock music.

Entering the arena, I see a number of other parents walking their children to the door. Most depart once the kids are inside. I note with some pride and satisfaction that I'm one of the few people older than thirty-five—one of the few cool enough to go in with the kids and brave the show. But once inside, I immediately feel out of place. The walkways of the arena are swarming with teens, the junior high hallway of your worst nightmare. Some ten thousand kids pack the place, pushing, bumping, grinding into one another. I've been to sold-out sporting events in this same building, but somehow these kids take up more space and create more congestion than fifteen thousand basketball fans.

I'm disturbed by this early bout of disorientation. Already this is not the same as taking the kids to the ballgame or the county fair—situations in which I have some control. I'm in foreign territory here, my past experience as a concert-going teen somehow irrelevant now.

The prevailing fashion alienates me as well: thousands of girls in black clothes, black lipstick, pierced countenances, colored hair. The boys are similarly pierced and dyed, pants sagging off their torsos, exposing underwear, their hole-ridden shirts advertisements for prominent rock bands.

My bewilderment and disorientation are further enhanced when we reach our seats and the show begins: immediately, overwhelmingly, the noise-level is way beyond tolerable. I knew it would be loud, of course. I'd been to the loudest shows of my generation, so I thought I knew what to expect. But I did not anticipate an unbearable, visceral torture pounding my head, reverberating deep in my bones. I'm trying to figure out whether the equipment is better than twenty years ago, or whether my sensitivity has grown with age. I look at my kids, remembering how they used to cover their ears and cry during loud fireworks displays. Now they're caught up in the general exhilaration, cheering, shaking themselves, glorifying in the noise. I remember one of my favorite anecdotes—how when The Who played *Tommy* for the first time at the Metropolitan Opera House in New York—the first rock show ever held there—the director of the facility, accustomed to opera and orchestras, hid in a closet and feared that the trembling walls were about to collapse. I've always loved that image; especially when I was younger, it seemed to me the perfect image of revolution, of the new and modern blowing away the old, desiccated pre-rock world. I identified then with Pete Townsend smashing his guitar. Now in the arena, I have a better understanding of what the director of the Met must have been going through. As the Pumpkins blast their way through what is supposed to be a song, I cover my ears and worry about the building falling down.

Still, the Pumpkins are putting on a good show, judging from the audience's reaction. As they play, random video images are projected onto a giant screen behind them: an eyeball, multicolored protozoa, a jettisoned booster rocket free-falling through hallucinatory space. At first, I think the images are meant to provide some content to the show, a substitute for verbal imagery since the singing is absorbed by the sonic blast and obscured by the snarling, whiny vocals. But then I notice that almost every kid in the audience, ten thousand strong, is standing (some on their seats) and singing, shouting, chanting every word to every song. I am amazed by their fervor, by what seems to be a commitment to the lyrics, a passion for the words. Intrigued, I strain to catch the words that exert this power. I am especially intrigued since my own boys are also shouting out the lyrics. I want to know what it is that has so captivated them.

The lead singer, Billy Corgan, alternates between adenoidal whining, snarling, and primal screaming. A lot of screaming. He has perfected the primal scream. What I catch of the lyrics seems to me to fit perfectly with his singing style. For the words, too, sometimes whine, sometimes snarl, sometimes articulate the angst behind the primal scream. On stage, back-lit, Corgan looks and sounds like the incarnation of Nietzsche's Last Man.

Up to this point, I have found the show mildly amusing, despite the din. But now as I listen, the lyrics trigger in me a stronger reaction, a deep-seated resistance to the whole spectacle. I have a strong urge to reject what I'm hearing, to recoil in both contempt and dismay. Years ago, I liked going to just this sort of show with its high-energy audience involvement—a kind of collective frenzy. And for this show, I've been trying to get into the spirit of it, but a growing sense of distress wells up inside of me. I cannot get into the spirit of it, and more than anything else, it's the lyrics that prevent me from doing so. Quite simply, they annoy me. Billy Corgan is expressing a fairly typical teen rage, nothing unusual in that. But what annoys me is that the rage is really not directed toward anything in particular. As I interpret it, Corgan just wants to say that his so-called life is lousy and that somebody else is to blame for it. He's not angry about anything specific—not injustice, not hunger, not war, not poverty—he's simply angry that certain unspecified forces have conspired to turn his life into a mess. All that's left to him is to whine and scream about it.

And by God he's going to whine and scream ad nauseam. I want to say, "Oh shut up already—and shape up. Stop whining and do something about this oppression you claim to feel." But it's not really oppression that concerns Corgan; it's *suppression*, all those things that suppress his yearnings and keep him from being and doing whatever he wants . . . the ultimate expression of petulant libertarian solipsism. Do something about it, I want to say, don't just wallow in it.

If it were just Corgan and the Pumpkins, I could dismiss this wallowing. But what dismays me most is that ten thousand kids have bought into it. Here is an arena full of teens singing along with him, apparently in the belief that Corgan's lyrics express what they themselves feel, an inchoate dissatisfaction and a need to blame everyone and everything else for their discontent. Of course, there's no way of telling whether they really believe in the Pumpkins' words, or whether they are just singing along because it feels good. Studies have indicated that teens are pretty much impervious to the lyrics, that they don't really give them credence even when they have them memorized—just as, when I was my sons' age, I didn't really want to blow the school to pieces when I sang along with Alice Cooper's "School's Out."

Still, when Corgan and his black-lipsticked legions shout—I'm mean really shout—with a querulous snarl, "Despite all my rage, I'm still just a rat in a cage," I have to sit back and shake my head, thinking, "Well, you're all just deluded. Your misdirected rage only furthers your impotence. You'll never do anything about your afflictions by gnashing and griping."

And so mid-concert, I've detached myself entirely from the event and dismissed what I'm witnessing, even though I'm still a little concerned that my own kids are part of what I'm dismissing.

But then, shifting the focus from the spectacle to my response to it, I have to wonder what has turned me into such a cynical curmudgeon. I recognize in myself something unpleasant—a smug aesthete who has to demean everything he sees. After all, I'm not really any less solipsistic than Corgan. Don't I feel a similar dissatisfaction and rage as I go through life? Don't I whine about things and believe someone else is to blame? And for that matter don't I still turn up the car radio when on the oldies station Mick and the Stones begin to snarl and whine that they can't get no satisfaction? Yes, yes, and yes. The truth is, we all must deal with the nothingness in some way or another. Youth often responds to its hurt with rage; but over time rage diminishes into mute discontent. Older, you confront this nihilism with a quieter weariness, even sorrow. Like Prufrock in T. S. Eliot's great poem, you become less concerned with rebellion, and more caught up with trivial matters like the roll of your trousers and the consequences of eating a peach.

I've reached that inevitable point—why, oh why is it inevitable?—when the aging generation finds the younger generation an abomination, the point when the nostalgia reflex leads you to believe that everything was all much better in the halcyon days of yore. Of course, it's all so much bunkum, a happy delusion we tell ourselves as we get older. What reasons do I have for believing that the bands I once listened to and celebrated were in any way superior to the Smashing Pumpkins? True, there was something more specific to protest then—a horrible war, civil rights violations—but only rarely did the music of the time truly engage itself with those problems. It only seems that the music was more engaged because the same four protest songs have been used over and over in the context-setting soundtracks of movies set in the 1960s. Mostly, the music of the time was about what rock has always been about—the young seeking freedom from the restraints that the older generation uses to shackle them. I know, sitting here in the arena, that I should like the Smashing Pumpkins. Twenty years ago, I surely would have liked them.

And in fact, there are some moments during the show when Corgan wins my respect. Just now, he has broken off a hard-driving song and launched into a more meditative guitar solo; he strolls slowly across the stage, hunched over the guitar as if weary with all of this, as if the show had suddenly palled for him.

But his young fans become bored and restless during this electric meditation. Some sit back in their seats and yawn. It's close to or past bedtime for most of the crowd. Some of them screech and scream, trying to call their cult leader back. Then, just when he seems about to leave them altogether, Corgan obliges their calls, returns to the microphone, and screams for them—a long, anguished scream, the primal scream to end all. It's just what the crowd wants. They're up on their seats again, gyrating, screaming in answer, knocking into one another.

And just like that, my spell of empathy for Corgan is cut short. With renewed ire for the inanity around me, I sink into the seat, disgruntled and derisive. Through one, two, three encores, my resistance mounts. I prepare in my mind how, after the show, I'll critique the concert to my kids, and then tomorrow to my class of college freshmen, some of whom are no doubt here in the audience. I'll lay it out for them, explain with irrefutable arguments just why the Pumpkins' performance is so wanting.

But leaving the arena, crushed in the crowd of enthused, howling teens, I realize that I haven't a prayer of convincing them. I'm deluded, a creature driven by vanity, if I think I can persuade them to my point of view. Seeing my ghost in the arena's plate-glass windows, I am forced to recognize that I am hopelessly out of place, the misfit in the scene. In the eyes of those around me, I'm just some old guy in the way, an old guy from a past generation who doesn't get it.

"Wasn't that great, Dad?" my sons say. "Awesome, huh?"

I leave the question unanswered. Still trying to be the cool dad, I fork over the money for T-shirts that commemorate this great occasion at twenty-five bucks—*twenty-five bucks?*—a pop.

On the drive home, I've recovered enough to put their enthusiasm to the test. Just for fun, I switch the radio to the classical station and immediately elicit yelps of protest from the back seat. I'm about to change it back to their preferred "alternative rock" station when something strikes me about the music: Hey, I know this piece. My father used to turn up the radio for this one. I can close my eyes and see him leaning forward, intent on the music, saying to me, "Listen to this. It's extraordinary. Hard to imagine someone could compose something so complex. You recognize this piece, don't you?"

And nearly thirty years later, I do recognize it. It's Beethoven's "Moonlight Sonata," the turbulent third movement. And my father was right, it's extraordinary. I hear something now that I somehow missed when my father tried to get me to listen all those years ago: depth of feeling, *earned* emotion, not the fabricated and readily marketed emotionality that has dominated the soundtrack of my years. It suddenly strikes me that Beethoven has captured the essence of what Billy Corgan was trying to get at with his screams, with his moody guitar solo, with his rat-in-a-cage grievances. And what the Stones were trying to get at in their rant on dissatisfaction. And what Alice Cooper was trying to get at in his angsty rumination on being eighteen.

In the backseat, the pleas to turn the station grow more emphatic. Instead, I turn up the volume and say, "You know what this is, guys? This is Beethoven. You should give it a listen. It's amazing."

And for a moment, everyone is quiet. We listen. Driving along the dark streets, we listen while Beethoven says something about what we all feel but have long struggled to express.

Father Knows Nothing

I'm standing at the kitchen counter cutting onions for dinner when my fifteen-year-old daughter says, "A boy at my school got shot over the weekend." This was in answer to my small-talk question about her school day.

I pause mid-slice. "Shot? That's awful. What—what happened?"

She shrugs. "Gang stuff."

I glance at her and immediately the paternal instinct kicks in, the same instinct that led me to rush out onto the playground to pick her up whenever she fell. The same instinct that caused me to feel her disappointment when she lost a tennis match. Now the instinct is telling me I'm supposed to say something to ease the trauma, something wise to put the boy's death in perspective, something to deflect the brutality of this world where teens are almost routinely killing one another. Go ahead, I tell myself, say it. But suddenly I don't know what "it" is. I hesitate and find I have nothing to say. I wrack my brain, but there's nothing there, nothing but an unexpected memory.

It happened the summer before my first year of high school. My two best friends got into a fight and one ended up with a broken nose. Like most of the teen fights I saw, it was puerile and pointless, this one having to do with disputed calls in a hotly contested game of "Peewee Ball," a baseball-like game of our own invention involving a rubber ball and a broom handle for a bat. I remember that day in great detail, a lazy hot day in August, the sky an electric blue against the pine tree tops, the air reeking of the oil that the county road crew had sprayed on dirt roads to keep the dust down. With the temperature pushing 100 degrees, we were surly, cantankerous, the small injustices of the summer—doubles that should have been triples, outs that should have been hits—finally swelling into outrages that could no longer be overlooked. Tom and Fred argued a line call, Tom threw the ball at Fred, catching him squarely in the face, just hard enough to produce a sting and a red splotch. Fred fired the ball back at Tom. Then Tom picked up the broomstick and smacked Fred on the arm. Like the conflict in Vietnam that we saw nightly on the news in those days, things escalated quickly and in a way we couldn't possibly have imagined.

Before I could react, Fred charged Tom, rammed him to the ground, and the two of them wrestled in the dirt until the taller, stronger Tom got enough space between them to throw a wild punch. Wild, but dead on. The blow caught Fred right on the bridge of his nose. There was a sick, crunching sound. I winced and opened my eyes to see Fred hunched over, blood pouring onto the ground.

When Fred's cartilage cracked neatly in two, I thought my world had cracked with it. I went home and lay on my bed, stunned and shaken by the violence I had witnessed. I wondered if things were ever going to be the same after the fight. Would my friendship with Tom and Fred end altogether? Would the two square off from now on as sworn enemies, dragging me into spiraling schemes of retribution? It seemed, for a few hours anyway, as if the fight had been a momentous event, the kind that would leave emotional scars for years to come. But, in fact, nothing much happened. My mother was duly shocked, but after a few calls to the other mothers—we all went to the same church—the parents took charge, agreeing to see to it that the boys made up, that peace was restored. Tom's mother made a cake and sent Tom over to Fred's house with it. I went with Tom to help with the reconciliation. Tom, contrite and chagrined, was only too eager to apologize. The fathers meanwhile seemed to find the whole business slightly amusing. "Boys will be boys," they said, as if fights between friends were a tradition, a rite of passage. "Every friendship involves a fight or two, nothing serious, just human nature. They'll patch things up right as rain." The joke was that no one would tangle with Fred come football season because his nose made him look as tough as Ray Nitschke, the famous linebacker for the Green Bay Packers. Fred's broken nose became a badge of honor. What had seemed at first a terrible event was shrugged off as commonplace, made to seem part of growing up, just another of life's little moments.

And that was it. We quickly put the fight behind us and went on being friends. To this day, that fight remains my most significant experience with violence, and yet I probably haven't thought about it in a decade or more.

So, when I'm standing at the counter cutting onions, listening to my daughter talk about a boy killed in a gang fight, I'm stymied. I know I'm supposed to say something, to be the comforter, but I draw a blank. Nothing in my experience has prepared me for this. My parents knew just what to say, knew how to handle things, because they'd seen schoolboy fights before and could put the little episode between Fred and Tom in perspective. Now a quarter-century later, I can offer no perspective on what is going on in my children's world. I have no words of wisdom for them when they tell me of peers killed, or of schoolyard arrests in which classmates are taken away in handcuffs. I have no words of wisdom for them. I grope for something to say, but only clichés come, and I know before I even utter them just how inadequate and hollow they will sound. So, I say nothing, feeling unworthy as a parent, feeling old and out of touch. I never imagined it would be this hard to talk with my children. I always assumed we'd be closer, that we'd share a greater understanding than my generation did with our parents. When I was a young father, I was confident there would be no generation gap between me and my kids, not a big one anyway. My parents were younger than those of my friends, but the gap was still significant; they listened to the Boston Pops while I was buying Led Zeppelin records. I thought Joe Namath was cool; my father considered him a showboat who had flouted the code of sports conduct. It would be different with me and my children, I was sure of it. I came out of the 1960s and knew about cool. I still listened to rock and roll and would be able to identify with my kids. We would go to concerts together and stuff. When my daughter was born, I had the idea that we would be more like siblings, that we would always be able to talk, understand one another.

So, I'm completely stupefied when I first perceive this gap that I didn't even know existed. But it gets worse.

I ask if the school plans anything—an assembly, counseling, class discussions—to help students deal with the boy's death (and I feel a twinge of guilt as I ask, as though I am abdicating my own responsibilities and hoping the school will take care of them for me). My daughter shrugs and says, "Same as last time, I guess."

Last time?

I now learn that the boy's death is related to the killing a few weeks earlier of another gang-involved student. Then there was a girl killed by a hit-and-run driver. And a boy who committed suicide. And a teacher killed in a drive-by shooting. And a recent alumnus and former football star murdered near a university campus. My daughter speaks bluntly. Six deaths this one semester.

"That's horrible, just awful," I say, mostly because I have nothing else to say.

She gives me this look that says, where have you been? What do you think it's like out there? I think of all the restrictions placed on the lives of my children—the bike rides they can't take, the walks in the neighborhood after dark they're not permitted, the heavy-handed curfews. I have to drive them to school—a distance shorter than what I used to walk in the third grade—not because they're lazy but because of safety. I feel sad for them, sad for the carefree life that they will never know. I wonder if I should be doing more about this state of affairs. Does she want to transfer to another school, maybe a private school? Should we flee the city for safer, gate-enclosed suburbs?

I ask her if she's scared about the things that have happened.

No, she says. It's not like anything has happened on school grounds or anything.

There it is. Complete role reversal. Instead of me reassuring her that things will be all right, she's the one reassuring me.

I feel like I've crossed over into some parallel universe where things are vaguely familiar yet incomprehensible. My daughter sits there doing her math homework. The problems are identical to those I struggled with in high school. When she has difficulty, she asks me for help, and we do the problems together—just like my father helped me. Her conversation is full of many of the same subjects that filled mine as a teenager: sports teams, dances, puppy loves, gossip. In every way, I think, she is the typical teenager and her life is little different from that of teenagers for decades. Except that, I now see, she's had to deal with what to me is a shocking amount of violence. From the time she was a child, I've tried to be prepared to confront all those "growing up" issues with her. I'm an open parent, not embarrassed to discuss drugs, sex, AIDS, relationship problems, career choices. But there's something about the violence that silences me. Pregnancy, addiction, disease—those are problems that can be confronted. If you know your choices, if you make the right, informed choices, then you can steer clear of the dangers. But violence nowadays is prevalent, sudden, and random. Drive-by, hit-and-run, caught-in-the-crossfire: violence claims the innocent as well as the corrupted. Standing here, cutting up the onions, I long for that simpler world when parents knew what to say.

Of course, the world I grew up in was not as simplistic as memory makes it. It was no family comedy where the only threat to bliss was an Eddie Haskell. But it was a world that could be ordered by the genteel wisdom of Ozzie and Harriet. Or so it seems to me now that I'm a parent trying to make sense of the world I've brought my children into. Back then, Fred McMurray could smoke his pipe, read his newspaper, and in a few pithy lines dispense tried-and-true wisdom that helped all three sons confront the burning problems of their lives. It was a world where my parents could help me deal with what seemed a traumatic situation, a world where they could put things right because they knew what to do and say. It was, in fact, a world where father knew best.

And what does father know now? Precious little, it seems.

Five minutes pass. Ten minutes. I still can't think of anything to say. All my reading, all my studying over the years—and still I have nothing wise to say.

"Dad, I need your help," my daughter is saying.

My hands clench. I feel tense, pressured. "Yes?"

She's got her history book open, a worksheet on the table.

"I don't get it," she says. "What was the French Revolution all about anyway?"

I feel a wave of relief; the tension eases. Here's something I can handle.

"The French Revolution," I begin, "can be summarized in three words ..."

"Hey, are you crying?"

"No, honey, of course not. It's just the onions."

On Jury Duty

It's seven o'clock on a beautiful February morning in Miami. As I step outside, I can tell it's going to be one of those wondrous South Florida midwinter days—temperature in the 70s, balmy breezes, relatively low humidity. Chamber of Commerce weather. A picture-postcard day. The kind of day best spent out of doors—strolling the beach, picnicking in the park, bike riding, rollerblading, playing golf or tennis, or just sitting at an oceanside bar with an ice-cold beer.

But for me no such pleasures are in store. Quite the opposite: I have been summoned for jury duty and am most likely doomed to waste the day stuck inside a gloomy chamber. I could be sipping coffee on the porch right now, reading the paper, listening to birdsong. Instead, I'm driving to the courthouse and dreading the tedious hours to come. I'm not in a good mood; but then few people bound for jury duty are in a good mood—in part because jurors have to arrive at the courthouse by 8:00 AM, and in part because jurors have to pay for their own parking, an indication of annoyances to come.

In fact, in America jury duty has generally come to be regarded as something odious. For weeks before the day you are scheduled to report, you mope about, filled with the kind of dread normally associated with a dental procedure. You plot strategies for avoiding it. Friends and colleagues give sympathy and advice. They help you refine—or hopelessly complicate—potential excuses:

"You could say that you suffered a work-related injury that makes sitting for long periods of time painful."

"Just tell them you're claustrophobic. Or highly allergic to the chemicals used in building materials."

"Act strange when they ask you questions, you know, jerk around a bit and give off-the-wall answers."

Those with some jury pool experience offer astute and sometimes contradictory advice: "Admit to every kind of hatred you can think of—homophobia, racism, everything."

"Act like a clueless idiot and they'll never pick you."

"Be pretentious. Act like an insufferable know-it-all and they'll never seat you on a jury."

It seems that avoiding jury duty has become the norm. According to studies, more than half the people summoned— around fifty-five percent nationally—shirk the obligation, either by filing an excuse or simply ignoring the summons. Add in undeliverable notices, and the typical yield from a given set of summonses is something like fifteen to twenty percent.

It's not supposed to be that way. High school civics classes teach us that the jury system is one of the "pillars of democracy," the very embodiment of the noblest democratic ideal: placing the power of the state in the hands of ordinary people. One federal judge likens it to "an ad hoc parliament convened to lend respectability and authority to the process." But lately the pillar has become pockmarked and weathered. Time has deteriorated it to the point that it's become more decorative— in a quaint, antique way—than functional. Like the other pillars of democracy—voting, for example—it has more currency as a principle than as a practice. In theory, we all subscribe to the value of trial by jury. We readily accept the notion that the jury is the means by which ordinary people play a direct part in the application of the law. We're apt to agree with Alexis de Tocqueville that "the practical intelligence and political good sense of the Americans are mainly attributable to the long use that they have made of the jury."

But for some time now questions have been raised concerning the efficacy of the institution. Some pragmatic critics, such as former Chief Justice Warren Burger, have argued that the jury system is an expensive anachronism. It wastes both human resources and government monies, burdens those called into service, and causes congestion and delay in the courts. Other critics decry the ineffectiveness of juries. Composed as they are of amateurs who lack the training to understand complex cases, juries too often make egregious decisions and administer varieties of justice that are uneven and unpredictable. Many countries—Israel, Germany, France—do not use the jury system. After World War II, Japan inherited the jury system from the United States only to abandon it. Gandhi, high-minded as he was about justice, rejected the institution for the world's most populous democracy.

In the United States, critics of the jury system argue that some trials, especially civil trials, would be better decided by a judge or a panel of judges. As experts versed in the intricacies of the law, judges would be better equipped to mete justice fairly and efficiently. As one disgruntled federal judge put it, "twelve men can easily misunderstand more law in a minute than a judge can explain in an hour." Defenders of the jury tradition respond that judges have limitations and prejudices that might not guarantee a fair result. For one thing they are elected, and, therefore, susceptible to the persuasions of contributors to their electoral campaigns. A judge is also less likely to represent the voice of the community than would a cross-section of the citizenry. Because a jury is supposedly resistant to corrosive influences, proponents argue that it remains the best possible system.

At least in theory it remains the best. But in practice its efficacy depends on people showing up to do their duty, and in America this duty is effectively voluntary. Little is done to hold accountable those who do not report. Officially, no-shows can be held in contempt of court. Fines are possible. But clerks I spoke to at the courthouse didn't know to what extent shirkers are pursued. No one could recall a single case in which a person had been fined or jailed for failing to respond. According to Stephen Adler, law editor for the *Wall Street Journal*, "in almost no instance does anybody suffer any consequences" for ignoring a summons.

As the dreaded day approached, I too contemplated ignoring the notice or inventing some excuse. I was leaning toward the claustrophobia line. I practiced a nervous twitch. But then as I thought about it, I wondered: how had something that had once seemed so essential to democracy, something that had been inculcated in our minds as a cornerstone of the American way, become so detested and regarded so cynically? Against my instincts, I decided to report on the appointed day, in part to do my duty, and in part out of curiosity: Why, I wondered, was jury duty held in such low regard?

From the very beginning, it was apparent to me that however hallowed the institution of the jury might be as an ideal, it surely isn't treated that way in reality. I found plenty of reasons why jury duty is despised. The role of the jurors might be sanctified, but the jurors themselves suffer rather shabby treatment. Criminals are put on trial at the courthouse; jurors, meanwhile, are put through a trial of their own.

For me, this trial began in the jury pool waiting room, which looked like the waiting area at an airport gate—and a rundown airport in some forsaken hinterland at that. For seats, jurors were consigned to rows of immobile chairs affixed to long metal bars. Hyperactive air conditioning chilled the dismal room. The overhead lights, covered by yellowed plastic panels, gave off a gloomy institutional glow, making the eyes water. Like many public buildings these days, the room was poorly maintained: broken furniture and defunct equipment stacked along the walls, empty cardboard boxes piled in a corner, odd pieces of wood and crumpled paper tossed on some unused shelves. Some of the ceiling panels were stained with water damage. Cords dangled. Metal bars protruded. The scuffed walls needed paint. The carpet was frayed and dirty. In the men's room, a hole in the wall between the urinals exposed the piping. The place had the look and feel of an underfunded mental institution.

The room was bad enough. Worse, nothing seemed to happen. Somewhere in the building justice was supposedly at work, but for all the jury pool knew, the entire criminal justice system had taken the day off. Stuck in the depressing room, you begin to think that you've been forgotten, or that you're being purposely ignored, or that—who knows?—you've wound up in an elaborate psychological experiment designed to study responses to utter, abject tedium. Anyway, something doesn't seem right.

Hours pass and little happens. You stand up to take an oath read over the barely comprehensible intercom. You are asked to fill out a questionnaire. You are given a plastic clip for attaching a juror's badge to your shirt and admonished to return the clip when your service is completed. "Do **NOT** leave without turning in your clip," the voice on the intercom warns. "Wait until the number on your badge is called." Movies are shown on the several televisions around the room. About mid-morning some numbers are called. The first movie ends, and another begins. A few more numbers are called. Everyone is released for lunch, then at one o'clock the waiting begins again. Another movie. A few more numbers called.

For most people, the jury duty experience begins and ends in the jury pool room, a long, pointless day of dozing, watching bad movies, chatting, reading. A hundred numbers might come up, but at the end of the day, several hundred people are still left in the room. Somewhere around four o'clock, they are dismissed and left to wonder what it was all about—eight hours of waiting around for nothing.

The first two times I was called in for jury duty, this was my experience. On the third go-round, however, my number came up and I was forced to experience tedium on a whole new level—specifically, the second level of the justice building, where the courtrooms were located.

Around 2:30, with twenty-five other weary people, I left the jury pool room, led by our bailiff down to the second floor, where he sat us on hallway benches beneath some beach-scene posters touting Miami's tourist attractions. Saying he'd be right back, the bailiff disappeared into the courtroom to see if the judge was ready for us. An hour later we were still stuck to those benches, still biding our time much as we had done upstairs in the jury pool room, but now without possibility of early release. The bailiff came and went several times, promising each time that we would shortly enter the courtroom.

We were playing the same waiting game, but at least it was in a new location, and the hallway was easily preferable to the jury pool room. In the hallway, you could observe a slice of the daily action in the criminal justice system. That's one of those phrases—"criminal justice system"—that comes readily to mind nowadays, perhaps because of its endless repetition in media. But it really doesn't call to mind any particular images, except maybe that of a split-screen newscast shot of a stern or appalled judge and the bowed-head of a defendant being charged with some nefarious crime. We speak of the "criminal justice system" rather easily, but most of us don't really know what it means.

My sentence of a few hours on the bench in the hallway outside the courtrooms in the justice building might not qualify as intensive research, but it did give me a closer look at this much discussed "system." I was impressed first of all with just how busy the place was. A constant stream of foot traffic coursed over the salmon pink and gray tiles of the hallway. Bailiffs and uniformed guards strode by us, their soft-soled shoes squeaking on the tiles, walkie-talkies crackling on the guards' belts. Lawyers spoke loudly into cell phones while we eavesdropped. "That's not the way to go about it," I heard one say. "It's got to go through the right channels or he's looking at five to eight, minimum." Now and then people came out of the courtrooms crying, attorneys and social workers trying to explain what the judge's decision meant for their loved ones.

Despite this noise and traffic, the hallway had a curious sanctity to its appearance. If the jury pool room resembled an airport lounge, the courtrooms seemed to have a church-like quality. A three-sided glass vestibule fronted the double doors—each decorated with three cross-shaped windows—that led to each courtroom. A glowing sign above the doors read, "Quiet please court in session."

Finally, we were led into a courtroom. Almost immediately we were led back out. For the next two hours, we shuttled between the action-packed hallway and the frigid, mausoleum-like courtroom. On our first trip in, the judge explained that the case involved some technical difficulties, hence the delays. He thanked us for our patience. Twice more we were brought into the courtroom only to have the judge change his mind when one of those technical difficulties cropped up, usually by way of a lawyer's motion. Whenever we entered the courtroom, the bailiff called out, "All rise for the jury." Everybody then stood—lawyers, defendant, court reporter—as we paraded in. By this point, however, the quaint display of respect appeared to us—the poor saps whose day had been wasted—to ironically underscore the treatment to which we were subjected.

At last, everything was in order for *voir dire*—a question and answer session by which the judge and the attorneys determine who will be chosen for the jury.

The original purpose of voir dire—to ensure an impartial jury—has long since been corrupted into a procedure that attempts to create the opposite, a biased jury. Skilled attorneys use voir dire to create that bias by asking questions that help them determine whom they want and don't want on the jury. They also attempt to influence prospective jurors before the trial begins. The object is to plant seeds in the minds of those who are eventually seated on the jury. Manuals for trial lawyers suggest that in voir dire the attorney should develop a relationship with the jury, expose the opposition, and prepare for summation—even though the trial has not technically begun. In voir dire, attorneys engage in subtle and not so subtle attempts to indoctrinate jurors by asking loaded questions designed to covertly influence jurors' thinking about a case—in essence a legal form of tampering. In the process, they also slow down the proceedings still further, forcing people to go through hours of folderol.

The manipulation and maneuvering on the part of the lawyers makes this phase of jury duty particularly tedious. In my case, voir dire went on and on, the same questions asked again and again. The lawyers, young and overly eager, seemed to be enjoying themselves, the jurors not so much. But sometimes the jurors themselves were guilty of delaying the process. Some gave long-winded answers that included unnecessary and irrelevant details. Others had difficulty grasping the lawyers' points. One of the supposed strengths of the jury system is its reliance on the common sense of regular folks. But it was clear in voir dire that common sense was at odds with fundamental trial procedures. "Do you understand the defendant has a right to remain silent?" the defense attorney asked a prospective juror. "Yes." "So just because the defendant doesn't testify, you won't hold it against him?" "Well, you gotta hear both sides, I always say."

Voir dire ended with a parody of suspense: the lot of us was sent out to the hallway—yet again—while the judge and the attorneys huddled inside the courtroom to determine our fate. Seven of us, or one in four, would be selected for the jury.

The others would be free to go home for dinner and a good night's sleep. We waited, restless and exhausted, in a hallway now emptied and devoid of its previous entertaining qualities, only a janitor remaining to sweep up the dust of the day's foot traffic. The decision took another half-hour, a long, fretful half-hour during which we yawned and yearned for release.

At 7:30 PM, the bailiff brought us back to the courtroom. The clerk somberly read out the names of those selected. One by one the chosen stood and trudged to the jury box. One name remained. The clerk paused, shuffled papers, cleared his throat, then read my name. Sighs of relief from the unchosen accompanied my solemn march to the box, where I joined the other six.

After that, things turned dreamlike. The judge thanked the unchosen for their time. The bailiff scampered around, collecting the apparently precious plastic clips that held their badges. Once dismissed, they bolted from the courtroom without so much as a backward glance at the lottery losers in the jury box. The bailiff swore us in. The judge popped a few pieces of nicotine gum in his mouth and told us that for reasons we couldn't know the trial must begin that evening, after we had a chance to eat. The bailiff led us into the jury room and left us with bags of cold burgers and soggy fries.

At 8:30, the trial began with the judge's instructions to the jury. The attorneys then presented their opening statements—plodding, slow, meticulous performances. There seemed nothing remarkable about the case—a routine DUI—nothing, anyway, that explained the endless delays and "technical difficulties." Fighting drowsiness, I took in about a third of what was said. Two hours into the trial, the court recorder announced that the battery on her machine was low. After a search for a replacement proved fruitless, the judge had no choice but to quit for the evening. But he said he wanted us back at nine o'clock sharp the next morning.

The bailiff hurried over to collect our plastic clips. We in the jury had spent fourteen hours at the courthouse that day. Just ten hours later we would be back for more.

During the second day—outfitted with a new plastic clip—I learned that the phrase "courtroom drama" is an obvious oxymoron to anyone who has served on jury duty. In fact, I came away puzzled about the public's fascination with trials and legal proceedings. I now find laughable all those best sellers, television shows, and movies that feature dramatic, riveting trials. Trials are not fast-paced and tense, as popular novels or legal-themed television shows would have it. Rather, they are necessarily deliberate and laborious. The proceedings lurch forward, full of silences while attorneys confer or gather papers or the judge contemplates a notion. Even the live broadcast of the O. J. Simpson case, which supposedly captured the attention of the country for weeks on end, attracted only a small audience devoted to the subtleties of trial procedure. Most people were content to catch a capsule summary on the evening news—and such a summary was possible precisely because so little had happened on any given day.

From the juror's perspective, trials are achingly tedious. Forced to sit in one uncomfortable place, jurors become in essence couch potatoes without the couch. And, of course, without the snacks, the bathroom breaks, the chances to stand and stretch. Moreover, much of the trial takes place beyond the juror's ken. The trial I observed involved numerous sidebars, during which the attorneys, the judges, the defendant, and the court recorder all huddled next to the judge's bench, whispering, nodding, arguing. The jury was not privy to these debates, and yet it was amply evident that the sidebars were a crucial part of the trial. Prohibited from speaking to one another during these lapses, we could do nothing but study the carpeting or doze.

Even during testimony, the pace is fairly slow. In the case I observed, the lawyers took too long to ask their questions and couldn't refrain from endlessly repeating themselves: "Um, so, could you tell us again ..." The witnesses—all police officers—spoke in the convoluted language of police reports ("I observed the odor of alcoholic beverage emitting from his facial area"). Looking for any kind of diversion, I found myself watching the strips of paper work their way through the court recorder's machine or studying the interpreter as he whispered translations of the proceedings into a little microphone connected to a headset worn by the defendant.

In short, by the end of the trial, it was more than evident to me why jury duty is so loathed. Not that it was a complete waste of time. I did learn something about the strategies that specialty law firms use to challenge DUI cases—in particular how it has become a matter of course for defense attorneys to try to put the police on trial, challenging their procedures, their veracity, their motives for arresting people. And I had the chance to participate in the administering of justice, which is what jury duty is all about—the chance, the privilege (rather than the obligation) to participate, to contribute to the fair and legitimate operation of democracy.

For a juror, the real moment of participation, the culmination of the experience, occurs during the deliberation. The trial over, six of us (the seventh, randomly selected as the alternate, was sent home) retired to a dreary little cubicle where we were to make our decision. It was after five o'clock on a Friday; we had spent more than twenty-two hours at the courthouse over two days; and yet, to my surprise given the constant complaining and cynicism that dominated our intermittent conversations, our panel took its time and discussed—at great length—the details of the case. Not that we replicated the scenario of *Twelve Angry Men* or anything (though we did have our Jack Warden double who wanted to convict and get the hell out of there). But our little cross-section of the community—a delivery man, a retired teacher, a construction worker, a student-housewife, an elderly widow—considered the matter more or less carefully and reached a unanimous decision. And so, in the end, the system worked. We did exactly what proponents of the jury system point to as the system's great strength and the main reason for keeping it: we, the representatives of the community, insured that justice was administered legitimately.

That's not to say there were no problems. After deliberation, we decided to convict, but it was not an easy decision. The case came down to the word of three policemen against that of the defendant. Without any other evidence, whom were we to believe? One of the jury system's most treasured assets is its reliance on the common sense of common people, who bring a lifetime of experience to judging whether other people's words square with their deeds. Supposedly, people have developed a knack for knowing whom to trust, whom to believe, whom to doubt. Yet lately, numerous studies have shown that jurors are rather inept at determining whether someone is telling the truth. Research shows that jurors overwhelmingly believe that an unappealing witness is more likely to be dishonest. Furthermore, the studies indicate that people tend to believe one witness over another on the basis of who appears more likable, assertive, and secure. In our case, we were given the choice of believing three police officers—adept at testifying after years of practice—or the defendant, who appeared in court both days wearing his muffler shop shirt and who struggled with English.

So, as we sat in the jury box for the final time while our foreman read the verdict, I wondered whether we had, in fact, conducted a search for the objective truth, or whether our efforts had merely reinforced what Mark Twain said long ago: "The jury system puts a ban upon intelligence and honesty, and a premium upon ignorance, stupidity, and perjury."

But as the judge came down to shake our hands and present us with our "Certificate of Appreciation" ("for the conscientious performance of an important duty of citizenship," it read), I had to feel that, despite the obvious flaws, the jury system still had value. It's certainly better than the trial procedures it replaced—ordeals by torture, such as carrying a piece of glowing iron or walking over hot coals or plunging one's hand into a pail of boiling water (if the defendants got burned they were found guilty; conviction rates tended to be high). So perhaps what Winston Churchill said of democracy applies equally well to the jury system: it's the worst system in the world, until you consider all the others.

It would be much better if jurors felt some dignity during their duty. Having the court stand when the jury enters, awarding certificates in the end—all that is well and good, but in between these dignified moments jurors go through an excruciatingly dull and demeaning experience not far removed from those medieval ordeals.

So, when I left the courtroom late that Friday evening and started down the empty hallway, I felt conflicted about the whole thing: proud to have participated in a noble tradition but also annoyed at the petty concerns that sapped the experience of its dignity. Just then I heard a shout. I turned around to see the bailiff chasing after me. "Hold on a moment, sir," he called. "You forgot to turn in your plastic clip."

House and Home

The house is completely empty.

I have never seen the place like this, not even when we assumed ownership years ago. I know it so well, this house. Every square foot of it. But it looks different now, its layout altered, the familiar made strange. It no longer feels like home.

When we first saw the house, it was cluttered with the discarded possessions of the previous owners. As we moved in, we had to deal with the leftover mess, emptying our belongings from boxes and refilling those same boxes with the former occupants' castoffs. The kids called it "the junk house."

Now, many years later, as we abandon the house, it is vacant for the first time in decades. The moving van departed this morning and is headed cross country. We have spent the last fifteen or so hours cleaning, effecting last-minute minor repairs, making sure all is in prime condition for the new owners. The closing is tomorrow morning, when we will sign the papers and hand over the keys. My wife has gone ahead to the hotel where we will spend the night. It is almost midnight, and I have stayed alone at the house to double-check everything, one final walk-through.

I start with the rooms farthest from the front door: upstairs, south side. First, my daughter's room, the corner of the house she occupied from elementary school through high school. In this room her favorite color (and the walls) changed from pink to lavender to baby blue. In here, she went from chatting on the phone with girls during middle school to flirting with boys during high school. In here, over the years, she listened in turn to Raffi, Madonna, Alanis Morissette, sometimes dancing or singing along. In here, her reading progressed from Dr. Seuss to the Babysitters' Club to Sweet Valley High to *Jane Eyre*. In the early years, she played with doll houses and princess castles. Later, she made dioramas for science class, mobiles and collages for art. She wrote journal entries and stories. She sulked over spelling and math homework. She cried into the pillow on several occasions (once because I had said no to something she really wanted to buy) and mooned over unrequited love. And night after night she dreamed—thousands of dreams, none of which a father can truly know.

And now, the room gets one final check to make sure we've addressed all blemishes and blotches: windowsills sullied by her pet parrot, spots left from the sellotape she used to affix photos to the wall. All spick-and-span now, the evidence of her presence in the room wiped clean, scrubbed from the surface. I flick off the light, stand a moment at the threshold, see the palm branches bobbing in moonlight through the window, close the door with a soft click.

Next: the boys' room, where the floor is strangely spotless. Normally, this room was layered with projects in varying stages of completion, abandonment, or deconstruction. The boys started with Duplos and advanced through increasingly complex Lego sets—castles, railroads, spaceships. There were always piles of Lego pieces on the floor, on desktops, on shelves, on windowsills. Adding to the clutter were stacks of baseball cards, board games, bats, balls, gloves, tennis rackets, piles of clothes, and shoes—everywhere shoes. In the early years, the boys had cassette tapes of Sesame Street songs, the voice of Bert or Kermit echoing down the hall. Later, they listened to CDs of Bush, Smashing Pumpkins, Nirvana, and Green Day, bass lines thumping the walls, teenage angst on high volume. How can this room be so empty, so quiet, all energy drained from it, the evidence of occupation removed? Where are all the ball caps, the T-shirts, the sports equipment? I find one token: the tiniest of Lego pieces trapped against the baseboard. I pocket it and continue with the inspection. My footsteps echo as I walk the room's perimeter, checking to see that every mark is gone, every dent smoothed over. Lights off. Door shut.

Down the hall to the bathroom. Who would guess that such a utilitarian space could inspire nostalgia? I linger at the threshold, remembering the scenes that took place here. Little kids in the bubble bath. Owies and boo-boos that needed bandages. Then, in later years, the farcical morning disputes over bathroom time before school. The self-conscious primping and preening. I remember, too, all the little malfunctions I learned how to fix, more or less. Toilet leaks, faucet drips. Figuring out how to caulk a tub, how to use a pipe snake. The things that home ownership teaches you, things you might not be inclined to do but that you learn to do in spite of yourself. Then the small measure of pride, the sense of accomplishment when spouse and kids are unduly impressed at what you've done. Now, taking one last look at my handiwork, I see that the caulking job was less than perfect. But the new shower head looks good. And the drains are working fine. New vanity cabinet installed. Tiles re-grouted. It's all part of my contribution to the care and maintenance of this house, just one of several caretakers during its lifespan. And, like the previous caretakers, I am soon to be anonymous, forgotten.

Next up, the master bedroom. Difficult to see this room so vacant and lifeless. It's not the missing furniture. It's the emotion that's been stripped from the room, the intimacy of a marriage. Physical intimacy, yes, but also all those discussions in the dark, the whispered conversations about—everything. Money. The kids. Careers. Impending travels and separations. Reunions. In this room, I spent hours staring at the ceiling while sick or in one funk or another. Bouts with depression or ennui that came and went. I can look up now and see the exact spot on the ceiling that I came to know so well, a spot that now seems to be fading before my eyes. I peer into the closet—barren without my wife's clothes. The floor seems cold and clammy, the overhead light too harsh. A strange feeling comes over me, a chill of sorts, and I have to hurry from the room, switching off the light, shutting the door.

Then down the staircase. Descending, I think of the first time we toured the house, the so-called junk house with its clutter and disrepair, the house that would become our home. Florida seemed foreign to us then, Miami a strange place that took us by surprise. Couldn't have imagined then that I would ever regret leaving the place.

Before the day we arrived, we knew nothing about Florida. Coming from the desert West, we were used to mountains on the horizon, a landscape shaded in brown hues, dry heat. We really had no idea what to expect in the strange new world to which we were headed. Didn't have much more to go on than reruns of *Miami Vice* and the impressions of a few acquaintances who had visited South Florida. What I saw and heard didn't entice me much. Miami appeared extravagant, exotic to the point of excess, a teeming landscape, muggy and disordered. I preferred the arid austerity of deserts. To me, the vast open spaces out west stood for clarity of vision, transcendent spirituality, a simplicity that seemed lacking in southern Florida's cluttered flamboyance. I was exchanging purity and clarity for a prolific, humid jumble.

As the impending move approached, my mind was filled with apprehension and second thoughts. All too soon the day came for us to head to our new home. The airplane took off. The mountains fell away. The Gulf waters sparkled. As we approached Florida, massive clouds sprouted in the sky, an obstacle course of thunderheads. Then came the turbulence of unstable tropical air. The plane pitched and rolled its way over the peninsula. Strong gusts played havoc with the descent. I watched the wings wobble and looked down on a riot of colors, a confused Jackson Pollock canvas far removed from the stark Georgia O'Keeffe land I had left behind.

We negotiated our way through a jammed airport loud with languages I had never heard before and passed through the glass doors into a steam blast, a quintessential June day in Miami, muggy and torpid.

The cabby glanced at us in the rear-view. Something about our appearance—sweaty, red-faced, gasping for air—gave us away: "First time in Florida?" he said.

We nodded.

"Great place to visit," he said with a chuckle. "Wouldn't want to live here."

The drive to our new neighborhood took us lurching through freeway traffic. I stared out at a cityscape that made no sense to me. There were buildings in a profusion of bright colors—pinks, yellows, purples, blues—colors I associated with Easter eggs, not houses. Wrapped around these colors was an entanglement of ostentatious verdure—trees, plants, vines for which I had no names.

The yard of our new home had been colonized by greenhouse plants on the lam. Shrubs, bushes, and flowers we had only known as potted houseplants here grew out of doors and in grotesque proportions. Inside, confronted with walls painted mustard and lime, we dropped our bags and tried to make sense of it all. Ants patrolled the countertops. Lizards scurried across the screens. A large roach lay overturned on the floor, legs pawing the air. We could feel the mold spores in our nostrils. The air smelled at once of rot and growth.

Then the grumbling began. It started with a low growl in the distance and grew louder as the crack and boom of a typical Miami thunderstorm bore upon us. The wind blew down branches and fronds. Rain pummeled the roof. Lightning crackled and detonated. Walls shuddered and panes rattled. The electricity failed.

"Is this a hurricane?" my daughter asked.

I couldn't bring myself to tell her a hurricane was much, much worse—something we would learn all too well in years to come.

Hours later, we went out for an evening walk in the sodden aftermath of the storm. Branches and fronds lay everywhere. Vast lakes inundated the streets.

But as we walked, I sensed a transformation. The black thunderheads yielded to pink and purple cirrus clouds, and a fresh breeze came in off the sea. Birds sang in dripping fruit trees. Most of this strange new fauna and flora we couldn't yet identify, but our vision was adapting. Whereas at first we saw only undifferentiated green stuff, now we began to discern one thing from another. Are those mangoes? Look at that tree with the wide canopy and the dangling roots. Look at the brilliance of those orange blooms. Who knew bougainvillea came in so many colors?

Passing a neighbor's house, we started at someone's shrill cry of *Mommy! Mommy!* Then we saw a cage on the porch, a macaw scampering in panicky circles. The kids laughed at the bird's antics, and my daughter asked if we could pretty please get a parrot.

A block later we came to the bay, a wide sheet of calm water. Right in front of us, a blue heron rested among the mangrove roots. A column of pelicans swooped in and skimmed the water. Overhead, a flock of parrots chattered in a royal palm. Beneath the surface, we spotted a school of fish and a manta ray. Music blared from a nearby house—a burst of horns and percussion that I would soon learn to recognize as salsa. But it was brand new to me at that moment, and we stood there in awe of it all: the birds, the fish, the music, the evening sky reflected in the bay water. Three dolphins breached the surface. A yacht drifted into view, and the drawbridge spanning the bay opened up, its platforms reaching into the sky.

"Wow," my son said. "Awesome."

It was, it was. Awesome and overwhelming. We had never been anywhere like this before, and now it was our home.

So here I am twenty years later, saying goodbye to the house where I have lived longer than anywhere else in my life. Downstairs now, I take one final look at the kitchen. It doesn't smell right. Fresh paint masks the scents of coffee, olive oil, garlic, beans in the crock pot. The familiar stains are gone, stains that told of recipes gone awry. Now the counters gleam, the floor shines, and as a consequence the room seems strangely inert. No radio delivering the news. No trail of ants to the sugar bowl. No gurgling from the coffee pot. No humming appliances. The fridge has been unplugged, the door propped open. The kitchen windows, which were usually open to the breeze, are now shut tight, no air from the patio, no scent of tropical foliage.

I shut off the kitchen light and retreat through the dining room, which seems to have grown bigger without the table, the buffet, the potted plants. Vacant, the space seems to lack definition. For many years, the kids' school years, we gathered around the table in this room to share news and events of the day over supper. After meals, we cleared off the table, turning it into a place for homework or games, a place for tears and laughter. But all of that is long past, as kids have become young adults and hurried off to college, careers, independence. Without the table, without voices filling the room, this space seems not only vacant but forlorn.

I pass into the study, a small space where I kept my writing desk, situated to take in the view of the backyard with its mango, avocado, grapefruit, lime, and carambola trees. Here I worked on poems and stories, writing and rewriting, fretting, pondering, occasionally catching flashes of inspiration. Some of these poems and stories have appeared in print, taking their place in the wider world, and yet for me their vitality is connected to this small room, as though for context they need a view of the backyard, with its fruit trees, busy squirrels, lazing dog, chattering birds, shushing rain. Without this context, what I've written here loses something, the energy somehow sapped from the words on the page. And now I have to leave behind this space that has been so central to my life. I shut off the light, stand a moment peering through the black pane to the shadowy yard, the poetic matrix occluded. I whisper something to myself, a line from a poem written here. Let that be the last word, the last of me in this space.

The Florida room is next, the family favorite with its cool tile floors, its windows on three sides letting in fresh, ocean-scented breezes, its morning light and afternoon shade. An ideal room for reading. Oh, how I cherished this space in the hour or so before dawn, when the air was what passed for cool in Miami. The house quiet, everyone else asleep. A book, a cup of coffee, a slight breeze rustling fronds in the darkness just beyond the window, the soft sound of moths brushing the screen, drawn to my reading lamp. Perfect. How many books did I read in this room? Hundreds, I guess, many of which will inevitably be linked in my mind with this spot, this corner of this room. Elizabeth Bishop's Florida poems. Gabriel García Márquez. Zora Neale Hurston. Annie Dillard. Joan Didion. Marjory Stoneman Douglas's surpassing depiction of the Everglades, *The River of Grass*.

For a few years, when the kids were young, we all curled on a rattan sofa to read together before bedtime. Those were the years of first readers and chapter books—*Frog and Toad, Ramona, The Phantom Tollbooth, Charlotte's Web*. But then we made the mistake of getting a new television and setting it up in here. Next came a computer, and the wonderful reading room was turned into a media room of sorts. The early morning hours were still available for books, but in the afternoon and evening the television took over, the space repurposed for viewing *Friends, The Simpsons, Beverly Hills 90210*, various sports. The kids became accustomed to the pitiful spectacle of their father wandering in, staring scornfully for a moment at some clamorous show, and then harrumphing off, book in hand, to find another—less pleasant—corner to occupy.

The living room, the first room encountered when one enters the house, is now the last one I pass through on my way out. Stripped bare, it looks dead, not a "living" room at all. But no matter how dead this space now seems, I know that it has been the scene of life's rich pageant. It has witnessed celebration: holiday gatherings, parties to mark achievements and milestones. It has witnessed tribulation: sit-down discussions to resolve disputes, make difficult decisions, break bad news. This room has been the scene of more mundane things, too: I think of all the hours spent on routine chores. Sweeping floors; dusting furniture; washing windows. We spent many hours on more complex tasks as well. Scraping old paint from walls and repainting those same walls; repairing doors that "just happened" to get dents in them who-knows-how; replacing screens that the dog had pawed through or that baseballs had compromised. Sometimes this was a room of rest—naps on the couch during Miami's midday heat—and sometimes it was a room of restlessness—fretful moments waiting for a child to come home from a date, tense hours enduring the rattling, rumbling, and lashing visited upon the house during tropical storms and hurricanes.

It's just past midnight when I step out the front door, crossing the threshold for the last time, pulling the door shut behind me. One last chance to survey the front yard, remembering games of catch with the kids and fetch with the dog, Easter egg hunts, science experiments for school projects, photo sessions on prom nights. I'll take with me memories of yard work, too: mowing the tough St. Augustine grass, hacking and yanking at the prolific weeds, picking fruit, planting hibiscus and bougainvillea, bromeliads and ixora. As I pass, I look up at the lovely bougainvillea, which over the years has grown prodigiously—higher now than the roof line. Tonight, the leaves shimmer in moonlight.

Driving away, I am suddenly full of misgiving. My chest tightens. There's a visceral sorrow—totally unforeseen—in abandoning the house. I did not think it would be so hard to leave it. I spent years hoping to escape Miami, yearning to return to the West. And now it's happening. I am going back to a new job—a dream job—in a high desert town with low humidity, a ring of mountains, winter snow. Yet, I feel—what? Bereft. Bewildered.

I stop the car at the end of the block and sit for a moment, my brow clammy, my breath short. It's such a strange sensation, this unexpected anguish, this deep-down hurt.

On an impulse, I find myself getting out of the car and walking back down the street—a walk I've made countless times—walking back to stand at the curb and take one long last look at the dark and empty house. Dark and empty but full of life.

II

Journey through the States

On Journeys through the States we start,
(Ay through the world, urged by these songs,
Sailing henceforth to every land, to every sea)
We willing learners of all, teachers of all, and
lovers of all.

—Walt Whitman

En Route: Iuka, Mississippi

There are good reasons for choosing the roundabout route, following the back roads: slower pace, better scenery, unexpected sights, sounds, tastes. A food you've never tried before. Birdsong you've never heard. An idea that hadn't previously crossed your mind. Something old, something new, confirmation that every day, everywhere there are new reasons to love the world. In small towns off the beaten track, wonders abound, particularly if you happen upon a local museum.

Consider Iuka, Mississippi. On Eastport Street, in between the Baptist church and the Methodist church, a row of storefronts occupies a block-long building of blue bricks. Barber shop, TV repair shop, antique shop. And here among the storefronts is the Apron Museum, a doll in a rocking chair on the sidewalk out front, two potted American flags on either side.

Inside is Carolyn Terry, curator, docent, and driving force behind the world's only museum dedicated to the humble apron. "Good morning, good morning," she sings out as visitors cross the threshold to enter the one-room museum. Aprons hang from clotheslines strung along the walls. More aprons are stacked on tables and arranged on department-store racks. All the different styles are represented: waist aprons, bib aprons, cobbler aprons, pinafores. There are bins of patterns for the sewing of homemade aprons. Craft books about aprons. Postcards depicting aprons. Dolls and stuffed animals dressed in aprons. More aprons than you've ever seen, by far.

Carolyn is sorting new acquisitions that have arrived in the mail: heirlooms donated by folks who have heard about the museum and want to contribute to the collection. These donations often have great personal value for those who have sent them to the museum; accompanying letters tell of their desire to memorialize someone—a grandmother, an aunt—who once owned the donated apron. Sometimes, the packages include photographs. Sometimes, there's a story or information about the garment's history. A big part of Carolyn's curatorial work involves cataloging the letters, photographs, even entire photo albums that she receives. It's one of the best things about running the museum: hearing the stories people have to tell.

To Carolyn, that's what aprons are all about—such an unassuming, ordinary, everyday item, yet there's so much history—family history, cultural history—associated with them. Just in today's mail there's this homespun gingham apron and what looks to be a depression-era photo of a woman outside a humble home, really nothing more than a shack. Someone's grandmother made the apron and wore it probably every day for years. Aprons. You see, they're intertwined with people's lives. That's their essence: they are practical items but also works of art. There's a historical aspect, too, Carolyn says. Aprons tell you about life at a given point in time.

And yes, aprons are mostly associated with women, but not exclusively. Many aprons in the museum are related to shop work or factory work. Here's Carolyn's husband wearing just such an apron, a leather apron from a Studebaker plant. Henry says that he had his doubts when this whole venture got started, but he's come to see the value of these aprons, what they mean to people. He truly enjoys meeting all the folks who stop in, just loves to hear their stories. It's a bigger deal than he ever imagined.

The aprons are arranged on racks, like items in a clothing store. Some, suspended from wires along the wall, are displayed with the skirt or bib spread for better viewing. Several decorate mannequin bodies. The collection is fitfully organized by themes, by eras, or by whatever connections Carolyn sees in them. Interpretive signage is limited, but many aprons are tagged with the donor's name and place of residence.

The best aprons, Carolyn explains, are those made before the 1960s. Back then, aprons were usually handmade. Starting in the sixties, aprons were mass produced on machines. But just look at some of these older ones, so nicely made, quality stitching and all. Some of the aprons on display are more than a century old.

In Carolyn's opinion, the 1950s were really the heyday of aprons, a time when there was a great variety in design and the craftwork was impeccable. She points out several examples: beautiful lacework; embellishments such as bells, ribbons, hand-stitched images and lettering; designs evocative of quilts.

Most visitors to the museum are drawn to the thematic aprons. Here's a set with funny sayings and cartoon illustrations ("How to keep your husband," "To hell with housework," "Eat, drink, and be merry, for tomorrow we diet"). One visitor browses through the aprons that tout a particular place, depicting its principal attractions, the imagery similar to what you once found on diner placemats and tourist maps. Foreign countries are represented—France, Canada, England—and pretty much all the states: Maine, Florida, Ohio. "Look at this one for California. It shows a bunch of tourist attractions, but Disneyland's not one of them. Must be pretty old."

Carolyn has been collecting aprons for more than a decade. She knew of some other apron collectors, and a common theme in their conversations was, "someone should start a museum." So, Carolyn did. She was at a point in life—early fifties, a little money set aside—when she could afford to do it. And wouldn't you know it's turned out to be her true calling in life, the thing she feels she was meant to do, the thing she needed to do. It's a blessing she could devote this stage of her life to this work. She thinks of the museum as her happy place.

Every visitor takes a picture of the quaint storefront, of course, with its potted flags and rocking chair. Photo-worthy, too, is the hand-painted signage on the window glass: a 1950s-era housewife in apron and high heels leaning against the "M" in "Museum." Carolyn is happy to oblige and stand out front for the picture.

Iuka is an out-of-the-way place—"off the beaten track," as guidebooks like to say. It is not located on any major travel corridor. Route 72 skirts the town, a two-lane highway that doesn't connect with any major destinations (from Iuka, it will take you to Corinth or Muscle Shoals). You either go to Iuka on purpose or you stumble upon it in the midst of a haphazard ramble. You could call Iuka a two-bit town, a no-account town, Nowheresville, or whatever; but in fact, like so many places in America, the local history is deep and telling. Once the site of a Chickasaw Indian village (long before the arrival of Europeans), Iuka was also the scene of a bloody Civil War battle (off Iuka's Battleground Drive, across from a McDonald's, a historical marker notes that "[t]he losses of the 11th Ohio at Iuka were the greatest of any light artillery battery in a single battle during the Civil War"). Later, the Iuka area experienced significant change with the advent of the Tennessee Valley Authority (TVA), part of the great transformation of rural America in the 1930s, when massive government projects altered the face of the land and the local way of life. Inevitably, in this part of the country, there are stories related to slavery, reconstruction, Jim Crow, and the fight for civil rights. Every Mississippi county borders in some way on Faulkner's Yoknapatawpha County.

There's one item of Americana unique to this part of Mississippi, the northeastern corner in and around Corinth, and that's the slugburger. It's a beef or pork burger made with filler of some kind (originally potato flakes, now usually soybean grits). The patty is deep fried in oil to a dark crisp and served on a bun slathered in mustard. Onions and pickles are optional. Slugburgers were introduced to the area around the time of the Great Depression, supposedly the invention of a man from Chicago, John Weeks, who somehow ended up in Corinth, Mississippi. The name apparently has something to do with the slang term for a counterfeit coin—a "slug"—though the exact connection is unclear.

According to locals, you'll find just about the best slugburger in Iuka at the Front Street Snack Bar, a tiny place a couple of blocks from the Apron Museum. Dating to the 1920s, the joint is now operated by two women, Genice and Maddy. They're pleased as can be when you stop by to sample the local cuisine, dispensing food and folk wisdom in equal measures and generally talking up a storm with out-of-towners. "Don't let your burger sit too long in the sack," they say. "Eat it while it's hot and crispy. You don't want a soggy slugburger, no, sir." A sack of slugburgers and onion rings, maybe a big cup of sweet tea, and you're on your way, headed for the next unexpected waystation on the American road, every mile a new wonder.

"Strange and Beautiful":
Ambrose Bierce at Shiloh

In the visitor center of Shiloh National Military Park, an interpretive display identifies renowned participants in the Battle of Shiloh, the first large-scale battle of the American Civil War. John Wesley Powell lost an arm at Shiloh (but still went on to chart the Green and Colorado rivers by boat, becoming the first to navigate through the Grand Canyon). Also present at Shiloh was Henry Morton Stanley, a Welshman fighting for the Confederacy; after the war he would become a journalist and famously search for and find Dr. Livingstone in Africa. James A. Garfield, who in 1881 would become the twentieth US president (and the second to be assassinated) was on the scene as well. Curiously, the display does not mention Ambrose Bierce, an odd omission given Bierce's stature in American letters and the significance of the Civil War in his works. In fact, no American writer saw more of the Civil War than Bierce, who was just nineteen years old when he fought at Shiloh. Subsequently, he participated in several other major battles and was severely wounded toward the end of the war. He was even, briefly, a prisoner of war. Later, as a writer, he would revisit his experiences in a series of short stories (including the well-known "Occurrence at Owl Creek Bridge"). Besides fiction about the war, Bierce wrote several essays that deserve greater attention and recognition, not only for their content but also for their contribution to the essay as a genre. First and foremost among these essays is "What I Saw of Shiloh," written nearly thirty years after the battle.

Under Bierce's influence, one summer, while traveling cross-country, I went out of my way to visit Shiloh. I wanted to see the topography of his compelling but under-recognized essay, a powerful piece that details the horrors of war and explores the psychological state of soldiers in battle. Located one hundred miles east of Memphis in rural southwestern Tennessee, Shiloh is more remote and isolated than most Civil War battlegrounds. Still, a fair number of people visit, including the usual enthusiasts of warfare, the kind of folks—mostly men—who carefully study the visitor center's relief maps and dioramas to analyze troop movements and battery placements. Since I was more interested in Bierce than in military strategy, I did not follow the tour group setting out to visit the battleground. Instead, I wandered off on my own, looking for places associated with the Ninth Indiana Infantry, Bierce's regiment.

What makes Bierce's essay on Shiloh so good? Start with the basics: description. Trained as a military topographer, Bierce developed advanced observational skills, not only for the details of terrain but also for military activity, weather, and something less tangible—the "feel" or mood of a scene. He was often sent out as a scout, and the stories and essays he wrote years later are packed with the kind of details that a scout might include in a report—albeit blended with more chromatic details that would strike an odd note in such report. Here, for example, is Bierce's description of the moment when his regiment crossed the Tennessee River to reach the scene of the battle, which was already in progress:

There were broad flushings in the sky, against which the branches showed black. Sudden flames burst out here and there, singly and in dozens. Fleeting streaks of fire crossed over to us by way of welcome. These expired in blinding flashes and fierce little rolls of smoke, attended with the peculiar metallic ring of bursting shells, and followed by the musical humming of fragments as they stuck into the ground on every side, making us wince, but doing little harm. The air was full of noises. To the right and the left the musketry rattled smartly and petulantly; directly in front it sighed and growled. ... There were deep shaking explosions and smart shocks; the whisper of stray bullets and the hurtle of conical shells; the rush of round shot. ... Occasionally, against the glare behind the trees, could be seen moving black figures .... They seemed to me ludicrously like the figures of demons in old allegorical prints of hell.

Upon arrival at the battle site, Bierce encountered a chaotic nighttime scene—"a confused mass of humanity" that included the wounded, the dead, and those desperate to escape the battle—"the cowards ... defeated, beaten, cowed" who "were deaf to duty and dead to shame." Pushing past "this abominable mob," Bierce's regiment marched through the darkness to find their assigned place in the line.

I followed them, walking through woodlands until I came to the place where the Ninth Indiana had encamped for the miserable, rainy night of April 6. (Signboards placed around the military park indicate where and when various regiments were stationed.) "A thunderstorm broke upon us with great violence," Bierce wrote. "The rain, which for hours had been a dull drizzle, fell with a copiousness that stifled us; we moved in running water up to our ankles." Here and there, he saw the bodies of dead and severely wounded soldiers: "Their clothes were soaken; their hair dank; their white faces, dimly discernible, were clammy and cold." Bierce heard the wounded calling out for water. He also saw "large tents, dimly lighted with candles"—the medical stations. "These tents were constantly receiving the wounded, yet were never full; they were continually ejecting the dead, yet were never empty," he observed.

Another passage describes the scene Bierce witnessed as the second day of the battle dawned:

> Here and there were small pools—mere discs of rainwater with a tinge of blood. Riven and torn with cannon shot, the trunks of the trees protruded bunches of splinters like hands, the fingers above the wound interlacing with those below. Large branches had been lopped, and hung their green heads to the ground ... or swung critically in their netting of vines, as in a hammock. Many had been cut clean off and their masses of foliage seriously impeded the progress of the troops. ... Angular bits of iron, concavo-convex, sticking in the sides of muddy depressions, showed where shells had exploded in their furrows. Knapsacks, canteens, haversacks distended with soaken and swollen biscuits, gaping to disgorge, blankets beaten into the soil by the rain, rifles with bent barrels or splintered stocks, waist belts, hats and the omnipresent sardine-box—all the wretched debris of the battle still littered the spongy earth as far as one could see, in every direction. Dead horses were everywhere; a few disabled caissons, or limbers, reclining on one elbow, as it were; ammunition wagons standing disconsolate behind four or six sprawling mules.

This passage displays all the qualities that we expect in a compelling description: evocative images, effective word choice, sonic echoes, specificity, implied empathy, and a catalog of objects that prompts an emotional response, something akin to

Eliot's objective correlative. Detailed description alone does not make for a great essay, of course. What else distinguishes Bierce's work? At certain points in the essay, the narrator (and with him the reader) enters into the moment, almost experiencing it in real-time, not just physically but psychologically as well. The effect—call it the "rhetoric of psychological presence"—is displayed in the essay's most startling—and troubling—passage, an encounter with a hopelessly wounded soldier: "He lay face upward," Bierce writes, "taking in his breath in convulsive, rattling snorts, and blowing it out in sputters of froth which crawled creamily down his cheeks, piling itself alongside his neck and ears. A bullet had clipped a groove in his skull, above the temple; from this the brain protruded in bosses, dropping off in flakes and strings. I had not previously known one could get on, even in this unsatisfactory fashion, with so little brain. One of my men, whom I knew for a womanish fellow, asked if he should put his bayonet through him. Inexpressibly shocked by the cold-blooded proposal, I told him I thought not; it was unusual, and too many were looking."

Beyond detailed observation and startling word choice, this passage is remarkable for the way that Bierce implies a range of complex and contradictory battlefield emotions, condensed in just a few lines—condensed so that it corresponds to the short passage of time, the handful of seconds it took to experience these emotions. Following the intense description of the dying man, Bierce shifts gears with a shockingly crass comment: "I had not previously known one could get on, even in this unsatisfactory fashion, with so little brain." Readers of Bierce's work might recognize here the acerbic, vicious tone that "Bitter Bierce," as he came to be known, developed as a newspaper columnist in San Francisco. To this point in the essay, however, there has been very little of this trademark Bierce tone, such that the example comes out of the blue and at a seemingly inopportune moment—a crude, inhumane wisecrack of the kind that detectives deliver over corpses in hardboiled crime fiction.

Bierce seems to cross a line here, indecency and bad taste becoming sheer meanness. Is there any possible justification for it? I think so. Looking at the passage as a whole, parsing the passage and noting the emotional swings, it's possible to see this comment as representative of a certain kind of gallows humor common in battle conditions, the kind of thing that is said out of shock in the presence of gruesome sights. It's a sort of coping mechanism helping to deflect the terror. Combat soldiers are certainly familiar with this kind of talk, as evidenced in the work of Heller, Mailer, O'Brien, et al. What's interesting about Bierce's presentation is that he doesn't assign the crassness to someone else. He doesn't couch it or preface it or water it down. He owns it and drops it in the text cold, raw, and unadorned— even if it doesn't present himself in a favorable light. Readers hear it and react just as they would while standing there over the horrific sight and hearing someone nervously say something crude and in poor taste. At inopportune times we sometimes have the urge to laugh or joke; when confronted with the shock and stress of a horrific battle, Bierce's narrator does the same. Now, granted, Bierce is writing this essay some twenty-nine years after the fact and could therefore be expected to refrain from spur-of-the-moment crudities; but throughout the essay he is insistently trying to get back to his feelings in 1862, the feelings he had at the spur of the moment. His presentation here conveys the young soldier's response in the heat of battle, and it does so without any hedging or qualification. We as readers thus experience the moment more authentically.

There's more. Hardly do we process our own shock at the image of the soldier and our dismay at the narrator's bad joke when there's a new development: "One of my men, whom I knew for a womanish fellow, asked if he should put his bayonet through him." The moment of gallows humor now yields abruptly to a sobering ethical dilemma: Should the suffering soldier, for whom there is no hope, be put out of misery? It's a question that soldiers on the battlefield are apt to face, and the dilemma was especially common during the Civil War when medical knowledge and technology were not advanced enough to help the severely wounded. Several years later, Bierce would return to this theme in a short story, "A Coup de Grace," which appears to be set at Shiloh. In fiction, Bierce's protagonist decides to administer a coup de grace—"blessed release, the rite of uttermost compassion"—to a fellow soldier dying in agony. In the nonfictional memoir, however, he could not countenance the thought, let alone the act. He was "inexpressibly shocked by the cold-blooded proposal." With this comment, the writer presents another huge emotional swing within the brief moment that the scene takes place.

Immediately, Bierce—who only seconds before had responded to the grotesque sight of the suffering soldier with a crass joke—is taken aback by the "cold-blooded" suggestion of a mercy killing. It's a strange reversal of sensibilities, but perhaps an accurate depiction of the roiled emotions and confused—even contradictory—thought processes of soldiers under the stress of war. Perhaps it is the suggestion of using the bayonet rather than a bullet that makes the proposal seems so outrageous. In any case, Bierce, as sergeant in charge—must make a quick decision, and he decides no, a mercy killing would not be right. His reason? "It was unusual, and too many were looking." He does not appeal to morality in rationalizing his decision, but rather to social norms and the presence of witnesses (who might testify or report). The decision is pragmatic. Once again, in the manner of Montaigne, Bierce does not shy away from presenting his thoughts and actions, however questionable, for the audience's scrutiny. Nor does he hide his faults or try to rationalize them. Rather, he seems more interested in capturing the emotional shifts, the psychology of a complicated and fraught moment.

At some point during one of the lulls, while his regiment was out of action, Bierce decided to venture on his own "down into the valley of death and gratify a reprehensible curiosity." In the midst of so much mayhem and destruction, Bierce wanted to see for himself the very worst of it (perhaps this was the kind of curiosity and desire for first-hand experience that would lead him a few years later into journalism). At Shiloh, the worst of it was a deep ravine—"the valley of death," as Bierce calls it—where on the first day of battle a regiment from Illinois "had been surrounded and refusing to surrender was destroyed." Finding himself near this ravine, Bierce took temporary leave of his regiment to tour the aftermath of the slaughter.

It seems like an unusual thing for someone to do in the midst of a sanguinary battle after a long night without sleep and a day without food under a constant barrage of rifle and cannon fire. Nevertheless, during this brief respite, Bierce descended into the ravine, "the valley of death." What piqued his morbid interest was the manner of death for many of the soldiers whose corpses he encountered. Something had happened in the ravine that, Bierce tells us, happened at many battles during the Civil War: the dead leaves of the forest floor caught fire "and roasted the fallen men." As Bierce explored the ravine, he kicked through an ankle-deep layer of ashes. There were bullet-riddled trees and charred stumps. He came upon bodies "half buried in ashes," contorted bodies whose "postures of agony ... told of the tormenting flame." The lucky ones met with "sudden death by the bullet." The unlucky included "scores of wounded who might have recovered" but who "perished in slow torture" as the flames advanced through the ravine. After examining the hideous corpses, Bierce turned away in disgust and with a cold, harsh, discordant comment dismissed the dead: "Faugh! I cannot catalogue the charms of these gallant gentlemen who had got what they enlisted for." The abrupt switch to present tense suggests that this is the observation of the writer Ambrose Bierce recalling the scene in 1881 rather than the thoughts of Ambrose Bierce the young soldier on the scene in 1862. The older "Bitter Bierce," renowned for his cynicism and sardonic wit, seems to interrupt to say that young men who choose to become soldiers are signing on for their own deaths and shouldn't be surprised when they "got what they enlisted for."

Shortly after this incident, Bierce's platoon found itself in the middle of the action. Many were wounded or killed—"a very pretty line of dead continually growing," as Bierce described it, again employing his trademark sarcasm. At this point, Bierce and comrades were exposed without protection, "lying flat on our faces." Meanwhile, the big guns of the artillery were pounding away, and the common foot soldiers were forced "to lie inglorious beneath showers of shrapnel darting divergent from the unassailable sky." Reduced to a passive role, they could do nothing, Bierce said, but "clench our teeth and shrink helpless" while the deafening cannons did all the work. This was not the glory of war, as romanticized notions would have it; this was sheer terror, the human sublimated to the mechanistic. Hours passed before Bierce's regiment escaped this helpless circumstance and fell back to the skirmish line. "For fifteen hours we had been wet to the skin," Bierce recalled. His comrades were "chilled, sleepy, hungry and disappointed—profoundly disgusted with the inglorious path to which they had been condemned. ...The spirit had gone out of them."

But there was still one more encounter to go: an enemy assault and another scene of noise and confusion, "a tempest of hissing lead that made us stagger under its very weight." Then, suddenly, silence. Just as the battle had reached its moment of fiercest intensity—or so it seemed to Bierce—it abruptly ended.

The Confederate soldiers were in retreat. Bierce looked around and saw new players on the field: stretcher-bearers, surgeons, and chaplains. Their appearance meant that "the battle was indeed at an end."

I walked around the Shiloh site for a few hours, visiting the places where Bierce's regiment had been, including a field near a ravine that could well have been the ravine where Bierce had come upon the holocaust scene that he so vividly described. Paths and traces of erstwhile roads took me through dense thickets and across fields. In many places the woods were particularly thick, and I broke through spider webs as I went. Now and then I had to brush off ticks. There were monuments and markers everywhere, including pyramidal stacks of cannonballs adorned with the names of fallen commanders, obelisks honoring this or that brigade, and many, many signboards indicating the locations of the various regiments, detailing where they bivouacked, where they charged, where they held a skirmish line. Some signs and granite markers indicated the sites of mass graves containing hundreds of bodies stacked several layers deep. There must be several hundred monuments scattered across the vast Shiloh site.

My walking tour took in the battleground's principal landmarks, including Bloody Pond and the Hornet's Nest, scenes of terrible death and devastation. Some landmarks were less ominously named—the Cloud Field, the Peach Orchard—but no less brutal and bloody during those two long days in April 1862. The Peach Orchard was notable because at the time of the battle it had been in full bloom—an incongruously lovely sight during the carnage. Although he had passed nearby, Bierce did not mention the orchard or the blossoms in his essay, perhaps because by the second day all the blossoms had fallen in the gunfire and the trees themselves were scarred and blasted.

Following the road in a roundabout loop back toward the visitor center, I stopped at the place where the Shiloh Meeting

House had once stood, the log Methodist church that had given the battle its name. In his essay, Bierce commented on the irony of "a Christian church ... giving name to a wholesale cutting of Christian throats by Christian hands." Ironic, but not surprising, Bierce said, given the "the frequency of its recurrence in the history of our species." This is the tone of voice most often associated with Bierce—caustic, acerbic, dismissive of religion, mordantly witty. This tone appears here and there in the essay—as in the crude comment on the dying soldier with "so little brain" or the scorn heaped on the "gallant gentlemen who had got what they enlisted for." Such sarcasm is expected of Bierce, American literature's avowed smart-ass.

But, surprisingly, this trademark tone rarely appears in "What I Saw of Shiloh." At the start of the essay, Bierce seems to distance himself from the writerly persona he had deliberately fashioned for himself in the San Francisco periodicals where his work had usually appeared. "This is a simple story of a battle," he begins the essay, "such a tale as may be told by a soldier who is no writer." With this opening declaration, Bierce indicates that he is trying to recover the frame of mind he had had as a young man—long before he became a writer—when he was just learning how to be a soldier, still somewhat inexperienced and a bit naive. When the Shiloh campaign began, he was already battle-tested, but Shiloh was still a baptism by fire for him in that it was a battle on a scale well beyond his previous experience (and well beyond that of any of Shiloh's participants, including the most seasoned generals). The narrative attempts to recover the mindset of the young man who could hear a call to battle as "exhilarating." For such a young man, "The bugle's call goes to the heart as wine and stirs the blood like the kisses of a beautiful woman. Who that has heard it calling to him above the grumble of great guns can forget the wild intoxication of its music?" The naive excitement voiced here at the beginning of the essay dissolves bit by bit as the narrator enters the fray and observes and experiences the horrors of war. It should be said that Bierce is somewhat ahead of his time in calling attention to these horrors and foregrounding them over the trite imagery and familiar platitudes of courage, honor, and glory. Skeptical of those abstract notions, Bierce won't allow his readers to hold onto their quaint notions about war and chivalry—this at a time when such notions were commonplace. Read this way, the essay succeeds in taking the reader through the stages of transition from wide-eyed innocence to bitter experience.

Given this thrust to the essay, it is somewhat perplexing to read the conclusion to the essay—essentially a postscript that Bierce added to a reprinting of the essay nearly eighteen years after its original appearance. This postscript is intensely nostalgic, the nostalgia expressed in purple passages that recall "when all the world was beautiful and strange." Bierce imagines that a "magic spell" has brought back the sights, sounds, and smells of the camps and battlefields he knew as a youth—"the dim valleys of Wonderland." It was a time, he sighs, "when there was something new under the sun." Bierce finds that he yearns to go back to those exhilarating days. This desire puzzles him because he knows full well that "evil," "desolation," and the "monstrous inharmony of death" are the true characteristics of the war. Even so, he finds it hard to recall "the danger and death and horrors of the time" and all too easy to recall "all that was gracious and picturesque." Now writing as an old man, thirty-six years after the battle and eighteen years after his first written recollection of it, Bierce thinks of "moon-gilded magnolias" and mockingbird songs and bright-burning constellations in the midnight sky. Even the memory of rifle shots stirs his blood.

Approaching sixty, he has discovered that old age is nothing but "drear and somber scenes." If he could, he says, he would go back to those days and willingly die in battle—as by rights he should have: "I will willingly surrender an other [sic] life than the one that I should have thrown away at Shiloh." Thus, he brings his memoir of Shiloh to a second conclusion, one that does not quite fit with the rest of the essay.

Bierce did not die at Shiloh. He went on to fight more battles for three more years in the Union Army, several times narrowly escaping death. But he survived it all, and the naive, enthusiastic youth transformed into a jaded, cynical writer who would not brook "hypocrisy, cant, and all sham" or the pretentions, stupidity, misprisions, and corruption of the powerful. For the rest of his life, he would "endeavor to see things as they are, not as they ought to be." That transformation occurred not in "the dim valleys of Wonderland" but on the real battlefields of the Civil War, most particularly at Shiloh.

Given the importance of Shiloh to Bierce's life and career—and given Bierce's extraordinary account of the battle—it is perplexing that his participation goes unmentioned in the Shiloh visitor center. I asked the park ranger manning the desk about it. He knew of Bierce and his role at Shiloh, but he couldn't say why Bierce was absent from the display. "Some sort of oversight," he shrugged.

In fact, Bierce is strangely absent—or only faintly present—in histories of Shiloh and the Civil War. Given the power and precision of his descriptions, his witnessing of major battles (Shiloh, Chickamauga), and his psychological insights into war, his work is particularly ripe for quotation. Yet several histories of Shiloh and Chickamauga do not even mention Bierce despite quoting numerous other participants. A few histories of Shiloh (such as Winston Groom's) mention Bierce only in passing and include a few brief quotations. Bierce does not make an appearance in the Shiloh segment of Ken Burns's long documentary film—magisterial and comprehensive though the film appears to be. Burns uses quotations liberally throughout the film yet does not include the American writer with the deepest experience of the war. If you wonder how Stephen Crane—author of the most celebrated Civil War novel, *The Red Badge of Courage*—compares to Bierce—well, there's no comparison. Crane was not even born until after the Civil War was over. *Red Badge* is a masterful work of the imagination, but it is not based on experience. Indeed, Crane probably took inspiration (and details) from Bierce; of Bierce's "Occurrence at Owl Creek Bridge," Crane said, "nothing better exists." As for his reputation among readers, Bierce is best known not for his Civil War writings (with the possible exception of "Owl Creek," which at one time was a staple of high school English) but for his amusing and sardonic *Devil's Dictionary*.

Before leaving Shiloh, I walked around the national cemetery established on the battleground shortly after the war. Row after row of white stones mark the resting places of the dead—nearly four thousand graves on twenty-two acres. Most stones are nameless, identification limited to regiments or states of origin. From what I could tell, the graves all (or mostly) belong to Union soldiers. Along the walkway some markers memorialize the dead in cliché-ridden verse, the kind that Bierce would have mocked: "Rest on, embalmed and sainted dead,/ Dear as the blood ye gave/ No impious footstep here shall tread/ the herbage of your grave." I think Bierce would have scoffed at those last two lines in particular and then proceeded to step impiously on the herbage.

The statistics for the Shiloh battle are grim. Nearly twenty-four thousand casualties during the two-day affair, more than the total number of American casualties for the Revolutionary War, the War of 1812, and the War with Mexico combined. Shiloh more than doubled the total number of casualties in the Civil War up to that point. The ferocity of the battle is hard to imagine when you visit the site today. The place is tranquil and even drowsy in the summer heat. Unlike other Civil War battlegrounds, Shiloh is isolated, and the area has almost no tourist infrastructure. The military park is beautifully preserved. The woods are dense, the fields are lush, and on a summer's day the air hums with insect noise and birdsong, making Shiloh a peaceful place to sit in the shade of a tree, dozing a bit on a warm, languid afternoon, with the Tennessee River flowing past and the gravestones gleaming in the sunlight.

If you read Bierce's essay, however, you'll know what the superficial calm conceals.

En Route: Quanah, Texas

"**B**link and you'll miss it." That's the sort of thing folks say about a place like Quanah, Texas. And, in fact, I passed through Quanah in no time at all as I traveled north on Route 287, bound for Amarillo and the heart of the Texas Panhandle. Two miles from end to end, that's all there was to Quanah, and it took me not even four minutes to cross it, Steve Earle's "Copperhead Road" playing on a local radio station devoted to "outlaw country."

The song was not yet over when I reached the northern outskirts of town, about to pick up speed again and head into the Big Empty, the dust-blown Texas Panhandle, on a raw, windy mid-March day. But something made me stop—a voice in my head, let's say, that told me to turn around, take another look at Quanah.

I had no good reason to stop. I had gassed up in Wichita Falls. I had a thermos full of coffee. But I wasn't in a hurry, I had no pressing business on the road ahead, so I turned around and headed back into town, thinking maybe there was something I needed to see or know about Quanah. Call it a modest hunch.

In truth, nothing much had caught my attention the first time through. Just another small town, the usual filling stations and drive-ins, a park with a water tower, several derelict commercial properties on the main drag—defunct businesses now boarded up and squatting amid pocked, weed-riddled lots. The one noteworthy sight was a property chockfull of yard ornaments—sunflowers, cacti, a pair of zebras, a flock of pink flamingos.

I tooled the two miles back across Quanah to the southern outskirts, but nothing seemed worthy of interest. The flamingos kept on bobbing in the strong West Texas wind, creatures out of place. Still, I had this sense that the town harbored something—maybe a curiosity, an anomaly, or some clue to help me understand what I was doing, where I was bound. You get such a feeling every now and then as you ramble around. An unfamiliar place you've never heard of before—a nondescript place at that—momentarily captures your imagination, and you feel compelled to stop, walk around the block, take a few photos of this or that, jot some notes, maybe venture into a diner or a bar to chat with someone you'll surely never meet again. Stockton, Kansas, for example. Or Decorah, Iowa. Tonopah, Nevada. Trinidad, Colorado. Waycross, Georgia. Ogunquit, Maine. Effingham, Illinois—man, oh man, what's with Effingham?

So: Quanah, Texas. A good place, possibly, to seek out something new, something unexpected. I turned into the parking lot of a grocery store—United Foods—and sat for a moment, watching as a woman exited the store and transferred several bags from the shopping cart to the bed of a pickup truck. A frozen pizza delivery truck entered the lot and jolted its way over potholes toward the store's loading dock. A long silver Cadillac drove up and parked next to me; a rancher got out and lumbered toward the store, holding on to his broad-brimmed hat in the wind.

The grocery store was adjacent to a park whose main feature was the town's water tower. At the edge of the park, a sign welcomed travelers to Quanah, "City of Legends," a decorative feather underscoring the town's name. The sign depicted two silhouetted horsemen, one a cowboy, one an American Indian.

Entering the park, I walked past a freestanding decoration: a pair of two-dimensional cowboy silhouettes stamped out of rusted iron and propped on either side of a plinth that supported a Texas-shaped chunk of granite. The two cowboys held lariats made of barbed wire above their heads, seemingly poised to lasso Texas by its granite panhandle.

There weren't many amenities in the park, just some benches and a couple of barebones picnic shelters set amid scraggly trees (pine, cypress, juniper). I sat in one of the shelters and watched the traffic flow by on Route 287. Tractor trailers and pickup trucks, mostly. No pedestrians in sight. No one in the park other than me. Overhead, the water tower spelled out the town's name. Beneath the letters, there was a picture: the likeness of an American Indian chief or warrior, a stylized noble savage.

Leaving the park, I headed up a brick road (one of several in Quanah) lined with one-story ranch houses, most of them well maintained. The yards were tidy, some enclosed by picket fences. Several of the houses displayed the Texas state flag. I passed the town's high school, a stolid, somber brick affair, the surrounding field cluttered with over-sized truck tires.

The brick road turned dirt then ended at a T-intersection with another dirt road. I turned the corner and followed this road, paralleling railroad tracks toward the town center. A few blocks over, the courthouse rose above the surrounding edifices. Here, the houses were no longer tidy: cluttered yards, peeling paint, collapsed porches, sagging roofs, boarded windows. They apparently weren't abandoned or unoccupied—vehicles were parked in the dirt drives—but they were in a bad way. The worst of them, nearly collapsed, had been spray-painted with optimistic messages: *God is Coming Back. God Loves You. He is the Way.* And, less optimistically: *Help.*

Near the town center, the road turned brick again, but the dereliction continued. Seemingly every building was abandoned, windows boarded up, piles of rubble in side lots. These were substantial buildings, block-long two-story structures, once stores or offices of some kind, maybe small factories, workshops, or warehouses. Like older brick buildings in other small towns across America, they displayed interesting architectural touches, such as ornamental facades, cornices, and parapets. Every entranceway, every window, every roofline displayed some flourish or embellishment, an indication that someone once took pride in the building's design and appearance.

Some brick walls harbored ghost signs—the faded images and lettering of advertisements from long ago. Coca-Cola. Goodyear Tires. One long storefront on Main Street bore the name Watkins in an elegant *art moderne* typeface.

I turned corners, circumnavigating several blocks, and found no sign of activity, encountered no one. There were vacant lots, the resting places of old farm equipment now sunk in weeds. Just as I was wondering if Quanah had become a ghost town, I came across city hall—an ugly prefabricated structure, windowless, the walls made from mustard-yellow metal paneling. Given all the many fine, empty buildings available in the surrounding blocks, it seemed odd that Quanah's city hall would occupy such an ugly, makeshift affair.

Most of the business activity in downtown Quanah, such as it was, was located in the blocks surrounding the courthouse square: tire store, auto supply store, body shop, farm bureau, chamber of commerce, Catholic services, bail bondsman, travel agency. In the middle of this hub of activity stood the county courthouse, a three-story blond brick edifice featuring a domed cupola and Ionic columns—far more attractive than city hall.

There was one other place in town to investigate: a few blocks over, amid abandoned and rundown buildings, the Hardemon County Historical Museum occupied a distinctive two-story stucco building adorned with a portico, a couple of turrets, and curving roofline facades. The windows were neatly trimmed with fresh red paint. This building—Quanah's depot on the erstwhile Acme and Pacific line—was a remnant of a bygone era, a time when even small towns well off the mainline featured an attractive railway station. The museum now occupied what had once been the depot. Decades had passed since passengers boarded or left trains in Quanah, and the nearest train tracks now were the freight rails a quarter mile away, but the refurbished Quanah depot retained an inkling of its previous glory. Inside the former waiting room, benches and a ticket window stood ready for passengers who no longer came. Instead, museumgoers wandered about, surveying a cluttered array of objects.

The place housed the usual serendipity found in local museums: odds and ends that had managed to survive the years tucked away in local attics, warehouses, basements, garages, and back rooms. There was plenty to contemplate: saddles and saddle-making tools; manual typewriters of different eras and makes (LC Smith & Bros.; Royal; Underwood); Singer sewing machines; phonographs; telephones; an antique switchboard; telegraph machines; guns; holsters; model trains; baby carriages with recumbent dolls; a cast-iron oven and stovetop; hand-operated washing machines; a bank safe; console televisions from the early years of broadcasting; wedding gowns; belt buckles; badges; hat pins; old law books; an official NASA astronaut suit; Native American shell necklaces. One room was dedicated to knickknacks: cups, saucers, Christmas decorations, lamps, pots, bowls, ashtrays, gewgaws of every sort. Any of the objects might well have had an intriguing history to it, but in the absence of information one could only stare and hazard a few guesses.

The displays of greatest interest in the museum had to do with the town's namesake, Quanah Parker, sometimes referred to as the "last chief of the Comanches." In photos and brief bits of text, the displays presented a somewhat haphazard account of Quanah Parker's story. Out on the courthouse lawn, a historical marker provided a more concise, easier to follow version:

> Quanah Parker, man of vision, fought against all odds to save
> the Comanche way of life. Then, he fought to survive and

prosper in a white man's world. His mother, a white woman captured by Indians at age nine, was raised a Comanche. When Quanah was a young boy, Cynthia Ann was recaptured against her will by Texas Rangers on the Pease River in 1860. He never saw her again. As a warrior, Quanah showed great bravery leading Indian forces especially in the Battle of Adobe Walls, he was never routed and never captured. Facing the encroaching civilization of the white man, he chose to lay down his shield and arms in the spring of 1875 at Fort Sill, Oklahoma. As he approached the fort, he dismounted and turned his horse loose saying "There goes the spirit of the Comanche."

Good story. Or rather, the essence of what sounds like it would be a good story. Like most historical markers, this one presented the outline of a story but no details. What made him a "man of vision"? What about the backstory of his white mother, Cynthia Ann Parker? What led to his decision to "lay down his shield and arms"? Readers of the marker would have to look elsewhere to find out.

Quanah Parker's story has a tragic tone—"last chief of the Comanches"—but does not necessarily have a tragic ending, depending on the value system you wish to uphold. Relocated to a reservation, Quanah Parker became a tribal judge, cattleman, and spokesman for his people. He traveled to Washington and met with President Theodore Roosevelt. In turn, Roosevelt traveled to Oklahoma to go on hunting trips with Quanah. His home, "Star House," was renowned in his day and is now listed on the National Register of Historic Places. Judged from the European perspective, Quanah Parker's story ends with success and contentment.

Nine years after Quanah Parker's surrender, a newly organized railroad town in Texas decided to adopt the name of the "last chief of the Comanches." Apparently, there is no record of what led to this decision. At least, I couldn't find an explanation in the town museum. The historical marker on the courthouse lawn did note, however, that in 1890 Quanah Parker visited the town and pronounced a blessing: "May the great spirit smile on your little town, may the rain fall in season, and in the warmth of sunshine after the rain, may the earth yield bountifully. May peace and contentment be with you and your children forever."

Quanah Parker's story stayed on my mind as I left the town named for him and headed north to Amarillo. Like many American Indians of his generation, he saw the demise of his culture and the transformation of his homelands into an alien world. When Quanah was born in 1845, the buffalo—source of life for the Comanche—was the most populous mammal on the Great Plains; by the time he reached middle age, the buffalo had been driven to near-extinction. Everything he knew from his boyhood and youth was gone. As he reportedly put it, "the spirit of the Comanche" had vanished.

How remarkably generous, then, that in 1890—the year of Wounded Knee and the effective end of American Indian resistance to the hostile takeover of their lands—Quanah Parker could find it in his heart to bless the town of Quanah and wish "peace and contentment" for those who had driven him and his people from their ancestral homelands. Did he really wish it? I had to wonder. It was certainly convenient for the citizens of Quanah to think so. But isn't it possible that this "blessing" was exaggerated in the news reports of the day? Indeed, the reported language of Quanah Parker's blessing has overtones of invented "Indian speech" commonly used in dime westerns at the time (and later in Hollywood westerns).

But who can say? History—as written by whites—reports that Quanah Parker blessed the town, and the story is likely to endure.

On the Oregon Trail

The landscape of the American West has to be seen to be believed.
And perhaps, conversely, it has to be believed in order to be seen.
— N. Scott Momaday

Midway through a long westward journey, I came to Fort Laramie in southeastern Wyoming.

To get there, I had followed a roundabout route, stopping here and there at historical sites and natural wonders. Months earlier, I had quit my job, canceled the lease on my apartment, dropped off most of my household goods at the thrift store, loaded what remained in the van, and set out on the road. I had a fuzzy idea that I could start over somewhere out west.

I proceeded slowly and haphazardly. I took detours to visit friends and see places I had read about, places that, for whatever reason, sparked my curiosity. Fort Laramie was one such place. In fact, I had long wanted to visit the legendary fort. In high school, I had read Francis Parkman's *Oregon Trail*, one of those books that you pick up with reluctance—no one likes "required reading"— and seemingly trudge through, only to discover years later that you remember many more details from the required book than you do from dozens of others that you had read eagerly and loved at the time. So it was for me with *The Oregon Trail*. Planning my own getaway, I remembered Parkman's desire to escape the stultifying east of his upbringing for what amounted to a research trip among the American Indian tribes of the high plains ("a summer's journey out of bounds," he called it). This urge to steal away—found in Thoreau, Melville, Steinbeck, Kerouac, and so many others—resonated with me, first as a restless young man and again as I faced middle age. Scenes and images in *The Oregon Trail*—bison hunts, thunderstorms on the prairies, long horseback rides without meeting another soul—came back to me and fueled my desire to escape, to undertake my own "journey out of bounds." In anticipation of seeing some of the places that Parkman wrote about, I re-read his book as I slowly traveled west. When I arrived at Fort Laramie, now a national historic site, Parkman's description of the place was fresh on my mind, and I entered the grounds expecting to find something at least vaguely reminiscent of what Parkman had described in *The Oregon Trail*.

But more than a century and a half after his visit, any trace of the trading post that Parkman described had long since vanished. Instead, the national historic site that I encountered memorialized the military facility that had eventually replaced the trading post in the 1850s. The place as I saw it looked a little like the campus of a military school. I walked around the grounds peering into officer's quarters, barracks, stables, stores, and the like—all reconstructions, the historic site having become a facsimile of the fort that had once existed.

To Parkman, visiting in 1846, Fort Laramie had seemed "less like a reality than like some fanciful picture of the olden time." The same could be said nowadays, especially during one of the historic site's "living history" days, when volunteers dress up in period costumes and engage in period-authentic activities. Soldiers march around the grounds. Stable boys, sutlers, even officer's wives stroll along posing for tourist photos. The conversations of the mock soldiers sound a bit like dialogue ripped from John Wayne movies. In the fort store, a replica of the original commissary, you can peruse the shelves to see what was available in 1880 (Tabasco Sauce, surprisingly) or you can order a sarsaparilla served up by a clerk dressed as an Old West saloonkeeper who will call you "pardner." Like many places along the western tourist trails, modern reconstruction has given Fort Laramie a movie-set atmosphere. In your head, you might hear Ennio Morricone themes, and you half expect Clint Eastwood or John Wayne to mosey out of the reconstructed barracks, headed for the parade grounds.

The fort—or some fanciful replica of it in a Hollywood backlot—did, in fact, serve as the setting for several movies, such as *Revolt at Fort Laramie*, starring John Dehner, and *White Feather*, starring Robert Wagner. There was also a radio show in the 1950s called *Fort Laramie*—described in the introduction to each episode as "the saga of fighting men who rode the rim of empire." Raymond Burr gave voice to the main character, whose job on "the rim of empire" was to civilize the region at gunpoint. The fort's role in empire building has remained a key theme in the historic site's interpretive materials. According to the audio tour that you can listen to on rented headphones, "Fort Laramie played a decisive role in the westward expansion," first as a trading post for fur trappers and westbound emigrants, then as a military post at the center of the campaign against the Sioux. At Fort Laramie, treaties were made and quickly broken, most notably the 1851 treaty recognizing Native American rights to the surrounding land—a treaty that the United States would soon ignore. At today's historic site, most of the focus is on the fort's military role—and this attention seems fitting given the intense militarization of the American West (then and now). On reenactment days, you can hear plenty of gunfire and cannon fire. During the time I wandered around the grounds, cannon firings seemed to come on the quarter hour, much to the delight of families on summer vacations.

Parkman saw nothing of the US military on his visit to Fort Laramie. At that time, the nearest army outpost was still seven hundred miles to the east. Instead, he saw Canadian trappers getting ready to head farther west on fur-hunting expeditions. He saw the arrival of pioneers, describing them as a "crowd of broad-brimmed hats, thin visages, and staring eyes . . . like men totally out of their element." The pioneer women, he said, had "cadaverous faces." Parkman also made several visits to a nearby Sioux encampment, where he and his traveling companion dispensed medicine and were treated to a feast of dog meat. The scholar noted the burial platforms of the natives and "mystic circles" of buffalo skulls. He also noted, somewhat suggestively, the "buxom young squaws, blooming in all the charms of vermilion." These "scenes at Fort Laramie" (as he titled the relevant chapter in *The Oregon Trail*) constituted what he considered a "fanciful picture of the olden time." It is striking to read this observation from someone writing in 1846—in the midst of what we think of as the heyday of the Wild West. More than a century and a half later, when reenactment and replica have become the rule, the picture is much more fanciful, by a long shot, than what Parkman encountered.

Outside of Guernsey, Wyoming, I came to Register Cliff, another site associated with the Oregon Trail. A dirt road led to a dust-blown parking lot and a historical marker at the base of a sandstone precipice rising one hundred feet above a bend in the North Platte River. According to the marker, the pioneers usually made this place their first encampment after leaving Fort Laramie. The soft, chalky sandstone of the cliff wall provided an opportunity for the pioneers to carve their names on the face; some seven hundred names have survived time and the elements. I wandered along the wall reading and photographing the inscriptions, including those left by:

G. O. Willard Boston 1855
R. Nesbit August 2 1855

J. W. Roll 1857 U.S. Post
S. H. Patrick June 6 1850

As the interpretive sign somewhat clumsily phrased it, "emigrants felt the need to leave their mark on the significant journey of their lives." For some, it was the last mark they left. One A. H. Unthank boldly inscribed his name on Register Cliff. He was nineteen and on his way to California for the Gold Rush, but he died of cholera only nine days beyond Register Cliff and was buried near present-day Glenrock, Wyoming. Some people did not make it past this point, as evidenced by three anonymous graves at the base of the cliff.

Other than the names and the graves, I saw little evidence of the erstwhile campsite. Once there had been a trading post and a Pony Express stop at Register Cliff, but no trace remained, as far as I could see. What else had vanished? According to the interpretive sign, Native Americans had marked these cliffs as well; pictographs and petroglyphs used to be visible, but "those images have been lost in the flood of white names on the rock"— just as the American Indian presence in this part of Wyoming had been all but lost in the flood of white invaders.

On the other side of Guernsey, I stopped to see a preserved remnant of the actual Oregon Trail, deep ruts of the kind that trail buffs (or "rut nuts," as they call themselves) love to ponder and photograph. In the mid-nineteenth century, tens of thousands of wagons passed over this spot, gradually wearing the limestone bedrock into grooves. Ever since the trail years, rainwater has coursed in these grooves deepening them into smooth ruts, like a plaster cast of the trail. It is one of the few places along the old route where the trail is readily visible, where it hasn't vanished beneath highways or plowed fields or development of some kind.

From the site's parking lot, a short winding path led up a steep hill to the ruts. A family followed behind me, two teenage girls and their father, who wore a white safari hat, his nose slathered with sunscreen.

"Here it is, girls," he said.

Staggering up the last portion of the path, the girls were not happy.

"It's too steep," one said.

The father jumped down into the ruts. "Wow, this is really cool," he said. "Check it out, girls." The girls were looking the other way, taking in the view of the parking lot down below. In the near distance, there was a small airport, train tracks, and various structures indicative of industrial agriculture; farther off was the town of Guernsey, looking like the toy towns that line miniature railroads.

"Look, there's mom." The girls waved. A woman down below, hand shielding her eyes from the sun, gazed up at the hill and waved back. "Hi, mom," the girls shouted in unison.

"Anything to see up there?" the mother shouted back.

The girls looked around, glancing over the ruts, then turned back to their mother.

"Not really." With that, the mother disappeared through the door of a motorhome. The girls turned to their father.

"Is this what you wanted to see, dad? Take a picture already and let's go."

Next to the ruts, a sign interpreted the site for visitors in a prose style so beautifully overblown that I just had to copy the text into my notebook: "Wagon wheels cut solid rock, carving a memorial to Empire Builders. What manner of men and beasts impelled conveyances weighing on those grinding wheels? Look! A line of shadows crossing boundless wilderness." It continued in this vein for more than two hundred words. I had read many a historical marker along the way; none could match this one for purple prose and tortured syntax (to wit: "Foremost, nimble mules drawing their carts, come poised Mountain Men carrying trade goods to a fur fair—the Rendezvous"). While I copied the words, the man in the safari hat came over to take a picture of the sign. Ignoring the historical marker, the girls continued to complain until dad couldn't take it anymore. "Hey, girls, what do you say we find a McDonald's and get some grub," he said. The girls responded with a perky cry of "Yippee!" and went skipping down the path with an enthusiasm not previously in evidence. I turned my attention back to the sign, writing out the last words: "Now the apparition fades in a changing environment. Dimly seen, this last commerce serves a new, pastoral society; the era of the cattle baron and the advent of settlement blot the Oregon Trail."

For all its bad prose, the sign was on to something with that last sentence. The word "blot" rang true to me, for I had seen many a blot and blight during my months-long ramble along the old roads and trails. In fact, exploring around a bit, I found a prime example of "blot" just a short distance from the interpretive sign. Following the wagon tracks, I soon came upon a barbed wire fence strung across the defunct trail. A sign read: "Private Property No Trespassing." Apparently, the Oregon Trail was now fenced-off and through-passage was not permitted.

Turned away in one direction, I decided to try the trail in the other direction, but soon came to another fence, this one even more forbidding, posted as it was with danger signs: "Do not enter—Bullet Impact Area." It was the boundary line for a military training facility, Camp Guernsey, where training for war in Afghanistan was being conducted. As I stood there, blocked from following the trail, an AC-130 gunship hovered in the distance, and every couple of minutes the sound of detonations and explosions indicated that training was at full bore: "the sound of freedom," as folks who live near military facilities like to say.

* * *

A detour took me away from the Oregon Trail out to yet another isolated historical marker. I didn't know what I expected to see, but I felt that I had to visit Teapot Dome simply because it was one of the few places in Wyoming mentioned in history textbooks. In those cursory American history classes that one takes in high school or college, Wyoming is rarely acknowledged, and then only briefly. Other than the Oregon Trail, what else is there? In passing one might learn that Wyoming was the first state to give women the right to vote, or that Yellowstone was the first national park. A few colorful characters, such as Jim Bridger, Buffalo Bill, and Butch Cassidy, had some connection to the state. At one time, students might have read Owen Wister's tales of Wyoming, especially *The Virginian*, but time has consigned the book to the backlist. Otherwise, Wyoming gets scant attention. But there was one historical moment when Wyoming was more or less center stage, at least for a scene or two: the Teapot Dome scandal in the early 1920s. In brief, the scandal involved the Secretary of the Interior (Albert Fall) accepting bribes for granting extraction rights to the oil on government lands, in this case an oil field in Wyoming that had been set aside as a reserve for the navy's oil needs. A government official in cahoots with a corporation was not a rare occurrence, but in this case it involved a cabinet-level official and the scandal threatened the presidency of Warren Harding. Several years later, Fall was eventually convicted and sent to prison. The oil company in question, Sinclair Oil, suffered no real consequences and over the decades became a prominent player in the oil game, its green dinosaur logo familiar to highway travelers.

Teapot Dome was Wyoming's most significant moment on the national stage, if you go by the record in the textbooks. Wondering what there was of Teapot Dome to see, I detoured from the Oregon Trail route I had been following to venture up State Highway 259, north out of Casper. What I found was a white promontory about a half-mile from the highway. The locale might best be described as "windswept." The large rock may have looked like a teapot at one time, but it no longer did, erosion having done away with the spout and handle.

The rock wasn't much to look at, but there were a couple of interpretive signs to read. Made of rusted metal, they were designed to look like oil derricks, complete with decorative gusher plumes emerging from the top. One sign told the story of Teapot Dome, concluding that "the result of the Teapot Dome Scandal was to open the public's eyes to the close relationship between government and big business." The companion sign, detailing development of the huge Salt Creek oilfield, noted that this development "accompanied the evolving interest in the West from a romantic wilderness to a resource of mineral wealth." In other words, exploitation eventually supplanted the frontier myth. But exploitation, in the view of the sign's sponsors, was not necessarily a bad thing: "It is responsible for the general prosperity and development of this region as well as the growth of Casper. Oil taxes have benefitted education, built good roads, and provided community services." Here, as elsewhere, the underlying (or in this case overt) message seemed to undercut the state's "brand message." In marketing materials geared toward prospective tourists, Wyoming—using the tagline, "Forever West"—promoted the imagery of a "romantic wilderness," but operations and reality on the ground were more concerned with exploiting the land as "a resource of mineral wealth." The message for tourists gave a nod to the idealized imagery, but the more material point articulated on the historical marker emphasized Wyoming's role as "an energy state and contributor to the nation's energy suppliers." Such are the contradictions of the Western myth.

Independence Rock, the famous Oregon Trail landmark, is now managed as a State of Wyoming historic site and rest area: toilets, vending machines, a small interpretive display, a picnic area, and a trail leading out to the distinctive granite dome. I met the caretaker of the facility, Mr. Long, inside the men's room, where he was stocking the soap and paper supplies.

Hundreds of people stopped each day, Mr. Long said. From his point of view, they were plain messy. They dropped trash, spilled water, and fouled the restrooms. Some people were "downright thickheaded, got shit for brains." It never ceased to amaze him.

"There are folks don't even see the rock 'til you point it out to them. They think it's one of them boulders out front by the picnic tables. They want to know where the names are."

Mr. Long lived in the trailer behind the rest area. He had been retired for years, but "couldn't sit still no longer." So, he contracted with the state to service the rest area. He mowed the lawns, cleaned the buildings, and picked up the trash people threw into the sagebrush. Even with the mess and all, he said, he loved being out on the high plains. "You got your open spaces, your clean air, your fishing in the reservoir. Way I see it, it's a little bit of heaven right here." It didn't bother him in the least to be far from the amenities of the city: Casper was a mess, ugly and congested. And he wouldn't even think about going down to Denver. "I'm done with city life. Done for good," he said.

After talking to Mr. Long, I walked out to the 130-foot-high domed rock to read some of the names carved there: *W. H. Collins 1862, R. McOord 1850, B. Garret 1853, P. Hollister, A. Power, J. L. Holland,* and on and on—hundreds of names. Landmarks and historical sites dotted the old pioneer trails I was following. At each site there were chiseled and scratched names, footprints, ghost voices whispering their longing to move on, move on in pursuit of the golden dream of the West. Somewhere up ahead at trail's end, we all wanted to believe, there was a promised land, the "Great West," as Thoreau called it, "enveloped in mystery and poetry."

I was hoping to climb to the top, as so many pioneers had done, for an overview of the Sweetwater River and the windswept plains of central Wyoming, but Independence Rock was fenced off. A sign warned that climbing the rock was strictly prohibited.

In Lander, I learned that the grave of Sacagawea, the American Indian woman who accompanied and helped guide Lewis and Clark, was located on the nearby Wind River Indian Reservation. Conscripted for Lewis and Clark's journey when she was only fifteen, Sacagawea smoothed the way for the Corps of Discovery as it traveled west. Many times, her linguistic abilities and her cultural knowledge proved invaluable. Because of her crucial role, schools, parks, and roads throughout the Northwest bear her name (often erroneously spelled "Sacajawea"). A dollar coin bears her likeness, and an entire mythology—but few facts—now surrounds her, the so-called Pocahontas of the West. The chance to see the grave of a legendary western figure—a veritable icon of western exploration and expansion—certainly warranted a small detour.

It was just a twenty-mile trip up the highway to the turnoff for the cemetery. The Wind River Indian Reservation, home to the Eastern Shoshone and Arapaho, was once quite large, but over the decades it had shrunk considerably as valuable resources (gold, coal) were discovered and white Americans encroached. Along with the loss of territory, the Shoshone were forced to share the reservation with their longstanding enemies, the Arapaho, the only other tribe remaining within Wyoming's boundaries. Other tribes that once called Wyoming home were moved elsewhere (such as the Cheyenne, who were forced to relocate in Oklahoma). To this day, the mainstream, largely white population of Wyoming is of two minds about the ongoing presence of American Indians in the state. Brochures in the tourist information offices tout the state's "Native American heritage" and promote numerous events—such as the "Native

American Heritage Fest" in Cheyenne—that celebrate this legacy in one way or another. But the man in the street—or in the bar, as it were—seems to have a different take. Such, anyway, was my experience at the Lander Bar the night before my side trip to Fort Washakie and the Sacajawea Cemetery. The friendly, talkative fellow on the barstool next to me was astute enough to gather that I was not a Landerite, and he wanted to know "what all" I had been doing in the area. I mentioned day hikes in the Wind River mountains, canoeing on the river, fishing at the reservoir—basically just making things up based on what I had read in the tourist brochures. In truth, I didn't want to admit that I was only passing through and more or less aimlessly drifting across the country. Similar admissions along the way had earned me puzzled looks—and a few knowing nods—whenever and wherever I entered into conversation. For conversation's sake, it seemed better to have an avowed purpose.

My drinking buddy in Lander was eager to talk at length about fishing, so I quickly switched topics, mentioning my intention to head up to the reservation to see Sacagawea's grave. This caught his attention. He had advice for me: "Watch your ass up there. Them Indians are a menace, bombing around drunk in their big ol' trucks. They'd as soon run you off the road as—, as—." He paused and thought for a moment and then let the thought go.

This seemed odd advice coming from a man who—according to the empty Collins glasses before him on the bar—was now into his fourth highball. Sometimes the temptation to play the devil's advocate—to goad a toad, as it were—is too strong and you just have to give in. So it was for me that night. I pointed to the empty glasses.

"Isn't that the pot calling the kettle black?"

He grinned back at me. "Tha's a good—good point. Tha's a very good point. But I'll tell you the difference, the difference between me and them Indians. I can handle—handle my liquor."

From the highway, back roads took me to the remote

cemetery. Arching over a cattle grate, an iron gateway bearing the name "Sacajawea Cemetery" framed the entrance to a dirt parking lot. No one else was visiting the cemetery that morning, but the graves had recently received plenty of attention, as most were adorned with colorful silk or plastic flowers, flags, wreaths, pinwheels, and other decorations. A path through the markers led to Sacagawea's headstone, a gray granite pillar about four feet high. The inscription identified her as a "guide with the Lewis and Clark expedition." A brass plaque said that the memorial was erected by the Daughters of the American Revolution in 1963. On either side of the pillar were smaller stones memorializing Sacagawea's two sons, Baptiste Charbonneau and Bazil. Close by, other headstones identified grandchildren of Sacagawea. At the foot of Sacagawea's memorial lay a rectangular dirt plot enclosed by decorative gardening bricks. People had placed small stones, shells, beads, coins, silk flowers, and American flags on the dirt and on the pillar's concrete plinth. A steady wind blew, rustling through tall grass and thistle. In the distance, I could see the snow-capped Wind River Range. It was a remarkable scene—intensely western in my eyes, with the vast prairie, the looming mountains, the isolated graveyard, the wind-blown grass. Sacagawea's presence seemed to sanctify the place. I found it moving in a way I had not expected.

I strolled around the cemetery to look at some other graves and memorials. Some of the stones had no words, only black symbols painted over whitewash. Other graves were adorned with antlers. A few were demarcated with old iron bedsteads. I saw the graves of several American Indian soldiers who had served in the Pacific, in Korea, in Vietnam. Curiously, one gravesite was dedicated to two white women, pioneers killed in the nineteenth century by Sioux raiders.

The path brought me back around for one more look at Sacagawea's gravestone. As I copied the words on it, the death date

gave me pause. Could it be right—1884? Nearly eighty years after
the Lewis and Clark expedition? That would mean Sacagawea
was close to one hundred years old when she died, a noteworthy
fact. What a remarkable life she must have lived: born at a time
when there was no real European presence in the interior West,
during her lifetime she witnessed the geopolitical and cultural
transformation of the region, a transformation that she helped
bring about through her participation in the seminal act of the
European invasion of the interior West. Born and raised in the
old ways, she saw those ways vanish. I wondered if any record
existed of her thoughts on the transformation, on the life she had
lived. Did any journalist or scholar interview her in her old age?
Surely someone must have sought out her story, one of the most
important in American history. Yet in all my reading about the
history of the American West, I had found no mention of such an
interview. In fact, I hadn't the slightest inkling about Sacagawea's
post-expedition life. I tried to remember what Stephen Ambrose
had said about her in *Undaunted Courage*, the recent bestseller
about the Lewis and Clark expedition. Only a few things came
to mind, first and foremost the general idea that Sacagawea had
linguistic skills and knowledge about the land that had helped the
captains immensely. Moreover, she carried a baby, a newborn
at the start of the journey, the same Jean Baptiste memorialized
on the headstone next to her grave and depicted with her on the
dollar coin. I remembered two specific anecdotes about her.
Somewhere along the way she joyfully encountered her relatives
whom she had not seen for quite some time. And in Oregon, she
was keen to see the ocean and a beached whale. I could not recall
reading anything more substantial about her, which seemed strange,
given her extraordinary role and her apparently long lifespan.

Back in Lander I stopped at the town library to review the account
in *Undaunted Courage*. Sacagawea does get some cursory attention

in Ambrose's book. Ambrose alludes to Sacagawea's backstory—namely that she was a member of the Snake (Lemhi Shoshone) tribe and that she had been kidnapped by the Hidatsa Sioux when she was twelve, held captive, and then sold at thirteen to a French-Canadian trapper named Toussaint Charbonneau. It was Charbonneau who had contracted as a guide with Lewis and Clark and, as part of the bargain, brought along his "wife," a boon to the expedition since Sacagawea could speak the language of the tribes that the explorers would soon encounter.

For the most part, Ambrose sticks close to the original, primary sources—specifically the journals of Lewis and Clark; surprisingly, neither captain had all that much to say about Sacagawea, even on those many occasions when her knowledge had proven invaluable. The captains were not even clear about her name. Lewis spelled it different ways. Clark called her Janie. Most often, they referred to her as the squaw or "squar." Ambrose does not provide a post-expedition account of Sacagawea (though he does so for most of the expedition's members), so he sheds no light on how she might have ended up in Wyoming. But Ambrose does make several astute observations about Sacagawea. He refers to her as "the most valuable intelligence source they [Lewis and Clark] had available to them" and he puzzles as to why they did not call upon her abilities more often. Ambrose also wonders how Lewis—"so observant about so many things"—could have been so unobservant about Sacagawea. Finally, Ambrose summarizes Sacagawea's peculiar situation: "A slave, one of only two in the party, she was also the only Indian, the only mother, the only woman, and the only teen-aged person." After the expedition, in 1806, Clark wrote Charbonneau (Sacagawea's French-Canadian husband) to say that "Your woman . . . deserved a greater reward for her attention and services on that rout [sic] than we had in our power to give her." Even in praising her, Clark did not use her actual name. One has to wonder how Clark could say that he had no "power" to give her something; he was, after all, one of the captains of the expedition. How much more power did he require? Yet Sacagawea received virtually nothing from the captains other than some cursory medical care when she was desperately ill. In fact, on several occasions she is recorded as giving presents to Lewis and Clark—Christmas presents, for example; and on one occasion she gave up her valuable beaded belt so that Lewis could trade with a chief for a fur coat that Lewis and Clark wanted to acquire for Thomas Jefferson. Lewis does not mention offering any compensation for the belt. Because of the captains' inattention to Sacagawea in the journals, she remains a cipher. Her life after the expedition—for all its apparent longevity—went undocumented.

As I was leaving the library, the librarian at the front desk asked if I had found what I needed. I told her I had been up to see Sacagawea's grave and was hoping to find out a little bit more about her and how she had ended up in Wyoming. It was surprising, I said, that so little was known about her, given how long she had lived. "Well, there's some dispute about that," the librarian told me. "Many folks doubt that it's her grave up in Washakie." Some accounts, she said, had Sacagawea dying of disease in North Dakota not long after the expedition. The Wind River version of her death emerged in the 1920s as a result of the investigations of a University of Wyoming scholar who claimed and tried to prove that an elderly Shoshone woman who had died in the 1880s was in fact Sacagawea. Apparently, some of the scholar's Shoshone informants remembered the old woman and specifically recalled her talking about going on a long journey with white men to see the ocean.

The evidence is too scanty to say definitively what happened to the real Sacagawea. The most certain thing that can be said is that Sacagawea vanished from history after the Lewis and Clark expedition (her child Jean Baptiste did not vanish, owing to

Clark's affection for him, but that is another story). What the explorers said about Sacagawea is all that is known. The rest is speculation and guesswork.

Westbound on Wyoming's Highway 28, I encountered more trail remnants.

A turnout led to a cul-de-sac where the unhurried traveler could learn about the history of South Pass and the Oregon Trail's crossing of the continental divide. Five panels arranged in a semi-circle gave brief accounts of the fur trade, the Trail, the Pony Express, and the geographical features visible from the turnout.

There was an austere beauty to the place—a broad, windswept sagebrush plateau with nearby buttes and distant peaks that called to mind William Henry Jackson's photographs from the 1870s. For a mountain pass—the continental divide, no less—it didn't look all that impressive, which was precisely why South Pass was so important. It gave easy and smooth passage across the spine of the Rockies. To reach the pass, mountain men and pioneers traveled with relative ease up the Platte and the Sweetwater, the trail climbing gradually to seven thousand feet. Wagons had no difficulty crossing the divide here, one of the few places in the rugged Rockies where such a crossing was possible. It must have been a grand moment when the pioneers arrived at South Pass, halfway into the journey, the East behind them, the vast unknown West ahead.

Some of their anticipation is reflected in the names given to the surrounding buttes, such as Pacific Butte and Oregon Butte. The pioneers were a long way from Oregon and the ocean, but crossing the divide seemed to put their goal in reach. They could now anticipate a successful arrival. Everything that lay ahead of them was truly the West, and they were thrilled to have reached its boundary at last. It was a premature thrill, of course, for the hardest part of the journey lay ahead, and by no means had they crossed the mountains simply for having crossed the divide. Terrible passages over far more grueling passes awaited them. But for now, they rejoiced, celebrating their success by halting at Pacific Springs to taste west-flowing water for the first time.

A steady warm wind blowing over the plateau gave me something of the same feeling. Looking west, I could imagine how the pioneers, suppressing any sense of foreboding about what was to come, chose to see the land ahead as inviting. That's how I chose to see it, too. Standing there in the warm wind, taking in the vista, I heard again Thoreau's refrain, "Westward I go free" and felt compelled to walk off the asphalt and onto a path that led out to more remnants of the actual Oregon Trail.

Some incongruities were strewn amid the sagebrush— automobile tires, the concrete platforms of abandoned projects, hundreds of broken bottles. Cows, having long since replaced the native bison, now grazed the range. These days, Bureau of Land Management (BLM) land is often leased for cattle grazing at a very low fee, and ranchers fiercely defend what they see as their right to use public lands at little to no cost. This insistence on government-funded exploitation clearly contradicts the notion of "rugged individualism" that circulates so freely in the West. When it comes to reliance on the federal government, many westerners seem to be in denial. In fact, many westerners seem to despise the government all the more because of this dependence.

Such contradictions and incongruities are part of the legacy of the Oregon Trail, which brought new patterns of land use to the region. The trail as I found it a century and a half later was a faint but tangible scar upon the land. A long remnant crossed BLM land just west of South Pass, but over the years this remnant had been used by cows and motor vehicles, so it was hard to call it the actual trail. Land use practices and modern technology had gouged and deepened the wound. Well, whatever it was, the path eventually led me to a stone marker commemorating the passage of Narcissa Whitman, one of the first women on the trail, a missionary who later died in a massacre near Walla Walla, Washington. That was another of the legendary trail's many twists: you might survive the hardships of the journey only to meet a more gruesome fate at your destination.

Back at the South Pass interpretive turnout, another traveler had arrived, a motorcyclist riding a Harley-Davidson. He nodded as he passed me then slowly toured the circle, glancing briefly at each of the historical markers. He stopped at the last one to read. He had all the accouterments: the leather saddlebags, the black sleeveless vest showing tattooed arms, the German army helmet over long black hair. It was all cliché, I knew, along with the gleaming bike itself, but it was a damn powerful cliché, and when he headed off, engine roaring, I felt a surge of yearning and envy.

A few miles down the road, I came to another historical marker:

> This point on the trail is called the Parting-of-the-Ways. The trail to the right is the Sublette or Greenwood Cutoff and to the left is the main route of the Oregon, Mormon, and California Trails. The Sublette Cutoff was opened in 1844 because it saved 46 miles over the main route. It did require a 50 mile waterless crossing of the desert and therefore was not popular until the gold rush period. The name tells the story, people who had traveled a thousand miles together separated at this point. They did not know if they would ever see each other again. It was a place of great sorrow. It was also a place of great decision to cross the desert and save miles or to favor their livestock. About two-thirds of the emigrants chose the main route through Fort Bridger instead of the Sublette Cutoff.

After reading the marker, I studied the map and saw that up ahead I would have to make my own decision about which direction to go.

That decision came at Farson, the crossroads point, the junction of two blue highways at a four-way stop sign. Which way to go? Angle for Idaho along the Sublette Cutoff, or head to Rock Springs, paralleling the original route of the trail? Different roads, different directions: Would the choice of one over the other make any difference, as Robert Frost had suggested? For a long moment I lingered in indecision until an oversized pickup truck came up from behind. In my rear-view mirror, I saw a young man already exasperated—no, pissed—before he had even come to a complete stop. He prodded with his horn. His lips shaped the word "asshole."

And so, I was forced off the road into a gravel lot. Which turned out to be the parking area for a small café, the Oregon Trail Café, with a sign in the window praising homemade pie. That simplified matters. Why not linger over coffee and pie for a bit and put off decision-making?

Inside the Oregon Trail Café, I sat in a booth and took stock: old calendars on the wall. Rodeo posters in the window. A stack of silverware on a table. Three seated women folding paper napkins around groupings of silverware. A row of pies on the counter. A percolating coffee pot. A coat rack with two pairs of boots at its base. A mop in a bucket. A newspaper from last week with a headline about school budget cuts and the depressed economy. Two pompoms on a lunch counter stool. Framed photographs of high school basketball teams. Reflective stars glued to the ceiling. A dog-eared trucker's magazine. Boxes of pancake mix. In my booth, I found a crumpled napkin tucked under the sugar dispenser. Unfolded, it revealed the words, "Cowboy, take me away" written with a pink pen. Yet another of the many enigmatic messages I kept encountering in my travels.

As it turned out, a flyer posted on a bulletin board near the entrance gave me the clear-cut sign that I was looking for: it promoted a "mountain man rendezvous" taking place at Fort Bridger the following weekend. That settled it for me—I would take the road heading southwest, bound for Fort Bridger and the rendezvous.

Historically, rendezvous were organized gatherings of mountain men, trappers, and other adventurers. Native Americans sometimes showed up as well. They all came together to trade and barter goods, share information and news, have a little fun, get rowdy, and generally reconnect with other human beings—a break from their mostly isolated existence in the wilderness. Some rendezvous were quite large, most notably the Rocky Mountain Rendezvous, held annually at various locations in Wyoming and Utah from 1825 to 1840. One mountain man described the principal activities of these rendezvous: "Mirth, songs, dancing, shouting, trading, running, jumping, singing, racing, target-shooting, yarns, frolic, with all sorts of extravagances that white men or Indians could invent."

These days, rendezvous reenactments are staged throughout the Mountain West. Like the living history demonstrations at historic sites, they feature activities, costumes, and entertainment germane to the Old West. A cross between a "cosplay" convention and a festival, rendezvous attract those who enjoy recreating some aspect of the mountain man lifestyle (shooting of antique rifles, primitive archery, tanning, trapping, teepee making, and the like) and those who want to observe the practice of these activities. Like any festival, food, music, and shopping are also on offer.

Today, Fort Bridger is a State of Wyoming historic site. A rendezvous reenactment is held every year on Labor Day weekend. It's a popular event, drawing people from around the world to southwestern Wyoming—an ideal location for a rendezvous since the historic site still looks much as it did in the nineteenth century. Moreover, the Bridger name is a huge draw, Jim Bridger being the most renowned of the nineteenth-century mountain men, the iconic figure of song, film, television shows, and dime novels. Bridger's name is writ large in the annals of the era and on the landscape of the contemporary West.

The drive to Fort Bridger took only a few hours, including a stop for coffee at Little America, a travel center off Interstate 80—restaurant, gift shop, motel, filling station—that was loudly advertised on scores of billboards along the freeway. My drive was uneventful; but for Oregon Trail pioneers, this was a long, bleak stretch over the seemingly endless sagebrush plains. Hardly any water was available along the way, and what water the pioneers encountered often proved hazardous. It was along this stretch, for example, that pioneers had to ford the Green River at a difficult crossing where deaths often occurred. After the river crossing, the drive to Fort Bridger was, for the pioneers, dry and desolate. I sipped coffee from a thermos and listened to Johnny Cash as I comfortably drove over the same bleak route.

Pioneers arriving at Fort Bridger found a rough-built log and sod structure where Jim Bridger and his associate Louis Vasquez operated a trading post. Bridger was often gone from the premises on one adventure or another, leaving Vasquez in charge; many pioneers on the Oregon Trail recorded their disappointment at missing the chance to see the renowned Bridger in person. Today's historic site features a replica of Bridger's trading post, and it was in the meadows behind this building that I found the latter-day rendezvous already in full swing. The event has been held annually since the 1970s, attracting hundreds of visitors and scores of vendors each year. There are demonstrations of primitive crafts (quill work, powder horn engraving). There are contests of various types (pistol shoots, a "hawk and knife throw," a Dutch oven cook-off). Tourists can take in storytelling sessions and musical acts or clap for the dancers in period attire at the buckskinners' ball. For those feeling a mite peckish, a "primitive food court" serves up pre-1840 snack food.

Participants and traders must abide by strict rules: Anything used in the camp area—clothing, gear, tools—must date from before 1840 or be historically authentic replicas of items from the period. The same goes for whatever is sold on traders' row. Inspectors visit each participant's campsite and each trader's tent, citing any violations of code. Repeat offenses can lead to expulsion. A rather specific rule sheet identifies forbidden items: no reconstituted antlers; no scented candles; no plastic honey sticks; no wind chimes or dream catchers; no zippers or elastic suspenders; and absolutely no sunglasses. Period clothing only, including period footwear. Non-participants, however, are permitted to wander around in Bermuda shorts and nylon Nikes.

I strolled around the site, observing demonstrations of obsolete skills, listening to musical acts run through the old-timey repertoire ("Shenandoah," "Clementine," "Old Paint"), and chatting with the costumed participants. No one would break character. Ask a question out of curiosity—"Where does one get buffalo bone awls these days?"—and you'd get a nineteenth-century answer: "Well, pardner, ye shoot yer own buffalo and make yerself a needle or ye trade with the Injuns."

Looking askance at the mummery, one might find it all a bit fatuous and over the top. But I was willing to play along. I was caught up in the spirit of the event and enjoying the show. There were folk dances, whittling activities, and games for kids featuring barrel hoops. In the primitive food court, bison stew simmered in an iron kettle. Then the call came for the flintlock shooting contest, and a crowd headed out to an open meadow. The guns pop-popped, the bearded and calico-clad crowd cheered, and merriment was general.

This is what I had encountered all across Wyoming: reenactment, costumed play, a desire to recreate a bygone era—the romanticized West of yore. From Fort Laramie to Fort Washakie to Fort Bridger, I had seen "fanciful pictures of the olden time," to use Francis Parkman's phrase. What was driving this enthusiasm for reenactment? People seemed to yearn for what the West—or better, the myth of the West—had to offer. They wanted to believe that the Old West still existed in some form. And in their yearning, they had turned to fanciful pictures and representations. They had embraced—to use a term fashionable in academia—*simulacra*: token imitations of long-lost originals. Throughout the region, there were pioneer pageants, covered wagon cookouts, staged shootouts, dude ranches for tourists. There were cowboy music revues, wagon train adventures, movie-set saloons, restorations of frontier hotels, and replica teepee camps. So many of us traveling around and across the West had come in search of something intangible, chasing an illusion, eager to believe in America's longstanding urge to head west for a fresh start, for renewal, for fulfillment, and for—well, for a manifest destiny, one that was individual as much as it was national. Lewis and Clark, the pioneers and gold seekers, the Boston Brahmin on a summer's journey out of bounds, the families on vacation, the dude on his Harley-Davidson, and the wanderer in his van who had quit everything for the lure of California—we were all seeking something that we believed the American West could give us. "The prevailing tendency of my countrymen," Thoreau called this westering spirit.

Nor was I immune to the spirit's allure. Who could resist the merriment of the Fort Bridger crowd as the guns blazed and the targets fell? Not I. I cheered with the rest. I downed a big bowl of "Indian-style" bison stew. And before I left the scene, I shopped the tents for a keepsake, perusing the displays of cookware, tools, clothing, and weapons all patterned after the objects of a long-gone era. In the end, I settled on an authentic replica of a mountain man shirt, a drop sleeve pullover—"totally period correct," the vendor assured me, "right down to the fibers and dyes."

En Route: Bingham Canyon, Utah

The state of Utah abounds in natural wonders, many of them protected within national parks and monuments renowned for their rugged, pristine beauty: Zion, Bryce Canyon, Capitol Reef, Canyonlands, Escalante, Bears Ears. The state also boasts several sites designated as National Historic Landmarks; some of these, too, are natural wonders: Desolation Canyon on the Green River, Emigration Canyon in the Wasatch Range, and the archaeological sites at Danger Cave and Alkali Ridge. Other landmark sites in Utah, however, might be more properly called *unnatural* wonders, including the Mountain Meadows massacre site and the remnants of the Topaz Relocation Center, where Japanese Americans were imprisoned during the Second World War. All these sites, natural and unnatural, are considered National Historic Landmarks (according to the Department of the Interior) because they are "places that hold national significance" and "illustrate U.S. heritage."

Among the National Historic Landmarks, the most unnatural wonder of all might well be Bingham Canyon Open Pit Copper Mine—the world's largest man-made excavation—located in the Oquirrh Mountains southwest of Salt Lake City. On approach from the east, the Oquirrhs present a dramatic profile. Part of the Sevier thrust belt, a belt that is "complexly folded and faulted," they run north and south, falling sharply at the north end, close to the shore of the Great Salt Lake, where they leave just enough room for a highway to squeeze through between range and lake.

According to geologists, this northern end of the range is made up of Pennsylvanian and Permian sedimentary rocks. The southern end, however, includes intrusions of Tertiary granite (molten igneous granite that intruded into older Permian sedimentary rock), and those intrusions contain rich copper ore, along with gold, silver, and lead. In 1863—sixteen years after the Mormons arrived in Salt Lake Valley—the ore was discovered, and the digging began. First gold and lead were extracted then, in the early years of the twentieth century, miners went after the copper, employing the new "open pit" method to get at the ore. During the course of the twentieth century, five billion tons of earth were excavated, yielding twelve million tons of copper and leaving behind a massive pit. The "scenic overlook" of the resulting pit is now a National Historic Landmark under the administrative auspices of the National Park Service. The mine itself is owned and operated by Rio Tinto Kennecott.

The drive up to the overlook goes through Copperton, a curiously tidy town in the midst of a degraded environment. Over the years, as it has expanded, the pit has swallowed up the towns that once existed in what used to be Bingham Canyon. Copperton, the company town, is just about the last one left. The "World's Best Copper Gift Shop" is there, along with a burger joint called "The Pit." After passing through the town, visitors come to a guard gate and pay an entrance fee. The drive up to the overlook involves negotiating a series of switchbacks and confronting an onslaught of descending trucks.

At the overlook and in the adjacent visitor center, interpretive signage boasts that Bingham Canyon is the world's largest man-made excavation, that the vast "bowl" could contain all of downtown Salt Lake City, and that the depth is double the height of two stacked skyscrapers. More than a half-mile deep. More than two and a half miles wide. It's "the richest hole on Earth," as one sign brightly says. More cumulative value than the California Rush, the Klondike Rush, and the Comstock Lode combined.

What's going on down below is a massive undertaking, given that the mined ore averages only 0.6 percent copper—one ton of ore excavated to get twelve pounds of copper. The pit's terraced slopes—"benches" in mining terminology—support railroad tracks and telephone lines. The electric shovels working the pit are outfitted with ninety-eight-ton buckets. From the overlook, they appear tiny—like toys gouging at the reddish floor. The yellowish-brown benches are crawling with huge trucks (250-ton capacity) hauling off the ore to the on-site ore crusher. Massive jet sprinklers keep the mounds and the dirt track wet.

Several towns once existed here when the canyon was still a canyon, towns strung out along a narrow road. As a historical marker at the overlook explains, the pit's steady expansion eventually swallowed the towns: "The land where the town [of Bingham Canyon] was located is now part of the Kennecott Copper Open Pit Mine. The 1970 census indicated that the population of Bingham Canyon, once a roaring mining town of 15,000, had dwindled to thirty-one people. On November 22, 1971, a special proposition to disincorporate the town was passed. After 123 years, Bingham Canyon was dead."

In the visitor center, displays avidly explain the multifaceted process of turning ore into copper, a process that involves drilling, blasting, hauling, and crushing—lots of crushing. Once crushed, ore is mixed with water and ground up "to a consistency of face powder." A "flotation process" concentrates the ore by removing unwanted material. What was once 0.6 percent copper is now 28 percent copper. Next, the concentrate is smelted until it is molten and impurities like iron and sulfur can be removed (sulfuric acid is a lucrative byproduct). By the time the molten copper is poured into anodes it is 99 percent copper—but still not pure enough. Once cooled, the anode plates "are subjected to an electrolyte process" that removes precious metals (gold, silver) and refines the copper to 99.99 percent. The result: copper cathodes ready for shipping to manufacturers of copper wire and sheeting. Home electrical systems, electric motors, communications equipment, and automobiles all require this copper.

The Park Service's interpretive signage reads like a promo for the mining company. Visitors learn that Kennecott has installed "state-of-the-art crushing, conveying, grinding, flotation, and filtration equipment." Conveyors haul crushed ore through five miles of mountain tunnels from the in-pit ore crusher to concentrators and smelters and refineries. Each day, 320 thousand tons of material is removed through the conveyors; half of it—the "overburden material"—is waste. Beyond the pit, on the other side of the Oquirrh range, Kennecott operates its "double contact sulfuric acid plant," its hydrometallurgical plant, and its cogeneration power plant. The smelter is touted as the world's cleanest, with 99.9 percent of all sulfur dioxide emissions recovered.

That claim is the only nod to environmental concerns that you will find in the display. For the most part, the visitor center of this national landmark celebrates excavation and extraction— and the visitors on this particular day seem to approve of that celebration. They hover over the glass cases and the miniaturized copper production facilities displayed therein. They discuss the finer points of the process and marvel over the miracle of it all. "See here, they do the flash smelting in this one here. State of art, says here."

There's no mention of it in the visitor center, but in 1973 renowned artist Robert Smithson (of *Spiral Jetty* fame) submitted a proposal to Kennecott's management for the repurposing of Bingham Canyon Mine into a monumental work of land art. For the bottom of the pit, he imagined constructing a rotating circular base and pools of bright yellow water created from toxic runoff. In effect, the artist wanted to make the unnatural wonder even more unnatural. Smithson died not long after he submitted the proposal, so nothing came of it. Meanwhile, mine operations have continued, an ongoing art installation, if you're inclined to see it that way.

I left Bingham Canyon by way of the oddly named Bacchus Highway, a road dominated by huge trucks. Pits and conical dirt mounds dotted the landscape. There were numerous A-frame structures, half-buried, whose purpose I couldn't figure out—storage sheds? Bunkers? The road headed north past several gravel pits. I swerved around roadkill, buzzards flapping up off a carcass as I sped through. Deer roamed the gaplands. Golf courses, railroad tracks, suburban parks, electrical dynamos, large Mormon churches, tract housing, and power lines were jumbled together. Pipeworks decorated a hillside. All along the way north to the town of Magna, Kennecott's infrastructure sites cropped up: a concentrator facility, a power plant, a refinery, several smelters, and some massive tailings ponds adjacent to suburban homes. Past Magna, the Bacchus Highway approached the interstate freeway and there, between Bacchus and I-80, I came upon a heap of black slag, another smelter, another tailings pond—all in plain view of the thousands of motorists passing by on the freeway.

The Oquirrh Range appears to peter out here (actually the range continues submerged by the Salt Lake's waters). Great Salt Lake State Park and its campground, where I had intended to spend the night, is situated directly across the freeway from all this industrial infrastructure, practically in the shadow of the smelter. Not exactly the view I had in mind when I read about a supposedly pleasant campground on the shore of America's largest lake west of the Mississippi. To me, it looked completely dismal, maybe the worst situated campground I'd ever seen.

I paused at the intersection and contemplated the landscape. It must have been austerely beautiful to the pioneers, at least to those who could look past the barrenness and see God's handiwork. But the pioneers also carried with them our culture's predilection for exploitation of the Earth. Sometimes they saw God's handiwork in nature, but they also heard the biblical dictum granting man dominion over the earth. We carry on the work to this day. What we see now—what we have inherited—is a topography altered by the culture that the pioneers brought. Our culture. And that is what makes Bingham Canyon a national landmark, a "place that holds national significance" and "illustrates U.S. heritage." In this case, it is the heritage of resource extraction, exploitation, and industrial blight. Bingham Canyon, once seven narrow miles long, has been gouged open into a massive, all-consuming pit. Even the towns that our extractive culture built were consumed as the pit expanded. Lark. Bingham. Highland Boy. Copperfield. They all vanished, along with any semblance of a canyon. In its place, there is a hideous, gaping pit. Unless you choose not to see a pit. One thing I learned in the visitor center is that the word "pit" is generally avoided in discussing the mine. The favored term appears to be "bowl." "A mountain once stood where the huge bowl is now," one interpretive sign enthusiastically states. A bowl that the US Department of the Interior and the National Park Service have endowed with landmark status.

Author's note: In 2013, a massive landslide occurred in the mine; 2.5 billion cubic feet of earth cascaded down, collapsing one side of the pit. The visitor center described here was destroyed. A new center opened in 2019.

Reading the Signs: Owens Valley, California

From Sherwin Summit, southeast of Yosemite Valley and Mammoth Mountain, US Route 395 descends precipitously into Bishop, a small town at the northern end of Owens Valley. Up ahead, for the next eighty or so miles, the southbound highway traverses a remarkable landscape: a valley that is anywhere from five to twelve miles wide, bordered on either side by impressive mountain ranges, each range cresting in "fourteeners"—peaks that top out at over 14,000 feet above sea level. John Muir's "Range of Light," the snow-covered Sierra Nevada, dominates the valley's west side, capped by Mount Whitney, the highest point in the continental United States at 14,505 feet. On the east side, the Inyo-White Mountains culminate at White Mountain Peak, 14,252 feet above sea level.

The lofty Sierra Nevada blocks moisture moving inland from the Pacific Ocean, putting the valley in a rain shadow. Average annual rainfall amounts to five or six inches. It is a dry land, austere and starkly beautiful with rocky outcroppings, exposed bedrock, petrified lava flows, basalt intrusions, and massive granite blocks. The principal crest of the Sierra Nevada, which includes the peak of Mount Whitney, is an immense granite wall fifteen miles long, one of the largest exposed granite blocks on Earth. The valley below is purportedly the deepest in the United States, some ten thousand feet separating the valley floor from the highest peaks.

Because of its dry climate, Owens Valley is sparsely populated—just thirty thousand people in nine hundred square miles. Nevertheless, it is a place rich in human history. "Owens Valley is a land between," writes landscape historian Rebecca Fish Ewan, "a place tucked behind high mountains, arid yet soaked in water history, draped in desert vegetation yet remembered for its verdant farms, sparsely dotted with towns—some no more than dreams on a map. It exists between stories, between vitality and decline, between granite mountains."

I passed through Owens Valley several times before I began to understand the forces that have shaped the place. During the years my grandparents lived in a Bishop mobile home park, I traveled up and down the valley, admiring the austere scenery: the river basin, the eerie remnants of the moribund lake, the little towns trying to get by on tourism, the scrubland ranches, the small herds of wild horses. There were side trips: one through the weird rockland of the Alabama Hills at the foot of the western range, and another up to the Ancient Bristlecone Pine Forest in the eastern range, home to some of the oldest trees on Earth. Given the place's stark beauty, I could readily understand why Ansel Adams had made numerous photographs of the valley, some of them iconic in his oeuvre.

As someone who likes to stop and read historical markers, I occasionally paused alongside Route 395 to take in the valley's handful of offerings. Not that the markers presented much detail. The texts were brief, sometimes suggestive, sometimes obscure. The markers provided a good opportunity to stretch muscles, take a photograph, feel the hot, dry wind on one's skin—but they did not provide much insight. That would have to come from further investigation in libraries and museums. Eventually, after the deaths of my grandparents, I revisited Owens Valley and the historical markers, armed with better information on the valley's remarkable but little-known history.

* * *

The first marker is in the town of Bishop, the valley's largest and only incorporated town (population: four thousand). The marker tells about the arrival of the town's namesake in the area:

> *San Francis Ranch*
> *In 1861, Samuel A. Bishop, his wife and party left Fort Tejon*
> *for the Owens Valley driving 650 head of stock. On August 22,*
> *Bishop reached a creek later named for him and southwest of*
> *this spot, established San Francis Ranch. There a peace treaty*
> *was signed by the settlers and the chiefs of the Paiute Indians.*

The brief text of a historical marker can tell only so much, just the tip of an iceberg, really. The rest of the story lies hidden beneath the surface. In this case, the marker leaves out quite a bit. Even though the valley's largest town would one day bear his name, Samuel Bishop stayed in Owens Valley for less than a year, leaving long before the town developed. Nevertheless, in bringing cattle to Owens Valley, Bishop introduced changes that would wreak havoc on the region.

Before Bishop arrived, very few whites had visited Owens Valley, not even the man for whom the valley was named. The first recorded visit was in 1834, when mountain man Joseph Walker entered the valley on a fur-trapping expedition. Walker would then pass through two more times—in 1843 and again in 1845 when he guided part of John C. Frémont's expeditionary party through the valley, "a winter trip of great hardship—low food supplies, little game, snow, bitter cold," as one account put it. Frémont did not see the valley himself, but he bestowed a name upon it, honoring expedition member Richard Owens by naming the valley, its river, and its lake after him. Like Frémont, Owens never saw the valley bearing his name.

In subsequent years, more whites visited but were generally skeptical of the valley's prospects. Few stayed for long. Meanwhile, in 1850 Owens Valley became part of the United States along with the rest of the new state of California. A government surveyor, mapping the area in 1855, summarized early American impressions of the valley: "On a general average the country forming Owens Valley is worthless to the white man, both in soil and climate."

But as more and more prospectors roamed California, probing here and there for the next lucky strike or bonanza, the mountains of Owens Valley inevitably attracted interest. Productive strikes were made just to the north and west, and soon small mining camps popped up in the mountains above the valley. Mining camps needed food, and that need prompted Samuel Bishop to bring his cattle to Owens Valley in 1861. A handful of other cattlemen had the same idea, and in a matter of months more than one thousand cows were introduced to a valley where previously there had been none. The environmental impact was immediate.

As the historical marker indicates, Bishop selected a site along a creek for the location of his ranch. Although little rain falls on the valley, some parts are well watered because snowmelt from the Sierra Nevada spills down the mountains in creeks that join the Owens River on the valley floor. Some meadows along the creeks can be quite lush, and Bishop naturally chose such a meadow for his ranch. His cattle did what cattle do: they grazed and trampled the meadows and fouled the creek. Without bothering about property rights, Bishop and other cattlemen simply assumed ownership of their selected ranch sites. They did not inquire about how the land was being used; to them it looked as though the land was not used at all, and there certainly were no titleholders in the legal sense.

But, in fact, the resident Native Americans, the so-called Paiute (a name bestowed upon them; their own name for themselves was and is "Nuumu"), relied on the meadows as a source of tuberous roots—a food source that was quickly destroyed by the cattle. At the same time, miners in the mountains were chopping down piñon trees for fuel, trees from which the Paiute harvested nuts, their primary winter food. Game (primarily rabbits and deer) that had populated the meadows moved off as the cows moved in, leaving the traditional Paiute hunting grounds devoid of game. Fishing in the now-fouled streams was affected as well.

Rather abruptly, the Paiute people faced a drastic change to their well-established way of life. Moreover, the winter of 1861–1862 turned out to be particularly harsh. The Paiute faced starvation. The newly arrived white settlers were not sympathetic, especially when desperation led some Owens Valley Indians to steal and butcher a few cows. The settlers retaliated with violence, shooting Native people and in one case raping three young women.

Obviously, this part of the story does not appear in the truncated account provided by the historical marker, which blandly relates that "a peace treaty was signed by the settlers and the chiefs of the Paiute Indians." Technically, this is correct, even as it leaves out any explanation of why the treaty was necessary. Moreover, "treaty" is a grander term than is warranted in this case. Details are sketchy, but it does appear that the ranchers and some of the Paiute reached some sort of accord in January 1862. The accord, however, did not address the root cause of the problems nor did it help the Paiute survive the brutal winter.

Whatever the treaty involved, it was short-lived, as suggested by another historical marker a few miles away:

Bishop Creek Battleground
On April 6, 1862, a battle took place around this site between
newly arrived citizens of the Owens River Valley and the Paiute
and Shoshone Indians, original inhabitants of the land. The

reason for this battle is lost in obscurity, but brave men on both
sides died here for a cause which they held to be inviolate.

This is a remarkable sign both for what it says and what it does not say. The text accords the "newly arrived" white people citizenship status, the word "citizens" conferring an automatic legitimacy on the new arrivals, the very legitimacy and sanctification that are implicit in the phrase "Manifest Destiny," the master trope of America's westward expansion. Native Americans, by contrast, are denied citizenship: they are merely "inhabitants" of the land. Their primacy as "original inhabitants" means very little when it comes to property rights because, the sign implies, they are relics of the past, their way of life now anachronistic. The language of the sign does grant the natives equality with whites when it comes to bravery in dying for an "inviolate" cause; however, for one party that cause is foredoomed while for the other the cause is not just inviolate but also ineluctable. This acknowledgement of Native American bravery draws upon the "noble savage" trope, so common in European discourse on the "original inhabitants" of the Americas—though not, it should be added, a trope commonly used in the discourse treating California's Indians, who were usually depicted as ignoble savages. The derisive term "diggers" was frequently employed to describe them—and the fact that the word rhymes with a derogatory term for Black people was probably not entirely coincidental.

Both Bishop-area historical markers assign a name to the "original inhabitants"—Paiute and Shoshone—but neither sign says anything about them. In fact, no historical marker in Owens Valley does (indeed, only one other marker mentions American Indians at all). What is known about these peoples? What is their history? The state historical markers do not provide any answers.

Evidence suggests that humans have lived in Owens Valley for eight thousand to ten thousand years, and possibly longer.

Throughout the valley, one can find evidence of prehistoric human presence: spear points, stone tools, house sites, grinding holes (for pulverizing acorns and medicinal plants). On rock faces, there are many fine examples of petroglyphs depicting spirals, circles, wavy lines, handprints, and various zoomorphic images. Not much is known about the creators of these objects, though some of the spear points found in Owens Valley resemble the distinctive style of spear points found in the Pinto Basin region of Riverside County. The Pinto sites date to between four and five thousand years ago.

The Paiute, or Nuumu, people had occupied Owens Valley several centuries before whites arrived. For hundreds of years, the Owens Valley Paiute lived a balanced life well-adapted to the valley's challenging conditions. Two-thirds of their diet came from vegetation, primarily tuberous roots gathered from meadows and pine nuts harvested from piñon trees in the Inyo-White Range. Each fall, the Paiute moved to camps in the mountains to gather nuts. They roasted and stored the nuts in special huts woven from tule reeds. Plants also provided them with medicine. For meat, they hunted deer, rabbit, and waterfowl. They gathered insects. They fished.

Down in the valley, the Paiute built shelters from willow and tule reeds and lived in small villages or clusters alongside streams. Of particular note: the Paiute were skilled at water management. They diverted streams, dammed creeks, and built irrigation ditches to water fields where wild plants grew, plants that they harvested. According to a journalist from Los Angeles who visited Owens Valley in 1859, "Their ditches for irrigation are in some cases carried for miles displaying as much accuracy and judgment as if laid out by an engineer, and distributing the water with great regularity over the grounds."

White settlers—the "newly arrived citizens" mentioned on the historical marker—were not as impressed as this journalist with Native land and water management. They did not recognize or acknowledge Paiute use of the land. To the settlers, the land was underused and unimproved—no cultivated crops, no domesticated herds. Because the Paiute did not use the land to maximum profit and fruitful industry, in the view of the white settlers they had forfeited their right to the land. Consequently, newly arrived citizens, such as Samuel Bishop, moved in and took over.

Given this background, one wonders how the historical marker could so ingenuously conclude that "the reason for this battle is lost in obscurity." In fact, the reasons were fairly obvious: the Paiute way of life, which had sustained them for centuries, was undermined in a matter of a few years. Threatened with loss of their lands and, in effect, cultural extinction, the Paiute people did what they could do to resist; as a consequence, conflicts and clashes took place all across the valley.

Only one other historical marker in Owens Valley mentions these "original inhabitants." The marker is found forty miles south in the town of Independence, Inyo County's seat:

> *Camp Independence*
> *At the request of settlers, Colonel George Evans led a military expedition to this site on July 4, 1862. Hence its name "Independence." Indian hostilities ceased and the camp closed. War again broke out in 1865 and the camp was reoccupied as Fort Independence until its abandonment in 1877. This fort made possible the early settlements in the Owens Valley.*

Interpreting this marker evidently requires some context. Following the 1862 Battle of Bishop, Owens Valley was the scene of numerous skirmishes and constant killings. Sometimes the skirmishes resulted in atrocities. Lending support to the settlers, vigilantes arrived from elsewhere in the state and from Nevada to advance what was, in effect, a genocidal campaign throughout California (for copious documentation of this campaign, see Benjamin Madley's *An American Genocide*). As the marker explains, settlers requested (or demanded) that the government do something about the "hostile" Paiute. Most of California's regular soldiers were back east fighting in the Civil War, so the government relied on volunteers to "pacify" Owens Valley. The pacification was vicious and brutal. The historical marker's bland language—"Indian hostilities ceased"—conceals what was a bald effort to eliminate the Paiute people from the valley by any means necessary, including extermination.

Colonel George Evans, who is mentioned on the marker, acknowledged that the Paiute had a "right by prior location to exclusive use of the valley." Nevertheless, Colonel Evans had instructions from his superior, Brigadier General George Wright, to confront the Paiute and "chastise them severely." Among army personnel engaged in the American Indian wars, *chastise* was a nineteenth-century euphemism for *annihilate*, as General Wright had done to American Indians (and their horses) a few years earlier in eastern Washington Territory. Evans did not shirk Wright's orders, reporting that he had "commenced killing and destroying wherever I could find an Indian to kill or his food to destroy." Evans did not exaggerate about the killing. For the next year, the army and paramilitary vigilantes (whose participation the historical marker ignores) went on a murderous offensive: According to one observer, the soldiers were "instructed to kill all the Indians they saw." A Sacramento newspaper reported a typical encounter: "Two companies of cavalry have been fighting the Indians four days and have killed 150. Two more companies have been ordered from Aurora and one from Visalia. They say they will kill all the Indians in the valley."

The army had superior firepower, of course, including the use of howitzers. Even so, the lay of the land made it difficult to engage in direct combat or to overtake Paiute encampments by surprise. As Evans noted, "the valley being open country, without a tree," the Native lookouts could spot "the appearance of troops for twenty or thirty miles ahead," enabling the Paiute to "scatter into the hills, where it [was] impossible to follow them."

In response to this situation, Evans adopted a scorched earth policy "so that [the Paiute could] have no opportunity of gathering and preserving their necessary winter supplies." Soldiers burned whatever food caches they could find, and constant army patrols made it difficult for the Paiute to hunt or gather the roots and pine nuts upon which they depended for survival. Rape was also used as a weapon; Colonel Evans noted that the soldiers and vigilantes "satisf[ied] their vicious lusts" by capturing Native women and "having carnal connection" with them. Evans issued orders to halt the practice, but Moses McLaughlin, Evans's successor as commander of Fort Independence, took no interest in protecting the enemy. McLaughlin intensified the campaign, reporting that "scarcely a day passed without two or three of them being found and killed, and everything destroyed that could be of use to the living." On at least two occasions, McLaughlin ordered the execution of prisoners. After subduing a Paiute camp, McLaughlin (in his own words) "had the bucks collected together." Those who were determined to be hostile "were either shot or sabered." McLaughlin believed that "such examples [would] soon crush the Indians and finish the war in this and adjacent valleys." The Paiute people, McLaughlin said, would "either be killed off, or pushed so far in the surrounding deserts that they [would] perish by famine."

Such is the fuller context for the statement on the historical marker that "Indian hostilities ceased," a statement that assigns all the hostility to the Paiute and ignores white hostility (which did not cease, even after the Paiute were suppressed). It is through language such as this—elisions and half-truths—that brutal supremacist actions are validated and upheld.

By June 1863, the Paiute people were effectively defeated, and nearly one thousand Paiute men, women, and children had been rounded up and held in an encampment at Fort Independence. What happened next was a calamity, yet another of the many inhuman events rarely mentioned in the sanctioned histories of the American West. Certainly, the historical marker at the site of the former Fort Independence gives no hint of it. On July 11, 1863, without any chance for preparation, the Paiute captives were removed from Owens Valley and forced to travel over the mountains to Fort Tejon, south of San Joaquin Valley. The 250-mile journey took eleven days. Most of the captives had to walk; soldiers whipped those who attempted to rest without permission. Those who faltered were peremptorily killed. Years later, one Paiute woman who had been a girl at the time of removal recalled the terror of the forced march:

> Some went on bravely, some were too feeble and weak and fell. I saw them lay down to rest or sit down to rest for want of water and food. I saw the white men with long knives stick the knife into their sides. . . . Our flesh was to be picked at by the hungry birds and coyotes of the wilds. Fear clutched my heart and mind. . . . My poor grandmother sat down for just a second, she was thirsty, she wanted water. Just then one of the men with the swords saw my grandmother sit down to rest. He was upon her in a second and stabbed her through the heart dead. In a pool of blood lay my grandmother, all alone, cold and stiff. . . . As small and young as I was I can still see the sight of my dead grandma back there.

The Paiute thus experienced what numerous other tribes, such as the Cherokee and the Navajo, also experienced: removal from homelands and a forced march of hundreds of miles.

Approximately 150 people died en route. The remaining 850 Paiutes (not counting those still hiding in the mountains above Owens Valley) were kept at the San Sebastian Reservation near Fort Tejon. Neither the government nor the military had made provisions for the influx. There was little food or water. Shelter was inadequate. The authorities did little to rectify the situation and in fact ignored the captives as best they could. With only a token guard in place, those Paiutes who were strong enough to do so escaped. Within six months only 380 Paiute people, mostly women, children, and the elderly, remained at Fort Tejon. These were soon moved to another reservation to languish.

Eventually, however, most of the Paiute returned to Owens Valley, revenants who tried to keep to themselves. But during the year or so of their absence many more settlers had arrived, along with more cattle, and these "newly arrived citizens" were not pleased to see the return of the valley's original inhabitants. Conflicts inevitably resumed—or as the historical marker would have it, "war broke out again." As before, the "war" was essentially a one-sided affair. While many Paiute people were killed in skirmishes, relatively few whites died. The climax came in early 1865 when unidentified Native people reportedly attacked a ranch south of Owens Valley. A white woman and her young son died when the ranch house burned down. In response, enraged white settlers and vigilantes went on a rampage, killing Paiute people in scattered attacks throughout the valley. A Paiute village was attacked, leaving as many as fifty dead. A newspaper report described infuriated vigilantes "slaughtering men, women, and children; those who escaped were overtaken and killed as they ran." The worst incident occurred on the shores of Owens Lake, where vigilantes attacked a Paiute camp and killed scores of people (reports varied as to the number dead—at least forty; more than one hundred according to one account). A newspaper correspondent wrote that "the whites are killing off the Indians on all sides." As the historical marker recounts, soldiers returned to Independence and reestablished the camp as a fort. The historical marker has nothing to say, however, about the consequences of the army's return.

After the slaughter of the second Owens Valley "war" in 1865, the Paiute people were effectively deprived of the valley, their traditional way of life disrupted and rendered obsolete. As one Paiute woman told an ethnographer years later, Owens Valley had become "a place where nothing could be raised. We lived there and watched the white man come in and fence the land where we lived and then like all Indians we had to move off the old homegrounds that we thought belonged to us." For the Paiute people, life had changed drastically—for the worse: "Nowhere can we gather seeds and herbs for medicine and food. We have to eat the white man's food entirely, we get sick—the white man's sickness, and get white man's medicine. Our lives are short compared to those of our ancestors."

Perspectives differ, sometimes radically. Rather than seeing the new economy and ecology of Owens Valley as inimical to a valid and viable way of life, the invading settlers believed that "white domination ... and its ability to make use of resources" provided the Paiute with opportunities for "comfortable living" that the old way of life could not. Such, at any rate, was the view of William Chalfant in his history of Owens Valley (*Story of Inyo*) published in 1922. Chalfant, a newspaper publisher and prominent citizen in the valley during the first half of the twentieth century, can be considered the "voice of Owens Valley," or at least the voice of "white domination" in the valley. In his view, this domination was beneficent, a blessing for the Paiute people.

Following military defeat, following removal and return to the valley, many Paiute people eventually became manual laborers and domestic workers on the farms and ranches that had spread across the valley. Ranchers came to rely on Paiute labor such that, in a curious twist, the whites of Owens Valley protested a federal plan to create a Paiute reservation outside of the valley, far from the farms and ranches. Needing laborers, whites now wanted to keep the "original inhabitants" in the valley after having previously sought their removal or extermination.

The Paiute people remain in Owens Valley to this day, living primarily on four small reservations outside the towns of Bishop, Big Pine, Independence, and Lone Pine. The Independence reservation contains the site of the former Fort Independence, headquarters for the military campaign against the Native peoples of Owens Valley. Though the Paiute participate in mainstream American culture, they maintain certain Paiute traditions, such as the gathering of herbal medicines and basket weaving. These traditions help the tribe survive. As Jesse Durant, a Paiute basket weaver, says, "Handwoven baskets are an integral part of our Paiute tradition. The baskets represent the relationship between our lives as a people and Mother Earth, who sustains our culture. They signify what we did to survive in our environment, how we used the plants around us, and how much time we spent gathering and carefully preparing our basket materials."

After 150 years of American education, the Paiute language has all but disappeared; as of 2010, fewer than fifty elderly people were using it as a first language. Nevertheless, projects are underway to preserve the language and Paiute mythology. Crucially, while living in a place that had suffered severe environmental degradation under the American economic system, the Paiute people hold fast to their traditional respect for Mother Earth, sustainer of Paiute culture. The tribe has safeguarded "the natural resources provided by land, water, and air," according to the Bishop Paiute Tribe's website. "Paiute culture remains deeply embedded with the valley's environment." In official tribal publications, the Owens Valley Paiute have explained their relationship to the land. Their own words tell the story that the historical markers deny them:

> The Owens Valley is sacred to the Paiute of Fort Independence, it is like our mother, who gave us life. It is spiritual, it is hallowed. It is not easy to put it on paper, but we will try for the sake of moving forward. The sagebrush, willows, grasses, and all plants that grow in the Owens Valley are sacred to us, they feed and heal our people for thousands of years. We use these plants for food, for medicine. We use these plants for shelter and for tools that we need to live. All of the animals, rabbit, lizard, deer, coyote and the insects, they provide for us. They are sacred to us. Without the plants, the animals and the land, we would not be. The Paya (Water), this is sacred. Paya is potentially an unrenewable resource, it must be protected. The rocks, creeks, lakes, lands, these are sacred to us. We lived in the entire Owens Valley, and beyond. This is our home. All of these are interconnected and without one, none could exist. Our people are buried here, their spirits speak to us, and they guide us. In order to keep our culture intact, we must protect her, and all her fauna and flora.

By 1870, with the army in military control of the valley, more settlers arrived to extend the economic hegemony of whites. Ranches expanded and prosperous farms sprang up. Building upon Paiute irrigation ditches, farmers created a canal system, and soon thousands of acres were under cultivation, producing apples, peaches, plums, apricots, wheat, corn, barley, and potatoes. Cattle and sheep roamed the ranches. Growing cities such as Los Angeles and Reno provided markets for the products of Owens Valley. Booster magazines gushed over the transformation of the valley into a land "where thousands of thrifty farmers have reaped a bountiful reward from the land of plenty." The valley was, according to the boosters, "a field so attractive, so varied, so rich in prospects, so inexhaustible in its resources, that the home-seeker, the investor or the capitalist will never tire of its exploitation." Though it received little rain, the valley seemed to have a prosperous future thanks to the abundant waters that tumbled down from the peaks of the Sierra Nevada, filling creeks and feeding the Owens River.

Passing through Owens Valley today, one wonders about those prosperous farms: the fruit trees, the fields of grain, the cattle ranches—where are they? One sees mostly desert landscape; there's little evidence of a "land of plenty" proffering "a bountiful reward." Here and there one might see an orchard of dead trees and wonder, what happened?

In brief, what happened was that the City of Los Angeles came and took the abundant water of Owens Valley, diverting it 230 miles via an aqueduct to city reservoirs. The story of this water diversion—or theft, as some would call it—is full of intrigue and subterfuge. But the historical markers in Owens Valley don't have much to say about it. Only one marker (not an official state historical marker at that) mentions the aqueduct and alludes to the strife that accompanied its construction and operation. Located off Route 395 on a dirt road that accesses the aqueduct, the low stone marker rests on the ground, the text partly obscured by grit and dust:

> ### Alabama Gates
>
> The Alabama Gates and gate house were constructed in 1913 when the Los Angeles Aqueduct was built to dewater the aqueduct when maintenance is necessary. On November 16, 1924, seventy or more local citizens seized the aqueduct at the Alabama Gates and diverted the city's water supply

through the gates into the dry Owens River to publicize the concerns of Owens Valley residents. Four days later the water was voluntarily allowed to again flow into the aqueduct. Over the years, attempts to reconcile the city's water needs and the concerns of valley residents have moved from confrontation to negotiation.

The marker hints at a backstory, one that has to be brought to the fore in order to understand the contemporary landscape of Owens Valley.

At the turn of the twentieth century, civic boosters believed that Los Angeles could and should grow into a major metropolis. It then had fewer than 100,000 residents but was expanding rapidly. The city could not grow any larger, however, without access to more water than the meager Los Angeles River could provide. To address the situation, Mayor Fred Eaton and William Mulholland, superintendent of the Los Angeles Water Department, devised a plan to secure more water for the city.

Eaton visited Owens Valley with an engineer for the Bureau of Reclamation, a new federal agency, which at the time was considering the development of an irrigation project in the valley. Eaton realized that the Owens River—even though it was more than two hundred miles from Los Angeles—could provide sufficient water for a city of millions. Eaton and Mulholland discussed the feasibility of an aqueduct from Owens Valley to Los Angeles. It would be a massive undertaking, but they decided building such an aqueduct was the city's best option. In 1905, acting at first as a private citizen (and pretending to be a rancher interested in ranch property), Eaton set out to buy land and the accompanying water rights. He would later transfer the purchases to the city, once the requisite bonds had been approved. In this way, Eaton was able to secure water rights without arousing suspicion in the valley. By the time the deception was revealed, it was too late for the valley. Los Angeles soon owned enough land to pressure more landowners into selling their property and the associated water rights to the city. In a relatively short time, Los Angeles owned most of the water rights in the valley. Marc Reisner in *Cadillac Desert*, the definitive account of water issues in the West, summarizes the city's efforts: "Los Angeles employed chicanery, subterfuge, spies, bribery, a campaign of divide-and-conquer, and a strategy of lies to get the water it needed."

The next step was to construct the aqueduct. Los Angeles voters approved bond issues in 1907, and construction began the next year. The engineering project was exceedingly complex, surpassed at the time only by the Panama Canal. William Mulholland's design for the aqueduct relied on gravity alone to carry the water from valley to city. To span the 230 miles, the city constructed canals, pipelines, covered-concrete conduit, troughs, a twelve-mile stretch of steel siphon, concrete tunnels (well over one hundred), and two reservoirs. Support systems such as power plants, roads and trails, telephone and transmission lines, and a cement plant had to be built, along with work camps for the aqueduct's more than five thousand laborers. The city also laid a 120-mile rail spur from Mojave to Owens Valley for the transport of supplies. The entire project took five years to finish.

Completion would not have been possible without assistance—and favoritism—from the federal government, particularly the executive branch. President Theodore Roosevelt and his close advisor Gifford Pinchot (founder of the US Forest Service) clearly favored the urban water needs of ever-growing Los Angeles over the agricultural needs of remote Owens Valley. Though both men were prime movers in the nascent conservation movement, they tended to take a pragmatic approach to environmental matters, an approach succinctly expressed in Pinchot's guiding principle: "The greatest use for the greatest good for the most people for the longest time." In fact, to pragmatic conservationists such as Roosevelt, favoring Los Angeles's rights to the water was the best option for conserving Owens River water, since the water would be put to maximum use rather than "wasted" through discharge into the saline (hence "useless") Owens Lake. By this logic, diverting the water to Los Angeles would save billions of gallons a year by preventing its loss to the saline sump. Roosevelt and Pinchot thus helped the aqueduct project proceed by granting rights of way across federal lands and ensuring that competing reclamation projects in Owens Valley were scrapped. Roosevelt did not conceal his favoritism: "The opposition of a few settlers in Owens Valley must unfortunately be disregarded in view of the infinitely greater interest to be served by putting water in Los Angeles."

That water started flowing into the city—or more precisely into the San Fernando Valley northeast of Los Angeles—in November 1913. At the ceremony staged to dedicate the aqueduct and to greet the arrival of the water, William Mulholland famously quipped to the gathered crowd, "There it is. Take it." The first "takers" were the investors in a San Fernando land syndicate. Acting on inside information, these well-connected and powerful men—"pillars" of the Los Angeles community such as Sherman, Chandler, Huntington, and Otis (readily recognizable names to anyone who has spent time in Southern California)—had bought up hitherto dry and worthless land in the San Fernando Valley. As friends and associates of Eaton and Mulholland, they knew before anyone else did that the aqueduct would terminate not in Los Angeles proper but in the valley beyond the outskirts where the water would be stored before distribution. The poorly watered and useless San Fernando Valley would soon be flush with water, and land values would soar. The syndicate bought the land when it was cheap and subsequently made a fortune.

The transformation of San Fernando's desert valley was particularly galling to the residents of Owens Valley, who now had to watch as water from their river was diverted into the aqueduct and transferred south to irrigate farms two hundred miles away. Meanwhile, their farms and ranches began drying out. Within ten years, agriculture was untenable in much of Owens Valley. Only the lands above the aqueduct intake (located a few miles north of Independence) could count on enough water for farming or ranching. But Los Angeles was still growing, and drought conditions in Southern California led the Los Angeles Department of Water and Power to acquire still more water rights. By then everyone knew what LADWP was up to, but the city held all the power. By obtaining water rights in a checkerboard fashion, the city could put the squeeze on remaining landowners, who eventually would be forced to sell. After taking still more of the river's water, Los Angeles then began pumping groundwater, further reducing the available water supply. Soon, farms and ranches above the intake failed as well, along with most local businesses. The population in Owens Valley dwindled.

Organized resistance to the city's actions was inevitable, although somewhat slow in developing. The first major acts of resistance did not occur until 1924. It is this resistance that is commemorated in the text of the isolated historical marker just off US 395. A few months before the events at the Alabama Gates, some valley residents dynamited a section of the aqueduct just north of Lone Pine. Still, Los Angeles refused to negotiate any compromise that would allow more water to remain in Owens Valley. In fact, the city continued to buy up water rights and pump even more groundwater. By the fall of 1924, valley residents were desperate. As the historical marker indicates, a large group showed up at the Alabama Gates on November 16, 1924, and cranked the weirs into position so that water in the aqueduct was re-diverted down a spillway back into the bed of the Owens River. The lower portion of the river had been dry for years at that point; for four days after the action at Alabama

Gates, water trickled its way down the dry bed, a paltry restoration of its former state. The restoration was short-lived. Los Angeles sent armed detectives to the scene, and a violent confrontation seemed inevitable. But a local sheriff intervened, telling the detectives that he could not offer them any protection if the large crowd of valley locals turned violent. The detectives stood down.

Meanwhile, Los Angeles obtained a court injunction ordering the valley residents to surrender; when served, the papers ended up in the spillway, drifting with the current down to the river. A rally followed, as whole families showed up at the aqueduct—women, children, the elderly—for a barbecue picnic. As it happened, a Hollywood movie was being filmed nearby in the Alabama Hills. Cowboy star Tom Mix expressed his support for the valley folk, sending words of encouragement and a mariachi band to entertain the protesters. The press turned it into a David and Goliath story. Even the *Los Angeles Times*, always an ardent supporter of the aqueduct, admitted that the valley farmers had "a measure of justice on their side."

Finally, the city resorted to its tried-and-true tactic of deceit. Word came that the valley would receive the compensation that it sought, or at least that there would be a hearing about compensation. The valley folk celebrated their apparent victory and closed the gates, letting the water return to the aqueduct (or, "the water was voluntarily allowed to again flow," as the historical marker somewhat awkwardly puts it). City officials had no intention of fulfilling the promise, however; they knew that the valley's remaining landowners were in financial straits, unable to make ends meet. The city held the upper hand and would dictate the terms it wished.

The resistance was not entirely broken, not just yet. On into 1927, valley activists took out their frustrations on the aqueduct's infrastructure, dynamiting pipes, conduit, siphons, power plants, telephone poles—anything they could access while the armed guards patrolling the aqueduct were out of sight. The city of Los Angeles effectively (but not legally) imposed a kind of martial law on Owens Valley. Floodlights lit up the aqueduct at night. Military police established roadblocks to stop and search vehicles and interrogate drivers. Machine gun nests were set up at strategic locations.

Through it all, somehow, no one died from violence. Financial ruin, however, continued to wear down valley residents and, in the end, it was the financial collapse of a local bank that put an end to the resistance, leaving Los Angeles in total control of the valley. Investigations had revealed irregularities at the valley's most important bank, Inyo County Bank. The two brothers who owned the bank, the valley's most prominent citizens and leaders of the resistance, were subsequently indicted, tried, and convicted of embezzlement. The Watterson brothers had resorted to accounting tricks, they explained, in an altruistic effort to keep valley businesses afloat. Valley residents accepted this justification, but there was no leeway in the law. On the day that the valley's five banks closed for good, a sign appeared on the door of the Bishop branch: "This result has been brought about by the past four years of destructive work carried on by the city of Los Angeles." When the dust settled, Los Angeles owned ninety-five percent of the valley's farmland and eighty-five percent of property in the towns.

The settling dust in this case was literal, Owens Valley having turned bone dry. Ruth Baugh, a geographer, visited the valley in 1936 and reported that drastic changes had occurred since the diversion of the water: "Land formerly productive has turned to sagebrush, and commodious farm buildings are now in ruins. Weed-choked irrigation ditches, abandoned farm machinery, and rows of stark bleached trunks identify the sites of former ranches."

Ghost farms. Ghost ranches. Swirling dust. Stands of dead trees marking the sites of former orchards: this is what desultory drivers on Route 395 saw in the years after Los Angeles diverted the water. Eventually, a second aqueduct was built, parallel to the first, to carry off still more water. Fred Eaton, the former mayor who had schemed to get that water, acknowledged—whether with remorse or satisfaction it is hard to say—what his scheming had wrought: "Wherever the hand of Los Angeles has touched Owens Valley, it has turned back into desert." In *Cadillac Desert*, Marc Reisner summarized the consequences: "In the end, [Los Angeles] milked the valley bone-dry, impoverishing it, while the water made a number of prominent Los Angeleans very, very rich."

The toll has been most noticeable at Owens Lake, where the Owens River once debouched. Formerly a sizeable saline lake of one hundred square miles, by 1926 it was all but desiccated, leaving behind a vast salt flat some fifteen miles long and four to eight miles wide—approximately the size of San Francisco. Ever since, winds have stirred the lakebed into clouds of alkali dust, choking the southern end of the valley and causing white-out conditions. The dust has been swirling for decades, a few million tons of it displaced into the atmosphere each year. The dust contains high levels of carcinogenic particulates, making the dead lakebed the largest single source of dust pollution in the United States and triggering frequent stage-one air pollution alerts for valley residents.

In the late 1990s, as a result of lawsuits, Los Angeles was ordered to mitigate the dust pollution. Over the years, the city's efforts to do so have cost more than a billion dollars. Los Angeles continues to fight court cases over its responsibility. Even so, the city is not reticent about touting its efforts to control the dust. In fact, the city's Department of Water and Power has put up a historical marker of its own:

Owens Lake Dust Mitigation Program
Owens Lake was once over 300 feet deep and part of a large

*ancient freshwater lake. As the climate changed over centuries,
the lake began to dry up leaving behind concentrated minerals
and salts. By 1905, diversion of water by farmers in the Owens
Valley, coupled with drought in the region, had shrunk the lake
even further to approximately 60% of what it was in the mid
1800's. In 1913, the City of Los Angeles purchased most of
the water rights in the Owens Valley and completed the first Los
Angeles Aqueduct to divert much of the remaining water in the
Owens River south to the city of Los Angeles. As a result, the
lakebed has been essentially dry since 1920.*

*Dust blowing from the dry lakebed became a problem for
the communities surrounding Owens Lake, and its presence
eventually constituted a violation of the Federal air quality
dust standard. In July of 1998, the City of Los Angeles and the
Great Basin United Air Pollution Control District entered into
a historic agreement committing the Los Angeles Department of
Water and Power to mitigate the dust conditions.*

*This marker signifies the first phase of a dust control
program—Shallow Flooding. This involves delivering water to
emissive areas of the lakebed until the soil becomes thoroughly
wet to the surface and is unable to emit dust.*

*This program is part of a series of actions in which the City
of Los Angeles and the Department of Water and Power have
taken positive steps to protect the environment.*

It's a nice-looking marker—bronze plaque set into a large
altar-like white rock placed at a turnout off Route 136. But those
who get out of their cars to read it might want to cover their faces
with a bandana or handkerchief. Eye protection would also help.
Even so, driving off they might find that their eyes are stinging
and their throats burning. The polluted air perpetually hovering
over Owens Lake brings to mind the sign that appeared on the
closed door of the Bishop bank decades ago: "This result has

been brought about by the . . . destructive work carried on by the city of Los Angeles."

To slake its insatiable thirst, Los Angeles did not neglect to go after the Paiute people's small share of the water. In 1912, the year before the aqueduct's completion, the federal government finally established a reservation for the Owens Valley Paiute, setting aside sixty-seven thousand acres. But it was not long before Los Angeles coveted Paiute lands and water rights. In 1930, Los Angeles Department of Water and Power produced a report with the provocative title *Owens River Valley, California Indian Problem.* Perhaps LADWP wanted to suggest that the Paiute Indians faced problems—which they did, including high unemployment and poor living conditions—but the subtext was that the Paiute were themselves the problem, or at least a problem for the LADWP.

In 1932, in response to the city's concerns, President Herbert Hoover used an executive order to give watershed protection status to a sizable chunk of the Paiute reservation. The Paiute were left with around three thousand acres, but this acreage, too, proved desirable to LADWP. In 1937, therefore, the federal government, now under Franklin Roosevelt, brokered an exchange: Los Angeles would take over the Paiutes' three thousand acres (along with the corresponding water rights) and in return the city would give the Paiute around 1,400 total acres in small parcels near the towns of Bishop, Big Pine, and Lone Pine. Only the land of the Fort Independence reservation (around three hundred fifty acres) remained untouched.

Walking along the streets of Independence, California (the entire town can be toured easily in under an hour), one comes across a historical marker at the corner of Market and Webster:

Mary Austin's Home 1868 – 1934
"But if ever you come beyond the borders as far as the town that

lies in a hill dimple at the foot of Kearsarge, never leave it until
you have knocked on the door of the brown house under the
willow-tree at the end of the village street, and there you shall
have such news of the land, of its trails and what is astir in them,
as one lover of it can give to another..."
—The Land of Little Rain

Other than the name, date, and apparent quotation, the marker offers no additional context. Who was Mary Austin? What is the significance of these words?

Writer Mary Austin was one of the more remarkable residents of Owens Valley. For a period of thirteen years (1892–1905) she lived in several places up and down the valley, including Bishop, Lone Pine, and Independence. She taught school and worked on stories and essays. In 1903, she published the first of her many books.

From obscurity in remote Owens Valley, Mary Austin went on to achieve literary celebrity, the renowned author of numerous books and hundreds of stories and articles. Without question, her most enduring work is found in her writing about Owens Valley, especially the book she wrote while living there, *The Land of Little Rain* (1903), a collection of essays that describe the unique natural and cultural environment of eastern California, particularly Owens Valley and Death Valley. The book's power stems from Austin's ability to describe the desert and inscribe the valley's flora, fauna, and human denizens with a strong spiritual quality. She remains the foremost literary figure associated with the valley. The title she gave her first book is now an often-used epithet for the valley and broader eastern California region. Gift shops and stores throughout the valley sell copies of *The Land of Little Rain* to tourists.

Born, raised, and educated in southern Illinois, Mary Hunter moved to the Bakersfield area of California when she was twenty years old. Although she had primarily studied science in college, she was an avid reader of literature and hoped to become a writer. She immediately found material for articles and stories in her new location and made California the setting for her first published works. Pursuing a writing career, however, proved challenging; she had married a man, Wallace Austin, whose many business schemes constantly failed, and Mary often had to set her writing aside while she worked as a teacher to support the family. The Austins had one child, a daughter, who was born with severe learning disabilities. The marriage was never a happy one, but Wallace's unsuccessful schemes did bring the couple to Owens Valley, whose austere beauty and extraordinary natural environment would inspire Mary's most renowned work. While living in the valley, Mary Austin became fascinated with Paiute culture and with the traditions of the region's Spanish-speaking people of Mexican heritage. A significant portion of her book on Owens Valley was devoted to these subjects.

While living in Owens Valley, Austin spent time with both Native and Mexican women, learning from them about traditional crafts, cooking, medicine, languages, songs, dances, and stories. Austin soon came to believe that mainstream American society, which in her view was too materialistic and capitalistic, should heed the wisdom of Native peoples. This belief emerges as a principal theme in *The Land of Little Rain* and would remain a key element of all her writing. During her years in Owens Valley, she became aware of the injustices perpetrated on the Paiute and Shoshone tribes. For example, she spoke out against the educational practices and regulations at the American Indian school in Bishop that were designed to suppress Native culture (such as forbidding the use of the Paiute language). She also called attention to the frequency of rape and sexual violence in the valley, crimes that were rarely regarded as such when the victims were Native women. Throughout her life, she advocated for Native peoples and the inherent value of their cultures. Her writing often focused on Native themes, expressing particular interest in American Indian religions and spirituality. Though her interest was sincere, it was, perhaps, misguided. For this reason, Austin is sometimes criticized for exploiting American Indian culture, appropriating and using it for her own ends.

The criticism may well be justified; still, it is important to recognize that Mary Austin was, for her time, unusually empathetic toward Native peoples. She believed in the vitality of Native and Mexican cultures, recognizing the wisdom and critical knowledge of nature that imbued these cultures and enabled them to be in a "right relationship" with the land. Her insight and empathy are most evident in two chapters of *The Land of Little Rain*. One, "Shoshone Land," tells about a Shoshone medicine man living among the Paiute. The other, "The Basket Maker," focuses on the life of Seyavi, an elderly Paiute woman. "Seyavi's baskets had a touch beyond cleverness," Austin writes. "The weaver and the warp lived next to the earth and were saturated with the same elements."

While dwellers of Owens Valley—people such as the basket weaver, the medicine man, a prospector, a muleteer, and landowning ranchers—receive due treatment in Austin's text, the bulk of attention is on nature—the flora, fauna, geography, and weather in the eastern California deserts and mountains. For this reason, Austin usually is classified as a nature writer in the tradition of her predecessors, Henry David Thoreau, John Burroughs, and John Muir (whom Austin met and disliked, perhaps because of his obvious disdain for Native peoples). She is seen as a forebear to latter-day female nature writers such as Gretel Ehrlich, Annie Dillard, and Terry Tempest Williams. Of Austin, Williams has said, "I view her as a sister, soulmate, and literary mentor, a woman who inspires us toward direct engagement with the land in life as well as on the page." A "protoecofeminist," Austin insisted on the primacy of nature and the need for humans to harmonize with the earth rather than seeking to establish dominion over it. This need is especially relevant in the desert, where "the manner of the country makes the usage of life there, and the land will not be lived in except in its own fashion."

Throughout *The Land of Little Rain*, Austin explores the ways that animals and plants have adapted to this seemingly intolerant environment. Austin's prose is infused with "the palpable sense of mystery in the desert air." At times her style seems almost archaic, the voice of ancient wisdom speaking from the sky or the burning bush. At other times, her voice is full of "delicate joys" and "great zest," enthusiastically celebrating "the restraining condition of Beauty in the arid West." Austin comes across as a seeker of deep truths, part storyteller, part scientist, part transcendentalist. Readers have responded to her unusual ability to combine precise description with a kind of mystical insight, as evidenced in passages such as this: "The beginning of spring in Shoshone land—oh, the soft wonder of it!—is a mistiness as of incense smoke, a veil of greenness over the whitish stubby shrubs, a web of color on the silver sanded soil." Austin admires "the rainbow hills, the tender bluish mists, the luminous radiance of the spring" in Owens Valley. She identifies the psychic effects of the desert landscape: "For all the toll the desert takes of a man it gives compensations, deep breaths, deep sleep, and the communion of the stars." In these descriptions, Austin refrains from distorting reality, yet goes beyond mere factual information. As she puts it, her focus is on things "patent to the understanding but mysterious to the sense." The reader comes away from the book with intimate knowledge of coyotes, buzzards, quail, creosote, various trees, the desert's seasons, the complexity of a watershed and the numerous ways humans have imprinted on it, and the awesome power of mountain storms.

She manages to articulate the very essence of the desert land and the life it supports.

To gather material for the book, Austin must have roamed around the valley, following human and animal trails into the mountains, surveying as much as she could. She evidently spent a good amount of time walking, waiting, and watching. She would watch animals at their watering holes, track down hard-to-find nests and burrows, and return over and over to the same places to observe seasonal changes. The book is as remarkable for its researches as it is for its writing. It represents repeated acts of keen observation, leading to an insightful "reading" of the desert landscape. Observation, for Austin, involves all the senses. She revels in not just the sights, but the sounds, tastes, smells, and feel of the desert. Here, as an example, she describes the sky then shifts to a catalog of odors:

> Out West, the West of the mesas and the unpatented hills, there is more sky than any place in the world. It does not sit flatly on the rim of the earth, but begins somewhere out in the space in which the earth is poised, hollows more, and is full of clean winey winds. There are some odors, too, that get into the blood. There is the spring smell of sage that is the warning that sap is beginning to work in a soil that looks to have none of the juices of life in it; it is the sort of smell that sets one thinking what a long furrow the plough would turn up here, the sort of smell that is the beginning of new leafage, is best at the plant's best, and leaves a pungent trail where wild cattle crop. There is the smell of sage at sundown, burning sage from campoodies and sheep camps, that travels on the thin blue wraiths of smoke; the kind of smell that gets into the hair and garments, is not much liked except upon long acquaintance, and every Paiute and shepherd smells of it

indubitably. There is the palpable smell of the bitter dust that comes up from the alkali flats at the end of the dry seasons, and the smell of rain from the wider-mouthed cañons. And last the smell of the saltgrass country, which is the beginning of other things that are the end of the mesa trail.

Given the strong identification of Mary Austin with the place, it is surprising to learn that Austin was something of a misfit in Owens Valley. Although a historical marker seemingly celebrates her residency in Independence, Austin's life in the town was troubled. In fact, wherever she lived in Owens Valley, her neighbors regarded the unorthodox young woman critically. In particular, she was criticized and gossiped about for her strained relationship with her husband and apparent neglect of her mentally disabled daughter. Many townsfolk regarded her as eccentric, especially when it came to her associations with Paiute and Mexican women. Her habit of visiting the American Indian villages and of entering Mexican homes caused consternation. On at least one occasion, a group of upstanding women confronted her for participating in Native dances. On another occasion she was criticized for delivering a cake to the Chinese laundry as a Chinese New Year gift. Her school-teaching offended some in the community as well, as she often compared Protestant spirituality unfavorably with Native American spirituality. Moreover, in her lessons she took a literary approach to the Bible, drawing the ire of local churchmen.

When *The Land of Little Rain* was published, many of Austin's neighbors formed an unfavorable impression of the book, some claiming that it was full of lies. The book that eventually would come to define Owens Valley—a book that is now sold in bookshops and stores up and down the valley—was not at first well received among the valley's residents.

For her part, Austin did not hide her dislike of the valley's "hot dull little towns" and the stultifying society she endured there. Although her book expresses a deep fondness for the natural setting of Owens Valley, Austin regarded it as a place of exile and found the towns "deadly, appallingly dull." She does not say much about this aspect of the valley in *The Land of Little Rain*, but later in life she detailed the dullness that she had experienced there: "The stark houses, the rubbishy streets, the women who went about them in calico wrappers, the draggling speech of the men, the wide, shadowless table-lands, the hard bright skies, and the days all of one pattern, that went so stilly by that you only knew it was afternoon when you smelled the fried cabbage Mrs. Mulligan was cooking for supper." Most of all, Austin could not abide the racial discrimination that she observed in Owens Valley. This contrast between town and outlands in Austin's depiction of Owens Valley is reminiscent of the contrast that Thoreau had perceived between Concord and Walden. Eventually, Mary Austin abandoned Owens Valley despite having commented in *The Land of Little Rain* on the way "this long brown land lays such a hold on the affections." Owens Valley is a place of "lotus charm," she concluded, "so that once inhabiting there you always mean to go away without quite realizing that you have not done it." Yet not long after writing these words she did go away.

The Owens Valley that Austin wrote about was the valley as it was before Los Angeles built its aqueduct and diverted the water from Owens River. Austin left the valley just as Fred Eaton was buying up land and plans for the aqueduct were being hatched. She knew something about the machinations of Los Angeles officials because her husband was involved in some local irrigation projects that were quashed in favor of the city's interests. Wallace Austin even wrote a letter to President Theodore Roosevelt protesting the situation. Later in life, Mary Austin wrote a novel (*The Ford*) that dramatizes a water-rights showdown similar to the

Owens Valley–Los Angeles confrontation (in the novel, the local farmers win). But beyond that, Austin did not directly take up the issue of water rights in the valley. Newspaper publisher William Chalfant later criticized Austin, saying that "she could have done more" to support the valley in its conflict with Los Angeles.

One of her biographers, however, claims that "she became something of a spokeswoman in the early days for fighting the Los Angeles takeover," and one account has her confronting William Mulholland in Los Angeles. After listening to her express her suspicions that Los Angeles would end up by taking all of the valley's water (rather than just the excess as the city was claiming), Mulholland reportedly said that Austin was "the only one who has brains enough to see where this is going." Maybe her prescience, her fear of the valley's doom, led her to leave the place, abandoning it to its sad, inevitable fate.

Despite this abandonment, Austin has long been recognized as the valley's true voice. Some years after her death, Ansel Adams—who had worked with Austin on a book about Taos Pueblo—put together an abridged edition of *The Land of Little Rain*, illustrating quotations from the text with his own photographs. In the introduction, Adams summarized the power of Austin's words: "The sharp beauty of *The Land of Little Rain* is finely etched in the distinguished prose of Mary Austin. Many books and articles have probed the factual aspects of this amazing land, but no writing to my knowledge conveys so much of the spirit of earth and sky, of plants and people, of storms and the desolation of majestic wastes, of tender, intimate beauty, as does *The Land of Little Rain*." As one of the several biographies about her concludes: "More than a century later, her book still attracts readers because of Austin's originality and prescience, and because she brought to Americans a new perspective on the Western desert, its people, its barren beauty, and its place in a complex and misunderstood region."

Ultimately, there is no more fascinating character in the history of Owens Valley, and the fascination has to do in part with her complicated relationship to the place. She loved it. She loathed it. She studied it, learned something of its capacious mysteries, and articulated both mystery and capaciousness to readers unfamiliar with the desert's delicate joys. She gave Owens Valley a voice. Because of Austin, the valley—now commonly referred to as "the land of little rain"—has a place in American literature. Yet she left the valley, abandoning it as soon as she could, and never returned. The quotation on the historical marker is a representative example of her gifts of expression, but it only hints at the full story of the valley's wandering adopted daughter.

Six miles south of Mary Austin's house, one comes across another historical marker just off Highway 395, a bronze plaque encased in a block of mortared stones:

> *Manzanar*
> *In the early part of World War II, 110,000 persons of Japanese ancestry were interned in relocation centers by Executive Order No. 9066, issued on February 19, 1942. Manzanar, the first of ten such concentration camps, was bounded by barbed wire and guard towers, confining 10,000 persons, the majority being American citizens. May the injustices and humiliation suffered here as a result of hysteria, racism and economic exploitation never emerge again.*

The text of this marker has sparked controversy from the moment it was unveiled. Veterans' groups and some valley residents objected to the term "concentration camp," arguing that the term was misleading, that the connotation of a concentration camp was too extreme for what had been, in the official government terminology, a "war relocation center" (at the time the camp was established, the *Inyo Independent* referred to Manzanar as the "Jap resettlement camp," and locals in Owens Valley took to calling it the "Jap camp"). Nevertheless, Franklin Delano Roosevelt, who signed Executive Order 9066, used the term "concentration camp" when referring to Manzanar and the nine other "relocation centers."

According to those who rejected the marker's language, Manzanar and the other centers were not at all like the concentration camps of Nazi Germany or Soviet Russia. Veterans' groups felt that the unpatriotic tone of the marker dishonored those who had died at Pearl Harbor and in the subsequent Pacific war against Japan, a war—they pointed out—that Japan had started. Some of the soldiers who had died were buried in the cemeteries of Owens Valley. Other residents of the valley had been wounded in the effort to thwart Japanese aggression. The text of the historical marker, opponents felt, dishonored them as well.

But if some thought "concentration camp" was too harsh, others felt that "war relocation center" was too soft, a typical military euphemism that disguised something pernicious and contrary to American principles. This point of view called attention to the punitive aspects of the relocation: Manzanar was, plain and simple, a prison, and the ten thousand people "relocated" there were prisoners, not one of whom had been charged with a crime, let alone been convicted of one. The majority of these people, as the historical marker notes, were US citizens.

For years after its unveiling in 1973, the marker was repeatedly defaced, the attempts to chip and hack it still evident to this day. Dissatisfaction over commemoration of the relocation center resurfaced in the 1990s when the federal government designated Manzanar a national historic site. The local newspaper, the *Inyo Independent*, received scores of letters opposed to the designation.

According to the letter-writers, it was an affront to those who had served in the war and an unnecessary dredging up of an episode best forgotten. The very act of remembering or memorializing Manzanar in any way has continued to annoy many people. Over the years, there have been periodic attempts to destroy displays and reconstructions at the site. Park Service staff have been threatened as well. And, according to the *Los Angeles Times,* one person called the offices of the historical site to say that he had traveled two hundred miles just to urinate on the historical marker. Some opponents of the site have argued that it perpetuates a falsehood. Manzanar was nothing like a prison camp, they insist. It was, rather, a safe space where Japanese Americans came of their own free will for protection. The most extreme opponents have argued that no one was forcibly relocated; there were no watchtowers, no barbed wire, these internment deniers have claimed.

In fact, some residents of Owens Valley, tired of the fuss made over Manzanar, have gone so far as to claim not only that the internees were well treated but also that they were better off for being in the camp. One interviewee for an oral history project said that she would get "really riled up when they tell how bad it was at Manzanar," concluding that "they had everything there." In some ways, it is understandable that residents of the valley during the Second World War came to feel that way. Owens Valley was a hard place to live in even in good times. Rationing during the war years made it that much more difficult. Valley residents knew that the War Relocation Authority (WRA) was providing food for the Japanese Americans in the camp. Moreover, the camp had access to water unavailable to valley residents; the internees were thus able to grow crops that could not be grown outside the Manzanar boundary. In such circumstances, valley residents could conclude that the internees did not face deprivation the way the "loyal" citizens outside the camp did. Viewed this way, the situation could seem galling.

This point of view still circulates in the valley, passed down to new generations who have heard it from their trusted elders. Calling attention to injustices that the Japanese Americans suffered continues to rankle many in Owens Valley, even those who were born after the war ended. However, the belief that the internees were well treated overlooks many details about conditions in the camp. Start with the food. Most of it was canned—hot dogs, spinach, beans—and much of it barely tolerable. Even the best of it was very different from the diet the internees were used to. There were no chefs trained in preparation of food for large numbers of people. And for every meal, the internees had to line up for their food and then eat it in mess halls in shifts with thousands of other people. There was no privacy, no family mealtime.

Consider, as well, the sanitary facilities. People had to share the latrine with others, around 250 people per latrine. There was no privacy for showers or toilet use (some people resorted to carrying large cardboard boxes into the latrine and setting them up as a kind of screen around the toilet). Moreover, the living quarters (built on a barracks model) did not have access to running water.

Then there was the surveillance: posted guards bearing arms and searchlights from watchtowers constantly crisscrossing the grounds, shining into the windows of living quarters even in the middle of the night. Over three years' time, these inconveniences and strictures would prove intolerable to most people; in any case, such conditions hardly qualify as "having it good."

Beyond all this, the most significant response to the notion that internment was not so bad concerns the losses that Japanese Americans suffered. In numerous cases, families were split up, never to reunite. In other cases, Japanese Americans lost everything—homes, cars, fishing boats, farmland, household goods—possessions and wealth that were never to be recovered (quite a bit of it was simply confiscated by white neighbors, their fellow American citizens). At the end of the internment, there were no homes to return to, no farms, no jobs. They had been relocated in a rush—five to ten days in most cases—without a chance to make arrangements for the safekeeping of their property. They had been forced to sell many of their goods for pennies on the dollar. When the camps were closed, many had nowhere to go, nothing to do, no way to make a living. The government did not offer assistance. Would the Caucasian residents of Owens Valley—would any American—accept such treatment from the country of which they were rightful citizens? And yet seventy thousand American citizens and their families were treated in exactly this way. Far from having it easy in the internment camp, they lost everything in the relocation and suffered long-term consequences.

The official justification was that internment served to protect Japanese Americans from hostile actions on the part of their fellow citizens. The rhetoric of the time suggests that many Americans harbored strong suspicions of their fellow citizens of Japanese descent. The *Los Angeles Times*, for example, editorialized: "A viper is nonetheless a viper wherever the egg is hatched—so a Japanese American, born of Japanese parents, grows up to be a Japanese, not an American." And General John L. DeWitt, head of the US Army's Western Defense Command said, "The Japanese race is an enemy race and while many second and third generation Japanese born on American soil, possessed of American citizenship, have become 'Americanized,' the racial strains are undiluted. ...The very fact that no sabotage has taken place to date is a disturbing and confirming indication that such action will be taken."

It is worth noting that no Italian Americans or German Americans were treated similarly.

* * *

In contrast to the harsh or euphemistic terms for the camp, the site's name—Manzanar—has a sonorous, even poetic quality (as do some of the other relocation camps, such as Heart Mountain in Wyoming and Topaz in Utah). "Manzanar" is derived from the Spanish word for "apple" and references the vast orchards that were developed at the site at the beginning of the twentieth century, just before the City of Los Angeles acquired the property—along with most property in Owens Valley—for its water rights. After the water was diverted to the city, the orchards were left to wither; by 1942, when the first Japanese American internees arrived, only a few trees had survived. To establish an internment center on the Manzanar site, the federal government had to receive permission from the land's owner, the City of Los Angeles, which granted it with great reluctance (for the city, there were two issues: one, that a settlement of ten thousand people would require more water than Los Angeles wanted to surrender; and two, that the city did not want suspicious people—potential enemies of the United States—quartered so close to the city's water source). Los Angeles was equally reluctant to surrender Owens Valley land fifty years later when the national historic site was created. Eventually, the federal government struck a deal and the city transferred eight hundred acres to the Park Service for the creation of the historic site.

Very little of the camp remains; the original barracks, latrines, mess halls, factories, guard towers, barbed wire fencing, hospital, and school are all gone, dismantled within a few years of the war's end. Only the high school auditorium, built by the internees themselves, still stands. After spending years as a maintenance shed, the auditorium was eventually converted into the historic site's visitor center, where interpretive displays detail camp life (the museum in nearby Independence has additional displays and artifacts). The Park Service has also been adding to the otherwise barren grounds, building replicas of a guard tower, a barracks, a latrine, and a mess hall.

The main point of visual interest at Manzanar is a memorial obelisk at the western edge of the site, where the camp cemetery was located. Constructed in 1943 by stone mason Ryozo Kado (who also built the sentry posts at the camp entrance), the obelisk in honor of the dead has come to represent the human suffering that occurred on this site. Painted white, the pillar stands out starkly against the desert scrub, while the snow-capped mountains of the Sierra Nevada loom above. Only a handful of people are buried here (most of those who died at Manzanar—about 160—were cremated in accordance with Japanese traditions). Nevertheless, the memorial has become the focal point for pilgrims to Manzanar, including former internees, their families, and those who are disturbed by the unjust imprisonment of the Japanese Americans. Many pilgrims leave items at the base of the pillar, such as coins, origami cranes, sake bottles, and sundry religious objects. The Japanese characters on the face of the obelisk read "soul consoling tower."

Apart from the obelisk and the auditorium, almost nothing remains from the original camp. The weather, however, is much the same today—windy, dusty—as when the camp opened. The ever-present wind-blown dust of Owens Valley constantly swirls, choking, blinding, and coating those caught in its path. In 1942, strong winds greeted the arriving internees, dust blasting and penetrating every building, coating every surface of the hastily built barracks, mess halls, and latrines. During the night, dust would cover everything and everyone. Upon waking, the internees had to shake out their blankets and sheets. With limited bathing opportunities, they constantly felt unclean and gritty. Years later, no one could forget it: "When the wind blew it was terrible. Everybody resented being put in such a place, especially when they were suffocated by sand," one internee recalled.

Most of the people had come from the coast; many had lived near the ocean. To them, the dust was otherworldly: "We got there right in the middle of one of those windstorms that were very common in Manzanar. The dust was blowing so hard you couldn't see more than fifteen feet ahead." The first task for the new arrivals was to block the gaps and cracks in the barracks walls, using tin can lids as patches. But keeping the dust out proved difficult, if not impossible. Eye and lung irritations were common. Everybody suffered one way or another. Today, the dust and sand still blow hard over the former camp, giving visitors a tangible idea of the harsh conditions that those imprisoned at Manzanar had to endure.

Having no choice, they did manage to endure. The internees adopted a Japanese phrase as their mantra, a guiding philosophy for surviving the worst: *shikata ga nai* ("It cannot be helped"). With impressive resourcefulness and ingenuity, they solved the pressing problems that imprisonment forced upon them. They combatted the dust. They built furniture from scrap lumber, including beds (for which they had only straw-stuffed sacks to serve as mattresses) and chairs and tables. They constructed and tended fine gardens. They trained morning glories and pumpkin vines to make the barracks walls more aesthetically acceptable. They set up beauty salons and barbershops and dental clinics. They built baseball fields and churches and temples. They staffed hospitals and schools. They put on concerts and organized scout troops for the children. They operated factories and made products, such as camouflage netting, to support the American war effort. Most impressively, they transformed dry fallow land into a fertile farm and grew crops so that they had something to eat other than canned food (at harvest festivals, the residents of Owens Valley came to the camp to buy some of the surplus).

In short, within one square mile, Manzanar became a fully functioning settlement of ten thousand people, the largest settlement that has ever existed in Owens Valley. To fit that many people in such a small area required a tightly arranged plat, especially since there were no structures (other than watchtowers) taller than one story. The camp was laid out on a strict grid of thirty-five blocks, with fourteen barracks per block (plus an additional structure serving as a latrine). The identical barracks—twenty feet by one hundred feet—were subdivided for four families each. Each latrine was shared by over fifty families.

Of all this, almost nothing remains except a hint of the grid and some of the building foundations. Here and there, granite stones encircle trees or form the semblance of a walkway or outline a long-vanished garden. Otherwise, the Manzanar site is a scruffy desert where saltbrush predominates. Standing at the memorial obelisk in the cemetery and looking east, one can only imagine what was here decades ago.

The imagination must conjure up not just the thirty-five blocks of barracks (490 housing units in all, along with their associated latrines and mess halls) but also the school buildings, the hospital facilities (where around five hundred babies were born), the community center, the gardens, the factories, the ball fields, the workshops, the golf course with its packed sand greens— all built or made by the internees themselves. One must imagine, as well, the separate structures comprising what was known as "Beverly Hills"—the section of Manzanar where the Caucasians who administered the camp resided (including schoolteachers, secretaries, health officials, and government bureaucrats). There was also a "Children's Village"—the orphanage at Manzanar where one hundred children of Japanese ancestry were housed, some of them babies. These were orphans who had been residing in orphanages in the so-called exclusion zone and were thus subject to Roosevelt's Executive Order 9066. Suspicion of persons of Japanese descent extended to one and all, no matter how young or old. So, orphans were removed from their orphanages and sent to Manzanar, where a makeshift orphanage had to be set up and operated. Orphans who had been living with foster families—

white or Japanese—were also banished from the exclusion zone and sent to the camp. Similarly, elderly and senile citizens in nursing homes or hospitals were removed from those facilities and sent to Manzanar.

Given such draconian measures, many internees found that the conditions of internment bordered on the absurd, prompting some to resort to humor as a coping device. For example, some Manzanar residents tacked up signs to give their barracks names such as Dusty Inn, Manzanar Mansion, and Waldorf Astoria. As Miné Okubo commented in Citizen 13660, her trenchant account of incarceration: "Humor is the only thing that mellows life and shows life as the circus it is. After being uprooted, everything seemed ridiculous, insane, and stupid. There we were in an unfinished camp, with snow and cold. The evacuees helped sheetrock the walls for warmth and built the barbed wire fence to fence themselves in. We had to sing 'God Bless America' many times with a flag. Guards all around with shotguns, you're not going to walk out. I mean ... what could you do? So many crazy things happened in the camp. So, the joke and humor I saw in the camp was not in a joyful sense, but ridiculous and insane."

Here and there around the grounds of the national historic site, interpretive signage helps today's visitors imagine what cannot be seen. One sign indicates the location of the eighteen-foot-tall factory sheds where internees wove camouflage nets in support of the American war effort. Nearby was a mattress factory that produced bedding for the internees. As the sign points out, Manzanar was "nearly self-sufficient by 1944" with industries "ranging from shoe and typewriter repair to soy sauce and tofu processing. A clothing factory produced uniforms and work clothes for the camp's nurses, mess hall workers, and policemen, while a furniture factory built desks, chairs, baby cribs, and toys."

The sign also alludes to "the Manzanar Riot in December 1942" without providing much detail. This "riot" occurred after low-paid kitchen workers tried to organize a union. The union's leader was arrested, which led to a mass protest. A crowd marched on the police station, whereupon military police shot and killed two Japanese men. Other protesters were taken into custody, branded as "agitators," and removed from Manzanar to more remote camps in Arizona and Utah. These events show how much the state and its authorities controlled the lives of the internees. Under such circumstances, the internees had no illusions that they were anything but prisoners.

The interpretive signage does not mention a memorial service that was held in 1945 at the flagpole outside the newly built high school auditorium. Virtually everyone still residing in the camp attended this service, watching as the American flag was lowered to half-staff and an honor guard fired guns in tribute. They were gathered to honor the memory of Robert Nakasaki and Sadao Munemori, two Japanese American men who had died in Italy during battle. Munemori was awarded the Medal of Honor for dying in the act of saving fellow American soldiers. The ceremony was held at Manzanar because the families of the two men were internees. While Nakasaki and Munemori were fighting—and dying—for America, America was keeping their families imprisoned behind barbed wire solely because of their ethnic background.

If imagination fails and visitors find that they cannot picture the site as an internment camp, they can turn to the work of three extraordinary photographers who documented life at Manzanar. Two are well known: Dorothea Lange and Ansel Adams. The third, Toyo Miyatake, should be much better known.

During the Depression years of the 1930s, Dorothea Lange produced seminal work in documentary photography and photojournalism for the Farm Security Administration. Many of her photos are readily recognized, such as "Migrant Mother," perhaps the most iconic image of the Great Depression. Following Roosevelt's signing of Executive Order 9066, the War Relocation Authority hired Lange to document the relocation effort. Why the WRA wanted such documentation is unclear—perhaps to demonstrate that the relocation was being done efficiently and humanely. If this was the government's goal, Lange was a strange choice. She deeply disagreed with the government's decision to relocate Japanese Americans, and as she worked on the project, she found ample evidence of the process's underlying callousness and inhumanity. Once commissioned, Lange energetically documented every stage of the relocation process, first photographing Japanese Americans at the homes, farms, and jobs that they were about to lose. She then followed them through the round-up, the forced removal to assembly centers, and finally the internment in the relocation camps. Lange spent several days at Manzanar during the summer of 1942. Her photos—especially those of the assembly centers, such as Tanforan in San Bruno, California—emphasize "rationalization and control, featuring the industrial and technological forces of domination," according to Linda Gordon, Lange's biographer. In the photos, people are kept waiting in lines then rounded up and herded about. They have been inspected and tagged, their names replaced with numbers. Old and young, male and female—all are subjected to various indignities and deprivations (both intentional and unintentional). Their faces show bewilderment, fear, anxiety, boredom, despair, with an occasional wry smile suggesting acknowledgement of the absurdity of it all. In Lange's photographs, the presence of a controlling authority is evident. This was a bureaucratic operation, the photos emphasize, with all the dehumanization that we have come to associate with such operations. The Manzanar photos reveal something else as well: defiance and determination to overcome the ordeal.

Somehow, Lange managed to convey this stark interpretation despite constant hassles and restrictions, particularly wherever the army had jurisdiction. She was not allowed to photograph barbed wire, watchtowers, or armed soldiers. An "escort" (or watchdog) followed her around, monitoring her activities, preventing her from interacting with the internees and denying her access to certain areas. Even so, the resulting photos were deemed too critical and too sensitive. Lange had to turn over all prints and negatives to authorities, who—recognizing the criticism implicit in the images—kept them from the public. Her photographs were not included in the "Final Report on Japanese Evacuation" issued by the US Army Western Defense Command—the military overseer of the civilian-led WRA. This report outlined the reasons for removing "the potential menace" that Japanese Americans supposedly presented. It also documented the removal process. Although photographs accompanied the report, none of Lange's images made the cut; the army apparently decided that they were too provocative in depicting the harsher aspects of the removal process. The WRA used a few of her photos; the army censored the rest, stamping them with the word "impounded" (a somewhat ironic designation given the subjects of the photos). Twenty years would pass before the photos, stored in the National Archives, were seen by anyone, including Lange. These images are, as Linda Gordon describes them, valuable as art and as statement: "These photographs exemplify Lange's mastery of composition and of visual condensation of human feelings and relationships. They also unequivocally denounce an unjustified, unnecessary, and racist policy."

Ansel Adams visited Manzanar more than a year after Lange. His photographs have a much different focus from hers. Manzanar was more developed and the conditions less harsh when Adams toured the camp. Moreover, as a friend of the camp's chief administrator, Adams did not face the hassles and restrictions that Lange had faced. Adams's photos, which comprise the only documentary project that the renowned nature photographer ever undertook, emphasize the remarkable resilience of the internees. In some ways, this focus reflected the wishes of Adams's friend Ralph Merritt, the director of Manzanar. Interestingly, Merritt did not agree with the rationale for internment, and he believed that the camps represented a grave injustice in violation of America's core values. He was determined to improve conditions for the internees; he also looked for opportunities to sway public opinion about Japanese Americans. He hoped that Adams could show them in a different light—as hardworking, loyal American citizens. This became Adams's focus as he worked.

Just as Lange had sought to do with her photographs, Adams wanted to present a contrast to the demeaning caricatures of the Japanese in American propaganda and media (imagery so prevalent that even beloved children's author Dr. Seuss produced such caricatures). At Manzanar, Adams turned to a genre he rarely worked in—portraiture—to draw forth the individual qualities of the internees. Adams stressed their resourcefulness, their ability to make the best of the situation. The photographs show them coping, enduring, and in some ways thriving despite the harsh conditions they suffered. In this sense, Adams's work captures "the spirit of the people of Manzanar," as he put it, and challenges the prevailing views of Japanese Americans as inherently disloyal, deceitful, and treacherous. It is hard to see the people in these portraits as traitors or enemies or incarnations of evil. Especially poignant are Adams's photographs of Japanese Americans in American military uniforms visiting their interned families. In her biography of Adams, Mary Street Alinder notes: "One particularly strong image reveals a simple still life of a tabletop in the Yorimitsu family's quarters covered with a small lace doily. A framed picture of a Caucasian Jesus leans against a portrait of their son, Bob, a PFC in military uniform, with three letters from him tucked to the side. Ansel quietly captured the irony of the son fighting for a country that had imprisoned the parents."

What Adams's images do not show—or show only minimally in comparison to Lange's work—are Manzanar's stark circumstances. Arriving some eighteen months after Lange's visit, Adams saw (or believed that he saw) a community that had succeeded in overcoming miserable conditions and cruel injustice. As it happened, Adams's approach to the project produced images that fit well with the government's desire to present the internment as humane. In Adams's photographs, the imprisoned Japanese Americans seem to have overcome adversity; they even seem to have thrived to such an extent that the internment comes across as tolerable, almost beneficial. In some ways, his photographs depict or can be interpreted to depict the internment as successful for both the government and the Japanese Americans. In effect, viewed a certain way the photographs seemingly present a justification of the internment. Whether Adams intended this interpretation is unclear; but his written text can certainly seem questionable in hindsight. For example, he wrote: "Manzanar is only a rocky wartime detour on the road of American citizenship." Such a blithe assessment led Lange and others to criticize Adams's Manzanar work as "shameful" in that it apparently glossed over the brutalities of internment.

This criticism is somewhat accurate concerning the photographs that Adams included in his book, *Born Free and Equal*, and in the exhibit of his work at the Museum of Modern Art in November 1944. Moreover, the text that Adams wrote for the book unconvincingly plays up the "positive" aspects of incarceration, namely that it had given the Japanese Americans a chance to prove their worthiness, a test they had passed, in Adams's view, with flying colors. The success of Japanese Americans in passing this test demonstrated, Adams somewhat fatuously wrote, "the immensity and opportunity of America."

In Adams's defense, he had to be cautious about the images that he included in the exhibit and the book, as authorities (such as MOMA's administration) fretted that images critical of the relocation would be viewed as subversive to the war effort. Adams's cautious approach is justified, one could argue, in that some of his photographs did get published and publicized, whereas Lange's did not. As a consequence, most of Adams's grimmer images—those that convey confinement, monotony, and authority—were not seen until the 1980s when Adams, approaching the end of his life, donated the remaining images to the Library of Congress. Late in life, Adams also came to regret the tone of the verbal text of *Born Free and Equal*; in his autobiography he called the internment "an obviously oppressive situation."

Given that Adams's photographs emphasize the achievement of the Japanese Americans in overcoming adversity, the governmental bureaucracy and the American public might have found the images reassuring. This was not the prevailing view, however, as Adams still took heat from those who wanted to see less positive images of the "perfidious" Japanese. Even Adams's positive images of Japanese Americans met with criticism and backlash from the military and others who insisted that the Japanese—no matter what their citizenry—were treacherous and evil. Representing them in any other light was shortsighted and compromised the war effort, these critics felt. Apocryphal stories circulated about public burnings of Adams's book; these burnings apparently did not actually happen (though Adams believed that they had). Even so, plenty of people at the time thought the book should not have been published.

What can be said, finally, is that Ansel Adams's fine photographs of Manzanar contribute another viewpoint to the debate over relocation and internment. They are an important part of the documentary record.

As revelatory as the photographs of Lange and Adams are, it is the work of a third photographer, Toyo Miyatake, that compels the greatest attention. His work stands out because of his unique perspective—his immersion in the life of Manzanar. Miyatake was an internee and thus knew the camp and the consequences of removal and internment from a perspective unavailable to Adams and Lange.

Born in Japan in 1895, Miyatake came to the United States when he was fourteen. He worked as a photographer in Los Angeles and owned a studio in Little Tokyo. He was friends with the renowned photographer Edward Weston. In 1942, when he was forty-seven, Miyatake and his family were sent to Manzanar. Cameras were banned at in the camp. Nevertheless, Miyatake smuggled in a lens. He then had woodworkers—fellow internees—make a box to encase the lens and a viewfinder, yielding a crude but functioning camera. It was well disguised as an ordinary box, enabling Miyatake to take illicit photographs for nine months before he was caught. The camp director, Ralph Merritt (the same camp director who had invited Adams to photograph Manzanar) decided to permit Miyatake to continue taking photographs as long as he was accompanied by a WRA employee. Eventually, Miyatake was allowed to work on his own and set up a darkroom with professional equipment.

Like Lange and Adams, Miyatake documented daily life in Manzanar: little girls receiving the gift of donated dolls; women seated under hair helmets in a beauty salon; children lined up at a barracks identified by a sign as a "Toy Loan Center"; two uniformed drum majorettes striking a pose with the Sierra Nevada looming as a backdrop. While the work of Lange and Adams is properly categorized as "documentary," Miyatake's photos go beyond documentation: they reveal to us the complex emotional and psychological effects of internment. As such, these are photographs of deep insight. They are photographs of witness and testimony. Because Miyatake spent not days but years in the camp, his photos bear witness in a way that Lange's and Adams's work could not. He was no mere visitor to Manzanar; rather, he inhabited Manzanar, an insider whose status allowed him to be present for scenes unavailable to visitors: boys swimming (illegally) in a pond just beyond the camp's perimeter; a soldier taking leave of his parents on the stoop of their barracks home; a ceremony taking place at the memorial for the dead. (Adams and Lange also photographed this memorial, but no people are present in their photos).

Some people see intimacy in Miyatake's photos. For others, the outstanding quality is *presence*. This sense of presence draws viewers in, making them part of the scene. Other photos of Manzanar, compelling as they might be, keep their distance; the scene is viewed as though through a pane, perhaps from an observation post (in fact, Ansel Adams made photos from a platform on top of his car, the camera a good ten feet above ground level). As an internee, Miyatake did not need to lurk or linger on the edges as an outside observer. He was an embedded photographer, on a par with his fellow internees, fluent with the language, life, and culture of the camp. He was thus able to make photos that were not only candid—Lange and Adams managed to make wonderfully candid photos at Manzanar—but also *involved*. A gardener, hat in hand, pauses by his meticulously cared-for terraced flowerbeds. Two children in a wooden shack stand neck high in an array of flowers admiring the blooms. A group of children and adults kneels on the ground to play games. In all these photos, the camera is at eye level with the subjects, as though the viewer is also standing amid the blooms, kneeling in the dirt, playing games.

As time went by, as Miyatake entered a second and then a third year of incarceration, he felt compelled to make bolder statements with his photography. Finally able to work on his own without interference or supervision from the camp administration, he looked for opportunities to include those aspects of Manzanar that had been elided from the sanitized photography produced under government sanction. In one series of photos, Miyatake's camera captured three boys standing near the camp's barbed-wire fence, peering through the wires at the world beyond, tentatively touching the wire. Another photo depicts a hand entering the frame close to the camera, extending a pair of wire cutters toward the barbed wire, a watchtower lurking in the background.

Ansel Adams is much better known, of course, for photographing the Sierra Nevada than for documenting the Japanese American internment at Manzanar. Ten miles south of Manzanar, at the edge of the town of Lone Pine, Adams made one of his more renowned photographs, "Winter Sunrise, the Sierra Nevada, from Lone Pine." Adams made his exposure just as the sun's first rays revealed the jagged peaks of the Sierra, Mount Whitney and its prominent pinnacles among them. In the foreground, sunlight touches a meadow where horses graze. Alternating bands of light and shadow give the image a mystical, fairyland quality. Magnificent as the photograph may be, it is odd that Adams made this the concluding image of his book on Manzanar—an image not obviously related to the internment camp other than by geographic propinquity. Perhaps he wanted to pull back from the discreditable affairs of humans to focus instead on the timeless, enduring beauty of nature. Perhaps he wanted to draw a contrast between the imprisoned people depicted in the preceding photographs and the free-ranging horses in the final image. Perhaps he couldn't resist ending with an image more in keeping with his aesthetic sensibilities than a documentary project and its attendant social commentary allowed for. In any case, the image is compelling and disturbing when considered in the context of Manzanar.

Similarly, the view of the Sierra—so awesome and awe-inspiring as one drives along the floor of Owens Valley—is disturbed and challenged by the fact of Manzanar. Leaving the national historic site and heading south down US 395 toward the location where Adam's made his "Winter Sunrise" image, one finds it difficult to contemplate the natural beauty of the mountains without also thinking about this human blot on the landscape. The nearby presence of the internment camp alters the scenery and complicates the vision of anyone—whether traveler or photographer—trying to focus purely on nature's splendor.

From the town of Lone Pine, the Whitney Portal Road heads west toward the Sierra Nevada Mountains and the highest point in the continental United States. Along the way, the road passes close to some of Owens Valley's most intriguing geological features. After crossing the Los Angeles Aqueduct, the road swings by some fault scarps left by a strong earthquake in 1872, one of the most powerful ever to hit California. The whole area is in a fault zone that has regularly "down-dropped," or sunk, while the granite blocks of the Sierra Nevada have pushed upward. This seismic activity makes Owens Valley what geologists call a *graben*, a depressed block of the earth's crust. The valley is getting deeper with time; even now, ever so slowly, the mountain ranges to the east and west are rising while the valley floor is sinking. The fault scarp west of Lone Pine looks like an embankment or cliff about twenty feet high—an indication of the vertical displacement that occurred during the 1872 earthquake, and just one small instance of the massive forces that have gone into the creation of the Sierra Nevada and Owens Valley.

Shortly after crossing the fault, the road enters the Alabama Hills, which are part of a massive granite block long ago shed from the Sierra Nevada and now mostly buried in the sand, gravel, and silt that have subsequently washed down from the mountain range. The hills are the portion of the block that protrudes from this alluvial fan. Because of erosion, the giant weathered boulders and crowns of the Alabama Hills have taken on weird and fantastic shapes. Most are smooth and rounded, their elongated, upright forms looking somewhat like breaching whales. Numerous natural arches appear here and there among the hills.

Following the road in and around the Alabama Hills, travelers might find themselves thinking that the landscape looks strangely familiar, as though they had been here before. Up ahead, a historical marker comes into view, and stopping to read it one discovers an explanation for this sense of déjà vu:

> *Movie Flats*
>
> *Since 1920, hundreds of movies and TV episodes, including Gunga Din, How The West Was Won, Khyber Rifles, Bengal Lancers, and High Sierra, along with, The Lone Ranger and Bonanza, with such stars as Tom Mix, Hopalong Cassidy, Roy Rogers, Gary Cooper, Gene Autry, Glen Ford, Humphrey Bogart, and John Wayne, have been filmed in these rugged Alabama Hills with their majestic Sierra Nevada background. Plaque dedicated by Roy Rogers, whose first starring feature was filmed here in 1933.*

Anyone who has seen a Western movie or television show has seen this landscape, has indeed come to regard these Alabama Hills as the quintessential landscape of the American West. This is the setting, as presented in films and television, of so many of America's archetypal stories and foundational myths. In hundreds of films and shows, Hollywood has used the Alabama Hills as a stand-in for the entire American West, the place we see in our imagination when we think or dream about the West (the only other terrain to rival it is Monument Valley in Arizona).

Interestingly, Hollywood has also used this same location for films set in India, the Holy Land, Spain, and even other planets; even so, these hills and weird-shaped boulders (along with the Sierra backdrop) are most immediately recognizable as the landscape of the Wild West.

Taking a walk on the many tracks made here by the vehicles of film crews—a despoliation that has resulted, ironically, from the near-reverent idealization of this landscape—one recalls iconic scenes and characters, starting with films made in the 1920s, such as *Riders of the Purple Sage*, starring Tom Mix. In the mind's eye, good guy Mix peers from a ridge, studying an encampment of horse thieves. Nearby, Hopalong Cassidy crouches behind a boulder, six-shooter drawn, ready for the inevitable shootout. Over there, the Lone Ranger and Tonto squat to examine tracks. Roy Rogers sits tall on Trigger, riding faster than possible in real life then dropping from the saddle to duke it out with bad hombres. Here comes Gene Autry singing "Down in the Valley" from the saddle of a trotting horse. There's Clint Eastwood taking on a crew of rough-riding bandits, one gun against ten. And there's revenge-seeking Steve McQueen at a crossroads beneath the high Sierra staring down the dusty tracks as he trails his father's killers. And over there, silhouetted against the dimming horizon, stands Barbara Stanwyck, who loved Owens Valley so much she had her ashes spread here, the place where she rode horses, fired guns, bested men at poker, held the dead and dying in her arms, and basically governed the whole show. No one could cross her, the maverick queen of the Wild West.

A host of other familiar faces manifest amid the boulders: Robert Mitchum, Kirk Douglas, Gregory Peck, Henry Fonda, Dennis Hopper, Gary Cooper, Tyrone Power, Spencer Tracy. Classic scenes recur before one's eyes. Posse after posse wends among the boulders, pausing over sagebrush, cutting for sign. War-whooping Natives appear on ridges, incongruously dressed in Plains Indian attire. Countless gun battles, bullets pinging and ricocheting off rocks, occasionally finding the target, bodies tumbling down slopes, falling from clifftops, rolling in dust, twitching in death throes: it all happened—and seems to continue happening—in these foothills just above Owens Valley.

Towering above all, John Wayne comes striding to the fore of the pack—the Duke, who rode, roped, and shot his way across Owens Valley in a dozen movies. Even today, the Duke's image is everywhere in Lone Pine—in store windows, in murals, on postcards, on every kind of souvenir imaginable, in bad art on the walls of tourist saloons. In his last appearance on film—a television commercial for Great Western Bank—Wayne sits on a horse and gazes around at these very boulders, the desert scrub, the snow-capped Sierra Nevada—the archetypal setting where his archetypal persona came to life. "Beautiful country," Wayne says with a sigh, as he contemplates the land.

The Duke's words might well come to mind as one wanders the trails through the boulders. At some point, inevitably, one arrives at a place where the panorama of Owens Valley stretches out below—the dusty, water-deprived bed of Owens Lake just to the south; the stark Inyo Mountains opposite, gashed with abandoned mining operations; the aqueduct glinting with water destined for Los Angeles; the trickling remnant of Owens River; the long, arrow-straight highway passing through hamlets, crossing fault lines, skirting reservations and internment camps, and cutting across desiccated orchards, farms, and ranches. It's easy to see why Hollywood came here to shoot—the scenery, the visuals are spectacular, despite the despoiling marks of man's handiwork. "Beautiful country," just like John Wayne said. Owens Valley is the perfect backdrop for telling the story of the American West, for Owens Valley is True West, and what has happened here is the quintessential Western story, a triumphant story in some ways, but also a story of conflict, conquest, exploitation, and degradation.

Hollywood, however, has more often been interested in telling only the story of triumph, transforming Owens Valley into a mythic place with a much different history from the history that actually played out—and continues to play out—in the "land of little rain."

Beautiful country. Should John Wayne have the last word on Owens Valley? His observation is true enough: it is indeed beautiful country. But if we only see the valley's beauty—what is left of it—we are apt to lose sight of a deeper, richer, and more emblematic story.

En Route: Elko, Nevada

A late-night arrival in Elko, Nevada, means no vacancy except in cheap dives like the Louis Motel on the far west end of town. At night, Elko seems rather joyless, even though the billboards on the approach to town promise good times in the form of casinos, brothels, and bars. The point is underscored by a song playing in the Horseshoe Club: "You're supposed to be feeling good. ..." But in the town's joy-spots, there's no evidence of good feelings, not on this night. Tonight, Elko is ground zero in a vast dislocated landscape, the place Emerson called "unapproachable America."

The bars are hazy and rank, with a lineup of men drinking hard and quick, their loud talk lapsing into expressions of resignation: *Yeah, but what you gonna do? That's the way it always goes. Same old, same old.* Around the corner, a gun shop sells "tactical survival" supplies. Just down the street, neon signs flicker in the desert night: the town's three brothels all in a row. Ghost-like in the glow, patrons pass in and out of a shabby door with squealing hinges. In the casinos, people play fast, pumping in money, mesmerized by slot machines or the numbers flashing on the keno board. Everybody's drinking. The historical marker in Railroad Park says Elko's always been a "rough, drinking, cowboy town."

In the light of day, Elko tries to strike an upbeat note. After all, it's the home of LeeAnne's Floral Design, Haley's Fine Gifts, the Cowboy Gear and Arts Museum, and a storefront Wedding

Chapel. And there's a bargain breakfast on offer in the coffee shop of the Commercial Casino: two eggs any style, toast, and your choice of sausage or bacon. A cup of coffee and things look a little brighter.

But for all that, it's not long before Elko's medley shifts to the minor key, the downbeat. Two elderly folks in a booth are discussing their gambling successes and failures loud enough for all to hear. She's losing heavily, it seems, and he says, "I told you, stop drawing to fill straights—it ain't gonna happen. Play for three of a kind and pairs and you might—repeat, *might*—come out ahead."

The waitresses, meanwhile, carry on their own conversation. "Feels like 11:30," one says. "Wish it was," her partner answers. Then some gossip: "You see that guy in here about six? Drunk and dropping money all over the floor? Thought he'd pass out right in his omelet."

In Elko, cigarette smoke and prosthetics are prevalent. People are not healthy. Everyone in the coffee shop is smoking, except for the guy wheeling around an oxygen tank, plastic tubes hooked to his nose. Another woman has a tube stuck in her throat. There are people with back braces, walkers, canes. Almost everyone looks decrepit; even guys in their twenties and thirties talk in old and weary voices, their shoulders slumped. Or is it just that it's early morning in a casino and what do you expect?

A trucker type comes in, takes a stool at the far end next to another trucker. The newcomer is a little too neat compared to most drivers—expensive aviator glasses, pressed jeans, shiny boots—and what's more he's a regular chatterbox. Goes on and on about the trucking business, tossing out buzzwords and trade talk: burning oil, liability, off-loading, air cylinders, hydraulic cylinders. His grittier and more taciturn interlocutor nods, blows cigarette smoke, and grimaces when the stranger pulls out a catalog of trucking supplies: another goddam salesman.

Pouring coffee, the waitress says, "Been winning?"

The question is directed at a young man with a faraway look. He chews his toast slowly, takes his time answering. "Not a player," he says, finally.

"I am," she says. "But I play too much. Some days I put all my tip money in, and that ain't good."

Across the coffee shop, a man gets up from a booth and says to his partners, "I lost it all, now I got to go back and start all over again."

They all laugh, another instance of the weird joviality about losing that predominates in these casino towns. People seem to regard their losses as inevitable, part of the fun they're supposed to be having.

A new arrival now engages the waitress. "Thought you'd be long gone from this place by now, baby doll."

"Nope. Just hanging on."

"Me, too. I keep trying to leave this place and I can't seem to make my break."

"Yeah, they keep me hanging around. Just to see what I'll do next, I guess."

"It's like the goddamned circus."

Time to move on. At the edge of town, Old Highway 40 seems to disappear into heat mirage and a vast searing sky. You're gaining speed, lifting off the cracked and ridged macadam—and it's like you're flying, flying into the great wide open and still not getting anywhere.

III

Travelers

Geographic curiosity leads me
on and on, and I can't stop.

—Elizabeth Bishop

Siboney

I was at a brewpub recently when a song playing on the sound system caught my attention. I knew the song from somewhere, but I couldn't quite place it. I wracked my brain, trying to recall the context—movie soundtrack? Warner Brothers cartoon? A record my parents used to play?

"Hey, what's that song?" I asked the bartender.

"Don't know, man. It's an Internet station. Big band or show tunes or something like that. Give me a second and I'll go back and check the screen for you."

While he was off checking, I suddenly remembered how I knew the song. Several years before I had heard it in a restaurant with my Uncle Joe. As usual, Joe had a story to go with the song.

Uncle Joe was quite the character—a world traveler, a raconteur, a nonconformist. He had been everywhere, it seemed, places you had never heard of, places you couldn't imagine. Hearing the song brought back Uncle Joe's voice and the stories he would tell on those rare occasions when he reappeared out of the blue to regale the family with his traveler's tales before abruptly disappearing again.

Every five years or so, he showed up unannounced—an enigmatic knock in the night while the household slept; and then the flicked-on porch light would reveal Uncle Joe standing there, stamping in the cold. When the door cracked open, we would hear his hearty growl, "Hey ya, sis, open up already will you? It's frigging cold out here. Where are those kids? Come here you little rugrats and give old Joe a hug."

For the next few days, Joe's booming, gruff voice and boisterous laughter would fill the house. My mother would fuss over him and prepare his favorite foods, feigning a frown whenever he ventured into vulgarity. We knew she wasn't really upset over the bad words; her joy at seeing her wayward brother again outweighed everything. Soon the frown gave way, and mother laughed—covering her mouth in embarrassment—at some quip or bawdy song, even as she warned Joe not to talk so coarsely and carry on like that in front of the children. On cue, Joe would roar, "Bull malarkey! Horseshit!" Whereupon we kids would fall apart with the giggles.

My father, too, would attempt—briefly—to show disapproval of his brother-in-law, whose capricious, adventurous, haphazard life contrasted so pointedly with father's own stable, staid businessman's routine. But Joe would always win him over. Despite father's outward consternation, he clearly relished the stories that Joe told. He would listen with frowns, nods, smiles—and then ask some question to elicit more information. "You say the islanders eat their octopus raw? Now, how did that taste, I wonder? Were you really able to stomach it?"

And that would get Joe going. "Oh, sure, your octopus is a first-rate delicacy. Raw, cooked, stewed, pickled. It's all good." He would then describe some truly weird food that he had eaten in Madagascar or Tasmania or somewhere. "Now that's something real nasty for you, near impossible to choke that crap down."

Men from the neighborhood would stop by to drink whisky-laced eggnog and listen to Joe's stories. Oh, those stories—tall tales full of brio and absurdity. They were so unlikely, over-the-top, and full of exaggeration. Everyone knew it, including Joe. But they were irresistible, like those Ripley's believe-it-or-not booklets we used to read in drugstores. Joe waxed on and on about ports of call, bar girls, gambling dens, Pacific atolls, typhoons, northern lights, killer whales, polar bears. There

were adventures with Galapagos turtles and Easter Island statues;
pygmies, cannibals, snake charmers, and belly dancers all showed
up in Joe's yarns. He alluded to the navy and the merchant
marines and told us all about the boats he'd been on—everything
from gleaming destroyers to rust buckets that barely stayed afloat.
A life at sea, a life on the road: Uncle Joe had been everywhere,
done everything, and he relished telling all about it. His voice
filled the room, and everybody was drawn in.

Throughout my childhood, Joe showed up sporadically to
enliven our house for a few days, generally looking none the
worse for wear. There might be a new scar or a new tattoo, in
which case we'd be sure to hear some crazy story about how he
got it. Then, after a few hyperbolic days he would disappear just
as suddenly as he had arrived, while we were left behind, stuck in
our routines.

The fourth or fifth time he appeared the rest of the family was
out of town. I was in college at the time, working the night shift
over the holidays to earn money for school. One morning I came
home and found him asleep on the porch swing. It was bitter
cold, and he shivered in his sleep. I shook him and spoke his
name.

He stared up at me, groggy, befuddled. "Oh, hey ya, kid.
How you doing? Now, which one are you? Davey? Christ, getting
so big."

Right away I could tell that he had changed. It was in his
voice—now raspy and feeble, no longer the gruff and muscular
storyteller's voice I remembered. He seemed frailer in body,
too, as he slowly unfolded himself from the swing and unsteadily
entered the house.

He dropped his duffel bag inside the door and listened without
apparent interest to my explanation of the family's whereabouts.
"That's ok, kid, that's ok. I just need a place to bunk for a spell."

For the next two days, he moped around the house, sullen and silent. There were no stories. He flipped through magazines or books, intermittently sighing or grunting.

On the third day of his visit, I sat with Joe in the kitchen. He had a can of beer and a magazine open on the table before him, but he didn't seem interested in either. This was the room where he had energetically told his wild tales—acted them out, practically—followed by robust guffaws when my mother scolded him for prurient vocabulary: "*Joseph*, the children!" (His rejoinder: "They're going to learn it one way or another. Probably at school. Might as well hear it from their old Uncle Joe.") I had never known anyone so full of life.

But now I had to lean forward to catch his words. I asked him what he had been up to since his last visit—must have been about five years previous. He was vague. "Oh, this and that, kid, this and that." He mumbled something about the merchant marines and a halfway house.

"What's that?" I asked. "A halfway house?"

He shrugged. "It's like..." The pause was long. "Like jail."

He stared at the beer can. "Anyway, what does it matter? Say, kid, I'm feeling good and goddamned peckish. What do we got for grub?"

We reviewed the contents of the pantry and the refrigerator. There usually wasn't much other than box meals or frozen food.

"Nah, this is all crap," Uncle Joe said. "We need something with a kick to it, something spicy. Real food. You got any spicy restaurants in this sorry-assed burg?"

There wasn't much to choose from. It was a typical Midwestern suburb—chain restaurants, bland fast food. I mentioned a couple of strip-mall Chinese joints.

"Szechuan or Cantonese?" Joe asked. "There's a big difference. Szechuan's got the heat, the flavor. But it has to be real Szechuan. None of this Americanized crap."

I didn't know what kind of Chinese restaurants we had, but it was a fair guess they were Americanized. I doubted they would do. Then I remembered the unincorporated area out by the county landfill where Mexicans and other Latin American immigrants had settled. There were some stores, some hole-in-the-wall diners, a butcher shop.

"Sounds like the ticket," Joe said. "Lead the way, kid."

We drove out to the edge of the suburban sprawl, past the incorporated limits. For five miles or so, Monroe Boulevard was a long strip of the usual shopping centers, gas stations, car dealerships, and franchise restaurants. With Christmas season in full swing, plenty of cars were on the road, jamming the parking lots despite the cold weather. Christmas lights twinkled on the storefronts.

After a while Monroe became State Highway 411 and the busy commercial sector gave way to a darker, sketchier stretch of road. Used car lots, industrial compounds, the county sewage treatment plant, then some fields interspersed with junkyards. Finally, we came to the ill-lit section of trailer courts and old barracks where migrant farmworkers lived.

We found a couple of storefront diners open, their windows steamed over. Joe sized them up. One looked a little tidier than the other, but Joe opted for the less kempt one on the theory that you get better food—"the real deal," as he put it—in a greasier joint.

And in fact, when we put it to the test, the food was, in Joe's estimation, "not too bad." He asked for the spiciest dish they had, which turned out to be a plate of goat meat swimming in a dark red sauce. We had some Mexican beer to go with it, and after a few bottles we were enjoying ourselves.

Joe told me a little bit more about his whereabouts since his last visit. Turned out there had, in fact, been a stint in jail. Double-crossed in Thailand, total frame job. But it wasn't the worst thing he'd been through in life. Some freighters he'd worked on had been real hellholes. Not that he ever wanted to do time again, "especially not in no third world country," but he'd survived, even made some good business contacts in Thailand. Something positive might yet come of his jail stint. Anyway, it wasn't a long stint. Someone had owed him a favor, got his sentence reduced.

"What kind of business contacts?" I asked.

"Who can say, kid. Who can say. You never know."

Music played while we ate and talked—Spanish radio. Trumpets. Accordions. Exuberant rhythm sections. Catchy stuff. The waitress sang along as she floated around the room. A new song started up and Joe said, "Well, I'll be goddamned. Haven't heard this one in years."

He was suddenly contemplative, his gaze focused on the tabletop. As the song proceeded, a smile came to his face, a sad smile. Wistful.

On the surface, it was not, in fact, a sad song but a lively dance number with a big band sound. The recording values were outdated, placing it in the 1940s or 1950s—the era when Latin dance music was enjoying some popularity in America. Despite the upbeat tempo, there was somehow a vague melancholia or despair in the music. The singer seemed troubled—unrequited love perhaps, or betrayal. That melancholy note seemed to affect Joe.

"Bring back memories?" I said when the song ended.

Joe nodded, still with the faraway eyes. After a moment, he sighed. "Used to hear that song all the time when I was stationed down in the Caribbean. Rosy Roads in Puerto Rico. Gitmo in Cuba. It was good then, in those days. Real good. Had the time of my life."

He fell silent a bit, then picked up the thread again. "Definitely the best time of my life. There's been some good times and some shit times. More shit than good. But the navy in those days, I loved every bit of it. And down in the Caribbean was best of all. The music, the rum, the cigars, the girls. It was hot as hell but didn't matter. It was pure paradise. Sounds crazy, don't it—paradise hot as hell? Still, I'd do it all again in a heartbeat. But let me tell you, kid, you don't get a chance like that but once or twice in life. Maybe not even the once for most people. I was stationed down there, what? A year or so. We used to go into the town next to the base. Crazy, crazy town. Bars, whorehouses on every corner. Beautiful girls, dancing, drunk off our asses. That was the high life, kid, let me tell you. Puerto Rico was great. Cuba was great. Damn shame what's become of the place, and now I'll never get back there, but if *you* ever get the chance, take it and go. Get the hell out of this frigging Dodge."

"So why did you leave the navy?" I asked him.

Uncle Joe moved food around on his plate and ignored the question. Something else was on his mind.

"Listen, there was this one night, we go to our favorite cantina, me and my pal, George. George is dancing all night with this gal, prettiest little thing. Late into the night this local dude shows up with his buddies and he thinks he has some claim on the girl. Girlfriend? Sister? Who knows? It gets a little pushy and before long the whole bunch of us are in a fight. Punches, knives. That's where I got this here scar, grabbing the knife as the guy went after George. But here's the funny part. One of us squids was this Mexican guy from L.A., Pedro. He starts talking Spanish to the Cubans and somehow what he says clears the air and before you know it, all of us—Yanks, Cubans, Mexicans—we're sharing bottles of rum and laughing and singing to the small hours. I think that song we just heard was one we sang. Or maybe it was one George and the gal danced to. Ah, hell, who can remember, so long ago. But Jesus, what a time."

That was all Joe had to say for the time being. He was silent on the ride back to the house, thinking about good times in the navy, I suppose. Or maybe he was thinking of his long, dark journey through life—the ships, the jails, the hotter-than-hell paradises. I had questions. I wanted to know more about his time in the navy and the merchant marines, but we didn't have the chance to talk further that evening. Still on the night shift, I had to go to work. I left him sitting on the sofa in the dark, can of beer on his knee, humming the song from the restaurant.

As it turned out, I never got the chance to ask those questions. The next morning when I returned from work, he was gone, and we never heard from him again. Presumably he's dead now. Did he die at sea? In jail? Murdered maybe, or just some burnt-out case wasting away in an expat hostel? No telling. Most likely, Uncle Joe ended up as one of the missing, the disappeared, the lost souls caught up in the maelstrom from which there is no escape.

The bartender returned with the name of the song on a piece of paper: *Siboney*.

I was grateful to put a name to it, as if merely knowing the name meant that I wouldn't ever again lose track of Uncle Joe. Later, I did a little research and learned the composer's name (Ernesto Lecuona, from Cuba), the artists who have recorded the song over the years (many), the versions that have charted, the movie soundtracks that have included it. I have listened to numerous versions of the song—big band, jazz, country, every Latin style imaginable—but in my head I hear it as a bolero played on acoustic guitar, background music to a scene in a film in which a man stands alone on a windblown deck gazing out beyond land's end to the open sea.

Small World

Traveling **twice the speed of sound** some sixty thousand feet over the eastern Mediterranean, most of the passengers on the Coors Light Concorde were savoring a meal of Caspian Sea caviar and salmon in champagne sauce. There were fine wines to choose from—a Bourgogne blanc, a Bordeaux red—and all the Coors Light anyone would care to drink. Despite the fact that they had been traveling for six hours now, having left New York that afternoon, the passengers were more or less enjoying themselves. But not Don Pevsner. As the plane hurtled toward the Middle East, Pevsner's tension grew. This was the second leg of a chartered Air France flight that Pevsner hoped would set the record for fastest global circumnavigation, and it was this leg that worried him most, this leg that might foil all his hard work.

Pevsner was fuming over a last-minute change in flight plans. Pevsner hated last-minute changes. After months of meticulous planning, he had plotted a globe-circling route that would maximize supersonic airtime. He had arranged for everything— landing rights, use of airspace, supersonic clearance. But as the scheduled departure date drew near, Pevsner had hit an unexpected snag in the Middle East.

To reach a scheduled fueling stop at Dubai in the United Arab Emirates, the Concorde would have to cross Saudi Arabia. But the Saudis had refused to grant supersonic clearance for the traversing of their territory on the customary airway, and to fly over the vast Arabian Desert at normal airliner speeds (600 mph) would mean a loss in time significant enough to jeopardize the record attempt.

Saudi authorities had proposed an alternative route to reduce the number of subsonic miles, a route that would require a flight "off-airways" into Dubai. The authorities in the United Arab Emirates initially agreed, but one day before the record attempt, the UAE suddenly revoked permission for the off-airways approach to Dubai. Despite last minute high-level negotiations on the part of Air France, the UAE would not budge. A 150-mile off-airways flight, even at subsonic speed, pushed the envelope too much in the sensitive Persian Gulf region. Despite a flurry of messages, the UAE was obdurate. "Nobody is permitted to fly off-airways into the UAE," the authorities said.

Pevsner was peeved. To him, the UAE's decision to revoke permission was arbitrary. The way he saw it, the "scurrilous behavior" of the UAE had "stuck a knife in the back of world aviation history." As the Concorde neared Saudi air space, he was in no mood to forgive the UAE for its intransigence, and he was in no mood for the "duet of strawberries and kiwifruit" that the cabin crew was just now serving.

His eyes flitted between the Machmeter on the cabin wall and the chronometer he held. Any minute now deceleration would occur, and the Machmeter would slip below 2, below 1.7, below 1, until they were traveling regulation subsonic speed. And then he would have to endure the slow crawl over Saudi Arabia. Nervous, tense, he knew the world record was in jeopardy. Staring into black space, he stewed over the way the United Arab Emirates had betrayed him.

Don Pevsner had a lot riding on this flight. The world record he coveted. His reputation. And then there was all the time—two years—he had invested in organizing and planning this excursion. Pevsner abhorred foul-ups and imprecision, and so he had micromanaged every last detail of the preparations, including planning the most efficient route and determining times of departure and landing. Pevsner was incensed that fickle bureaucratic fools on the ground could so callously, so arbitrarily exercise their petty authority and thus ruin his history-making project. He glared at the Machmeter. A minute passed, then two, then three. Still no deceleration. Something was going on.

Organizing trips came naturally to Don Pevsner. Growing up in New York, he was fascinated by geography and transportation. At first, he favored trains. Air travel, especially on prop planes, didn't excite him. But when as a boy he first saw 707 jets taking off and landing at Idlewild Airport in New York, he was enthralled. He hung out at the airport just to watch the planes. In 1963, when he was nineteen, he flew BOAC from London to New York and rode in the cockpit. The cockpits of jet planes fascinated him, and from then on he always asked for permission to visit the cockpit, at least on European flights where such visits were legal. He began a lifelong hobby of collecting the business cards of pilots.

When he was in college, Pevsner—now hooked on travel—got a summer job working with Hertz in Europe. In order to get a free ticket to Rome, he got the idea of organizing an excursion of fifteen students. The next year he repeated the scheme for a free ticket to Amsterdam.

When he returned to the United States, Pevsner attended law school in Florida. He didn't like it much and soon determined that he had little interest in practicing law. But upon finishing his degree and relocating to Miami, he realized that he could put his legal training to use by advocating for the rights of travel consumers. He established himself as a class action attorney, specializing in travel industry cases. Skilled at both polemics and promotion, Pevsner soon scored some notable victories with his aggressive, badgering style. In the early 1970s he went before the Civil Aeronautics Board to fight against the airlines' practice of charging fliers for luggage weighing more than 44 pounds. Later, he took on motel chains and even Disney World for practices that Pevsner considered draconian and abusive. It infuriated him to see big corporations ripping off unsuspecting consumers, and everywhere he looked he saw the same sort of swindling, the big guys robbing the little guys blind. Pevsner saw himself as a crusader. Much of his legal work was pro bono. His Florida license plate read JUSTICE.

After a spell as assistant general counsel for Air Florida, in 1982 Pevsner turned to consumer journalism. He wrote a UPI syndicated column called "Travel Wise" informing travelers how to save money and avoid scams. He contributed editorials to major newspapers on issues such as airline deregulation, airfare inequities, and the 55-mph speed limit. Along the way, he made some enemies who could not appreciate his persistent, in-your-face bulldogging. He took on Alfred Kahn, former chairman of the Civil Aeronautics Board, in what the *New York Times* called "a dogfight over deregulation." Pevsner claimed that the deregulation of the airline industry was "a shell game." Kahn called Pevsner "choleric," but in Pevsner's view his criticism of deregulation had been "admirably restrained."

But restraint wasn't really Pevsner's strong point. In between dogfights, ideas for grandiose projects kept popping up in Pevsner's mind. He fired off letters to influential people like William F. Buckley Jr. outlining plans for restoring an abandoned railroad bridge over the Hudson River and building an elaborate hotel and restaurant complex on it. Another Pevsner idea proposed delivering unused airline meals to needy people. Pevsner prided himself on being a doer, someone who turned dreams into schemes.

By the mid-1980s, he started organizing tours again. In 1985, he chartered a British Airways Concorde from Miami to Aruba, stayed overnight on the island, and returned to Miami aboard the Concorde the next day. It was the Concorde, not Aruba, that interested him. From the first, Pevsner was enamored with the Concorde, a beautiful bird—sleek, aerodynamic, its afterburners shooting out cones of flame. A true engineering marvel. But more than anything else, Pevsner liked the speed. To him, only supersonic long-distance air travel made sense. Once you'd flown at Mach 2, conventional-speed flights became tedious. Three hours, Miami to New York? Ridiculous. Five hours, New York to Los Angeles? No way. And why sit through an eight-hour flight to Europe when the Concorde could have you there and back with time to spare?

For Pevsner, supersonic travel became part hobby, part cause, and he mulled over ideas to cultivate both the hobby and the cause. In 1989, he developed a project that would be the prototype for his future enterprises: he chartered a British Airways Concorde for an around-the-world flight. Pevsner envisioned a twenty-three-day luxury tour at supersonic speeds. He got his friend William F. Buckley Jr. to sign on as host, and then Pevsner sold seats on the charter for thirty-nine thousand dollars each.

It was a hell of a joyride, a tremendous kick, thirty-five hours of flight time to indulge in the beauty, the thrust, the swift efficiency of the Concorde. It was also a profitable venture, though he refused requests to reveal just how profitable. But it was lucrative enough for Pevsner to put together a sequel, hosted by astronaut Frank Borman, for nearly forty-four thousand dollars a ticket. This time around, he sold three-fourths of the seats, not enough to make money. Pevsner was more forthcoming about his losses, claiming the Borman trip cost him more than two hundred thousand dollars. He could have canceled and lost less, but he gritted his teeth and went ahead with the flight. "I do projects," he said. "Sometimes they pay off, sometimes I lose my shirt."

But eventually Pevsner wanted to do something more than mere luxury tours. He wanted something to commit to, something to achieve. That's when he discovered that records existed for round-the-world travel. Long gone were the eighty-day trips postulated by Jules Verne. Today's Phileas Foggs flew not in balloons but in jets, and by 1988 the record time had been whittled down to thirty-six hours, fifty-four minutes, and fifteen seconds (in the competitive world of speed circumnavigation, seconds were counted). Captain Clay Lacy set the record in a Boeing 747 SP and declared it unbeatable. But a few weeks later, just to prove Lacy wrong, Captain Allen Paulson flying a Gulfstream IV shaved forty-five minutes and forty-one seconds off the record. It now stood at 36:08:34.

Pevsner studied the times. They were beatable, very beatable. All you needed was a Concorde. A few more technical stops would be necessary because the Concorde must be refueled more frequently than a 747 or a Gulfstream IV. Lacy had needed only two stops, Paulson four. The Concorde would require six. But with efficient ground handling and a reasonable turn-around time, the Concorde at Mach 2 would easily make up for time lost on the ground.

Pevsner wanted that record. Shattering it would be a perfect way to promote SST travel. He also wanted the record because the people already in the game of round-the-world record setting—people like Paulson, the billionaire CEO of Gulfstream Aerospace, and Lacy, who owned a Learjet operation, were high society pilots, men with deep pockets. Men who could afford to be players in the speed game. Pevsner saw himself as an outsider infiltrating this elite ring. Just a regular guy with more ambition and drive than money disrupting the rich boys' game. He wanted to stick it to them. Beating someone like Paulson at his own game would be the sweetest achievement of his life.

But big money was obviously a prerequisite in order to charter a Concorde. In 1992, for an attempt at the westbound round-the-world speed record, Pevsner sold seats on a chartered Air France Concorde for 23,800 dollars each, "less than a dollar a mile," he noted in promoting the event. He dubbed the flight "Sunchaser One," and claimed it was "the most exciting aviation event since Lindbergh crossed the North Atlantic in 1927." On October 12, 1992—the five hundredth anniversary of Columbus's New World landing (Pevsner relished that sort of symbolism)—"Sunchaser One" took off from Lisbon, Portugal, and circumnavigated the globe westbound in 32:49:03, the fastest flight ever around the Earth.

But Pevsner wasn't content with that accomplishment. He also wanted to beat the *eastbound* record. This time, he intended to do things differently. To pay for the flight, he no longer wanted to depend on selling seats to ultra-rich people looking for a novelty luxury trip. That tack had proven uncertain on "Sunchaser One," when Pevsner had trouble scaring up paying customers. He sold only thirty-two of the seventy seats and barely managed to break even after Air France picked up the remaining tickets. Nor did Pevsner exactly enjoy kowtowing to CEOs and their ilk— the very people that the crusader in him had always wanted to challenge. He was tired of the prima donnas on the luxury tours. He preferred to fly with aviation buffs, people in it for the record chases. He wanted the events to be more egalitarian.

So, Pevsner turned to corporate sponsorship. At first, he tried to interest the major marketing and PR firms in the idea. But to Pevsner's dismay, befuddlement, and ultimately his anger, he found no takers. He was dead serious about his schemes, and he chafed when others didn't share his commitment. Pevsner rankled at the complacency of "self-satisfied executives and corporate giants;" in his eyes, they were "too bureaucratic and tunnel-visioned to see the possibilities" in his project. They had listened, given a big yawn, and gone back "fat, dumb, and happy on the train to their suburban homes in Connecticut."

In the face of their self-satisfied apathy, Pevsner was all the more determined to succeed, if only to show up these dull fat cats.

Pevsner contacted a small Miami-based marketing firm, NatCom. Unlike the major marketing firms, NatCom saw potential in the project. Griff Siegel, a young vice president for program development at NatCom, recognized that Pevsner could be a little too zealous and demanding, a style that didn't work well when it came to winning over Madison Avenue types. You had to look past Pevsner's aggressiveness to the project itself. Siegel thought Pevsner's proposed event had "promotion" written all over it. He considered an around-the-world trip on a Concorde intriguing enough, but the crucial element was the record chase—and the chance to participate in what would become an entry in the Guinness record book. That hook made Pevsner's project a sweepstakes natural. The right company with the right product could cash in on the glamour of this history-making event with catchy in-store displays that would really drive up sales.

Several companies were interested, but the right company turned out to be Coors Brewing Company, which wanted to give away seats on the Concorde as part of a sweepstakes promotion for their light beer product. The way Siegel saw it, the Concorde image would play well with the beer's "silver bullet" trademark. The plane had that sleek, bullet-like look, the very embodiment of the concept that advertisements had developed for the product: fast, lean, aggressive, trendy, hip. And what a cool thing to do, zip around the world at Mach 2, touching down here and there to check out airports on different continents; thirty-two hours of killer party in the sky. Who wouldn't leap at the chance? It would be one awesome promo.

With the Coors promotion in full swing, Don Pevsner went to work planning routes and times for the big event. For Pevsner, putting the whole thing together was a tremendous kick, the most energizing thing he could think of doing. But the real thrill came when he saw the plane on the JFK tarmac in New York. There it was: the Concorde in all its glory, a gorgeous thing. Then came the call for boarding. Ninety-nine people would make the trip, including two celebrity guests: former astronaut Tom Stafford and racecar driver Kyle Petty.

The Air France Concorde that Pevsner dubbed "Sunchaser Two," sporting the Coors Light bullet logo outside the nose cone, pushed back at 11:44 AM, New York time, on August 15, 1995. From the moment of pushback, Pevsner was absorbed with tracking and recording the data of the flight. Assiduously precise, he recorded to the second the Greenwich Mean Time for not only the pushback, but also the start of the takeoff roll (11:48:20) and liftoff (11:49:10). Then, in flight, he noted the precise moment that the main gear got airborne, the precise moment of transonic acceleration, the precise moments of attaining Mach 1, Mach 1.7, and Mach 2. As the flight progressed, he would record the exact instants of deceleration, the return to subsonic speed, and the touchdown. All this data would later be corroborated with the onboard observer from the *Fédération Aéronautique Internationale* (FAI), the body that sanctions aviation speed records. For each leg of the trip, Pevsner kept scrupulous track of the data. He computed the total time for each leg, the total flight time above Mach 1, the total time at Mach 2, as well as the flight's average speed and the total distance traveled in statute miles. He made his calculations as the flight progressed, and over the cabin intercom he recited the statistics for the benefit of the passengers.

The rest of the travelers settled in for the ultimate late twentieth-century tour. Caught up in Pevsner's data drama, they eagerly anticipated the first breaking of the sound barrier—announced by two minutes or so of shuddering thrust after the pilot activated the afterburners. Then they cheered and celebrated their supersonic initiation with a champagne toast.

From that moment on, the alcohol flowed freely, and the eleven-mile-high party was underway.

On this first leg, New York to Toulouse, France, the cabin crew served a lunch of lobster salad and potato croquettes with truffles. With the abundance of gourmet food and alcoholic drinks, the Atlantic crossing passed quickly (three hours, twenty minutes, and two seconds according to Pevsner's chronometer), and the supersonic passengers found themselves in France at dusk.

A crowd greeted the plane at Toulouse, the city where the Air France Concordes were built. Flashbulbs popped in the French night, and the throng cheered as the airplane landed and the passengers entered the terminal. There, they found the next phase of the ongoing party waiting for them, courtesy of Air France: food, music, photo opportunities, handshaking. Griff Siegel, NatCom's VP, got to work recording the festivities for a documentary video about the flight.

After an hour on the ground in France while the airplane was serviced, Pevsner and company re-boarded the Concorde and took off for Dubai. Sixty thousand feet up, Pevsner recorded the data and glanced through the porthole at the dark Mediterranean. The lights of Sicily and Malta glided by on either side. The Middle East drew near, and Pevsner grew anxious. He'd pretty much resigned himself to a subsonic flight over Saudi Arabia, a big disappointment because the loss in time just might quash their chance at the record. But when the time came for deceleration and the Machmeter stayed at two, Pevsner felt a surge of excitement.

After twelve minutes he could no longer bear the suspense and rushed forward to the tiny cockpit. The pilots greeted him with the incredible news: the first Saudi air controller had given them permission to proceed at Mach 2. Fifteen minutes later the second controller also gave them the OK. Incredulous, Pevsner listened as the voice of the third Saudi controller crackled up from the black hole below. An argument was underway amongst the controllers, the voice explained, but the upshot was that Air France Flight 1995 could proceed at Mach 2. Pevsner was ecstatic: they'd crossed Saudi Arabia at supersonic speed. The record chase was alive. He still had his shot at history. He had no idea what went on down below that night, whether the controllers had granted permission on their own or whether higher-ups had given their approval. Whatever had happened, Pevsner now felt profound gratitude to the Saudis. The United Arab Emirates, however, he vowed never to forgive.

Dubai, 4:00 AM local time. Despite the hour, another crowd showed up to greet the plane. Now eight hours into the journey, the supersonic passengers emerged from the cramped jet into the shockingly spacious Dubai airport. The terminal seemed to gleam, but some of the supersonic passengers were disturbed to find restrooms with mere porcelain holes instead of urinals. Griff Siegel, accompanied by a sheik in flowing burnoose and a pack of security guards, scurried around the airport filming for his video. He was surprised and amused to find that here, halfway around the world from home, there was a Baskin-Robbins right in the Dubai airport, open at four in the morning!

Air France had arranged for another reception, a fête with mounds of traditional Arab food. One of the airport officials, looking up at the Concorde, asked Siegel what "Coors Light" meant. Siegel offered to bring him a sample of the beer. The official declined; alcohol was forbidden in the Muslim country, he explained, and he could not be seen in public holding a beer. But he gave Siegel his address and asked him to send a case. Now *that*, Siegel thought, was what a successful promotional campaign was all about.

After an hour and thirty minutes in Dubai, the Concorde rose up and over the Gulf of Oman. Following the drama in the Saudi night, Pevsner was rewarded with a spectacular vista: sunrise, the jet hurtling forward, pushing the Machmeter needle. Up ahead was this stunning band of colors, a vibrant spectrum like God painting the sky. A fluffy carpet of clouds spread beneath the plane all the way to the distant curve of the horizon. Even through the Concorde's tiny windows—barely bigger than a snorkeling mask—it was incredible. This was what Pevsner liked most, getting "up and over the dull, prosaic, cruel world" and looking down on it from above: the age-old dream of Icarus. Between glances at the Machmeter to monitor the plane's approach to Mach 2, Pevsner stared at the blinding spectacle. Griff Siegel saw it, too. In fact, the whole cabin went silent for some ten minutes in the presence of the awesome display.

Then the cabin crew came down the aisle with champagne and smoked salmon, lamb medallions Provençale, stuffed eggplant and broccoli, mango mousse, and pastries. Down below was the Arabian Sea, streaked with clouds and glassy like a marble. And there in the distance was the ghostly tip of India, and there was Sri Lanka. They were cruising right over the trouble spots of the world, places that you read about in the newspaper or saw in horrible news clips on TV. Hard to believe from sixty thousand feet up that it was all going on right down there, maybe at this very moment—civil wars, riots, famine, whole countries run amok. Next came the Andaman Sea, a monotonous blue. And then Myanmar, hazy and brown—lots of bloody business going on there.

Now Pevsner saw the fields of Thailand, an opaque green, growing more intense and more startling as the jet descended. The Concorde circled over Bangkok's chaos—snarled traffic, teeming slums, glittery strips of prostitution and opium—and circled again. The air traffic controller had put them sixth in line for approach, a ridiculous delay, Pevsner felt. Everything had been arranged ahead of time. The Thais knew what was going on, what was at stake, and yet they'd put him sixth in line, as if he had all the time in the world. Pevsner did not enjoy traveling to the so-called developing world anymore, precisely because of foul-ups like this. All the crime, strife, tribal warfare and the like. You only had to look at Rwanda falling apart, that was the future of Africa and the "developing" world. Nasty. Brutish.

And then it was ground again, Bangkok, noon, fourteen hours into the trip. Sure looked hot and humid out there. Another crowd had come out to see the plane, the faces and clothing noticeably different. Pevsner liked this aspect of the trip, too, the transition between cultures, between continents, between climates. It almost seemed magical, it happened so fast.

In the airport, Air France had yet another gala awaiting the supersonic travelers, some of whom were uncertain where they were. Thailand? Taiwan? Was there a difference? Another banquet, another dance troupe in native costumes gyrating to strange music. For Pevsner, stops like this were interesting but also a bit nerve-wracking. After all, it was on the ground where things could go wrong: mishandling of the refueling operations, slow and inefficient local maintenance crews more interested in gossip than the pursuit of world records, meddlesome bureaucrats. In the sky, the Concorde took over, Mach 2 a given, just pure unadulterated speed. If the record were going to be lost, it would be here, on the ground. He kept an eye on the passengers, leery lest one wander off into a duty-free shop and get lost, cause a delay.

Siegel, on the other hand, was having a blast. Here in Bangkok, like every other port-of-call, he dashed around with his escorts, videocam whirring away—a totally cool experience, the thrill of a lifetime, because here he was talking to people all over the world in just one day! It was like this great opportunity to meet people, experience the world, which when you thought about it really was a small place after all, just like the Disney song.

After an hour and a half, they said goodbye to Asia. On the three-hour flight to Guam, sandwiches came down the aisle, along with more drinks. Someone wanted to know if there would be any movies, but the short duration of the flights wouldn't allow it. A few people tried to read or sleep. Some put on headphones and listened to music. The plane hurtled ahead, passing Mach 1, Mach 1.7, settling in at Mach 2.02, some 1,498 mph. But now no one toasted the occasion. The passengers had rather quickly become accustomed to supersonic speeds, jaded even. Hardly anyone except Pevsner bothered to look at the Machmeter anymore.

They'd been traveling for sixteen hours and the smallish Concorde seats, two on either side of a narrow aisle, were not terribly comfortable. A passenger on a previous Pevsner excursion had likened the experience of twenty-plus hours in a Concorde seat to a cross between a root canal and a hemorrhoid exam. You could maneuver up and down the aisle, peer into the cockpit, try like everybody else to buttonhole the celebrity guests, maybe hear Stafford, the former astronaut, quip that this was the *slowest* flight *he'd* ever made around the world. But the too-narrow aisle on the Concorde made moving around difficult, what with the ubiquitous serving carts advancing and retreating. Well, if there was little else to do, at least there was an abundance of food and drink, and the supersonic passengers indulged themselves. Crapulous, one passenger retched in the restroom, rendering it temporarily unsuitable for further use.

Don Pevsner had no trouble finding something to do. He had his data to record, which as he now figured it, looked better and better as far as the record shot was concerned. He also found that supersonic travel provided serene moments conducive to contemplation. It had to do with the altitude Concordes flew at, and with the smoothness of the ride, like being on a magic carpet. Now high above the Pacific Ocean, he thought about aviation's pioneers: Smith and Arnold, the first to circumnavigate the globe in a plane. Took them five and a half *months* back in 1924; and Lindbergh, of course, whose nonstop New York to Paris flight took two hours longer than the Concorde needed to circle the Earth; and then there was Amelia Earhart, lost since 1937 somewhere down there in the blue vastness that the Coors Light Concorde now glided over. It was true, Pevsner thought, that there were old pilots and bold pilots, but no old, bold pilots. Now sobered by the thought of Earhart's quixotic daring, he saluted her memory. Compared with the real heroes of aviation history, the only danger the Concorde's passengers faced was overindulgence from lobster and champagne.

Guam was incredible. They landed at dusk in a humid rain punctuated by the flash of servicemen's cameras. Then came an official reception presided over by the commanding general for the Western Pacific, but there was little time for pleasantries or pomp. The air force personnel, all gung-ho for the record chase, turned in a record themselves; in 1:16 they had the Concorde serviced, rolling down the huge runway, and airborne.

Pevsner was impressed and grateful. He was now feeling confident that the record would be theirs. While the cabin crew served breakfast (poached eggs in Mornay sauce with croissants) the Concorde soared over the International Date Line, and the supersonic passengers began the sixteenth of August all over again.

But three hours later in Honolulu everything went wrong. For some odd reason, the airport crews had not been prepared for the Concorde's 4:00 AM arrival. First, the boarding stairwell wouldn't reach the cabin door. Then there was no electricity, so the Sunchaser passengers were forced to remain on board the darkened jet while the Honolulu crew plodded at their tasks. To Pevsner, it seemed that the ground crew were deliberately dragging their feet. It was either gross incompetence or willful subversion. Next there was a problem with the pumping of the fuel: the idiots were using too small a hose. Stewing aboard the dark plane, fretting over what this foot-dragging might do for the record shot, Pevsner suspected that something political was going on: Could the ground crew be doing this to an Air France plane on purpose, as a way to protest France's recent Pacific nuclear tests? If so, it was a stupid thing to do, with aviation history in the making and a major US corporation paying the tab.

And now it seemed there was some problem with the delivery of the catered meals—a further delay. This was too much to take. "To hell with the red snapper," Pevsner shouted. There was a record to set. They'd just have to wait until Acapulco to eat. Out in the terminal, luau girls were waiting to hula dance for the supersonic passengers, but there'd be no party in Honolulu. The Concorde had already been sitting on the ground for an hour and forty minutes. Still, the Hawaiians had one more delay in store for Pevsner: inadequate ground power tripped the circuit breakers during engine-start. It took the concerted efforts of the Air France crew, "consummate professionals," in Pevsner's estimation, to save the day and get the bird off the ground.

Up over the Pacific again, the Concorde banked hard right, and the passengers could see Diamond Head to port, mantled by the dark velvet sky and crowned by a few glowing clouds. On the same side of the plane, the sun rose from the ocean: their second sunrise on August 16.

Having endured a flight without food, the supersonic passengers descended in Acapulco to the strains of a mariachi band. Griff Siegel and the film crew got to work shooting the festive bash, another killer party, complete with an authentic Mexican buffet. A relieved Pevsner saw to it that the Mexican crew was all business. They would have a good turnaround time, almost as good as Guam. The passengers were herded aboard, mariachi trumpets blasting *adiós, qué le vaya bien, andale, andale.*

And now the excitement began to build. They'd been on the plane and in airports for twenty-nine hours straight, but who could feel tired now? They were going to be in that Guinness book! The second, maybe the third wind kicked in. A pumped-up Pevsner went into the cramped cockpit where he could see the pilots' confidence in their grins. Captain Michel Dupont gave him the thumbs-up and predicted they'd whip the old eastbound by a good four hours and the westbound by at least an hour. Dupont and co-captain Claude Hetru, both fifty-eight years old, were crack pilots, two of the best. They had the right stuff, all right—Dupont was pilot of France's presidential Concorde, the very jet they now rode in, specially selected for this world record flight—and Pevsner admired the hell out of them. Concorde pilots belonged to an elite club. You couldn't find any better. DuPont and Hetru would go down in Guinness as the record-holders; Pevsner was honored to be the one who put them there.

Now everyone was having a good time. Pevsner and the pilots smiled as a confused Mexican air controller down in Yucatan asked in broken English where the jet was going, and at *what* speed? But they were already at Mach 2 and out of Mexican airspace before the Mexicans could figure it out. Back in the cabin, the passengers, fresh from the feast in Acapulco, were served a dinner of ceviche, sautéed tournedos in truffle sauce, and roast potatoes. The champagne flowed like water.

As the Concorde curved around South Florida, obscured because of cloud cover, Pevsner thought about his mother, an invalid in Fort Lauderdale. His greatest regret was that she had not been able to go with him on his excursions. Bedridden from a stroke, she would never be able to experience the thrill of these flights. The thought brought tears to his eyes. It also made him realize what motivated him to go to such great lengths to pull off these schemes. You had to do things while you could, you had to seize the day. Nobody ever got what they wanted out of life by waiting or putting it off until the right moment came along. His stepfather, for example, had waited until retirement to travel around the world, but during his journey chest pains hospitalized him in Tokyo and ended those dreams. Then there was Pevsner's lifelong best friend, only a day younger than he, who had just died from metastatic melanoma. No, you couldn't wait for the "right moment" because it might never come. You had to take advantage now.

And here he was, doing just that, fulfilling his dream, the Concorde decelerating, fifteen minutes to touchdown in New York. It was all academic now. The only question was the final numbers. With touchdown at 07:16:59, Pevsner started totaling them. The media awaited, and he wanted to have everything figured out and ready to go for the press conference. Even as he walked off the plane, Pevsner was punching in numbers, translating the final mileage to kilometers.

On the ground in New York, Pevsner informed the media that "Sunchaser Two" had eclipsed the official eastbound round-the-world record by 4:40:45, and the Guinness Book 1992 Concorde record by 1:21:14, with a total elapsed time of just 31:27:49 for the 25,252 miles, New York to New York. Pevsner declared the new record unbeatable by any commercial airplane on the planet. Then he delivered the same message he had reiterated everywhere on the trip: supersonic travel was superior to conventional-speed air travel, even though issues concerning the sonic boom limited Concorde use to transoceanic flights. But the first generation of SSTs was nearly twenty years old now—still great planes, but in danger of becoming obsolete. A new generation of SSTs was needed, one that would correct the Concorde's deficiencies. Dismayed that only a few SST routes were still operating, Pevsner called for governments and the airline industry to begin work on jets bigger than the Concorde, jets that could carry the masses— two hundred fifty people a flight—at a more affordable price than the prohibitively expensive Concorde. These new planes, built from conventional aluminum alloy, would be more fuel efficient and have a greater range—six thousand miles as opposed to four thousand—allowing them to cross the Pacific nonstop. Finally, the new planes would have to be more environmentally friendly, somehow solving the noise-pollution problem on the ground that kept the Concorde out of widespread use. Pevsner strongly advocated for research and development of new SSTs. He for one wanted no more "long slogs" on slower jets. He had no interest in the over-hyped Boeing 777 with its "puffery" like enlarged overhead bins. Speed: that's what truly mattered.

Griff Siegel raced around JFK getting the last bit of film footage for his video. He couldn't believe how phenomenal from a PR standpoint this stunt had been. Given all the media exposure, the news clips, the wire photos, and the crowds greeting the plane itself, he figured that the event had generated four billion worldwide media impressions for Coors—and those were *free* impressions, Siegel noted. No doubt about it, Coors had gotten their money's worth and then some. It was truly a boffo promo.

When the filming was done, Siegel found himself alone looking at the Concorde as it sat regally on the runway in the golden light of dusk. Just then it hit him what an incredible experience this had been. It was totally surreal. Just yesterday at noon he had been right here, and now, evening the next day, here he was again having gone completely around the world and talked to people in all those different places. Wild. Awesome. In the promotional video, he would want to capture that idea. The video would commemorate the flight, but he also wanted it to serve as a social commentary, demonstrating that with supersonic jets it is indeed a small world.

It was like the Epcot Center, where you could simulate a trip around the world by going from pavilion to pavilion. But

"Sunchaser Two" had done it for real, the whole world terminal-to-terminal, and with a show and a buffet at each stop. Basically, they had just zipped around Epcot at supersonic speed, and what a ride! Exhausting, but a total blast.

With the record chase over, Don Pevsner wasn't ready to take it easy. It wasn't in his nature to take it easy. First, he had to fly over to France on the Concorde to return the chartered jet. Then it was another of those damn slow slogs on a commercial flight back to Miami. In a couple of weeks, he'd be on board an old Russian research ship taking a tour around the icebergs of the Northwest Passage. After that? He had some ideas. The Coors deal had proven profitable for Pevsner, though once again he refused to say how much he had made. It was "nobody's damn business." But it was lucrative enough for him to begin planning more high-profile events. What about a chartered Concorde over the North Pole? Or maybe the first supersonic circumnavigation of South America ... or a westbound Concorde flight on New Year's Eve, 1999. If timed right, he calculated that you could actually see in the millennium no fewer than four times, as the Concorde gained time on each leg while traversing the time zones. He already had exclusive contracts with Air France for these projects if he could get them off the ground. Given the success of "Sunchaser Two," Pevsner was sure some corporation would want to sponsor these high-profile events or one of the other ideas that were constantly popping into his head. He felt like he could go anywhere, do anything. All he needed was someone to pick up the tab.

An Immigrant's Story

Born in the Soviet Union exactly at midcentury, Leonid Yelin has been shaped in turn by the two ideologies that have dominated the post-World War II world: communism and capitalism. The Cold War between these two competing ideologies had a profound impact on the course of his life. The history of the period will tell of Stalin and Truman, Khrushchev and Kennedy, Brezhnev and Reagan—the big players in the geopolitical game. But the real meaning of the game is most tellingly revealed in what novelist Graham Greene called "the human factor"—that is, in the lives of ordinary people like Yelin who have survived and even thrived under the *isms* inflicted upon them.

Yelin's parents were Romanians who fled their native country in 1940 when the Romanian fascist Ionescu joined forces with the Nazis then signed away a third of the country's territory to the Germans. His parents did not know each other at the time; both were among the thousands of refugees who headed for the Soviet Union and the protection of Stalin, Hitler's enemy. They fled by rail, by cart, and by foot, first crossing into the Ukraine. But Hitler's invasion of the Soviet Union forced the refugees farther and farther west, across southern Russia and the Kirghiz Steppe of Kazakhstan into the sandy wastes of the distant Soviet republic of Uzbekistan—2,500 miles in all. They finally settled in the city of Tashkent, and Hitler finally stalled in Stalingrad on the Volga River, a thousand miles behind them. But life for the refugees remained difficult. The normally xenophobic Russians were now doubly suspicious of foreigners, especially Romanians, since Romanian troops were part of Hitler's invasion force. Not permitted to join the Red Army, Yelin's father was sent instead to Siberia to cut trees for the duration of the war.

After the war, Yelin's parents found themselves unable to return to Romania because the USSR had annexed their home province. They eventually met and married in Tashkent. Leonid was born in 1950, just as the Cold War was intensifying. Stalin was in the twilight of his rule, but his totalitarian system was firmly established. Far away in the Pacific, the Americans were blowing apart atolls with hydrogen bombs, and in Siberia Russian scientists were busy catching up, closing the gap in the arms race so well that by the time Leonid was ten, American politicians were nervously claiming the Russians had taken the lead.

Like American schoolchildren of the 1950s, Yelin grew up fearing the Cold War enemy and believing that its military machine was out to rule the world. While American children were watching filmstrips and movies about the communist menace and learning to duck and cover beneath their desks in case the Russians dropped "the big one," Yelin was attending school in Tashkent and learning about American belligerence. Portraits of a smiling "Uncle Lenin" decorated the classroom walls. Leonid and the other students watched films about America. But Yelin saw nothing of Manhattan skyscrapers or amber waves of grain or busy freeways or tidy suburbs with a car in every driveway. Instead, the Soviet films depicted a nightmare America where homeless and jobless masses roamed the streets, where the police clubbed and kicked Black people, where thousands and thousands of children starved in filthy city slums and in hovels on barren stripmined mountains while a handful of tycoons battened on the slave labor of the poor children's parents.

Yelin readily believed that what he learned was the truth. He was only a child, and the teachers made it all sound so believable.

Yelin felt truly sorry for the American children growing up in such a cruel system; sometimes he was moved to tears in class as he read about impoverished children deprived of food because the rich capitalists horded everything. The teachers even took up collections: every child earnestly contributed a few kopeks to a fund for the American kids. Now, decades later, Yelin wonders with a wry grin what actually happened to all the money that was collected.

Much of the curriculum was devoted to learning about "Uncle Lenin" and patriotism. They read countless stories lauding heroic devotion to the Soviet state. Some of the stories concerned a young boy named Pavel, whose patriotism was so devout that he reported on his own father for stealing grain from the state farm. The moral of the story was clear: you should put the fatherland before even your own father, and you should report those who disobey the state. In school, children were encouraged to report on one another. Each row in the classroom had a "leader" designated by the teacher. That leader had to report each day on which children had arrived late or failed to do their homework or were not dressed in the proper uniform—gray suits for the boys, black dresses with white aprons for the girls. Such tattling thus became an ingrained habit, one that persisted in Soviet citizens beyond the school years.

Like all other Soviet children, Leonid belonged to the Young Pioneers, a Scoutlike program emphasizing good deeds and the study of communist ideology. The goal of the Young Pioneers, according to one manual, was "the formation of communist, all-people morals." A properly educated youth should be "a convinced collectivist, a person who does not think of himself outside society." Yelin was, as he puts it, "a total believer" in this ideology. Of course, there really was no choice. The government controlled all sources of information. The Communist Manifesto was like the Bible: it could not be doubted. There was no way not to believe.

And, in fact, Yelin had good reasons for being a believer. True, his father, a cobbler, complained that life was too austere. "They say this is the greatest country, bah!" his father would grumble. "I've been to Bucharest. In Bucharest, they had everything. Here there is nothing!" But Leonid dismissed his father's gripes. Their life in Tashkent was pretty good. They had work, food, and schooling. They also had sports. A promising athlete, Leonid was growing up with all the benefits of Soviet athletic training, perhaps the best in the world. Early on, he displayed exceptional athletic ability and excelled at several sports before dedicating himself exclusively to volleyball, at seventeen. Although on the small side for a volleyball player, his exceptional vertical leap allowed him to play outside hitter, a position normally filled by taller players. His skill at the sport earned him opportunities not easily come by in Soviet society. At eighteen, when he, like all Soviet males, had to enter military service, Yelin was able to get into officers' school and avoid the harsher boot camp simply because he was a good volleyball player. The military sponsored sports teams, and the best young players from local clubs were allowed to fulfill their military obligations by playing for these teams.

At first, Yelin liked the officers' school. The uniform and the drilling appealed to his teenage sense of adventure and glory. Like other Soviet youth, he had been taught to revere the military. All his life he had heard patriotic stories of Soviet heroism in the Great Patriotic War, as the Soviets called World War II. And indeed, some measure of reverence was understandable. From the Soviet perspective, the Red Army had done the most to defeat Hitler. The Soviets had suffered over twenty *million* casualties and had fought off a Nazi invasion (America, by comparison, lost 400,000 soldiers in the war and did not fight on its own territory). It was natural for a Soviet boy of Leonid's generation to want to participate in that glory.

But while in the military Yelin underwent a mild transformation. For the first time, he became aware of double standards and hypocrisy in the military and in society at large. It was, however, a subtle transformation, and at first Yelin wasn't even aware of it. But others were. Unbeknownst to Yelin, the KGB began compiling information on him.

Somehow, a series of random and innocent details caught the attention of the internal surveillance bureau. At the time, Yelin didn't recognize the significance of these details; after all, he thought he was a loyal patriot. But in the mind of some bureaucrat of domestic espionage, certain random incidents formed a suspicious pattern.

First, his father was a discontented foreigner. Despite Leonid's political orthodoxy, his father's discontent was enough to mark them both. Second, Leonid neglected to join Komsomol, a mass organization that prepared youth for membership in the Communist Party. Membership in Komsomol was important. Failure to belong jeopardized acceptance into institutions of higher learning and dimmed career chances. His neglect was nothing more than a fluke, typical teenage procrastination. It wasn't that he didn't care to join, he just kept putting it off, what with the distractions of sports and schoolwork. Nevertheless, the oversight earned him another demerit.

Then, during his military service, Yelin attracted attention by criticizing procedures or policies that he thought wrong. Yelin has always been the kind of person who speaks his mind; if he considers something wrong, he says so. All his life, he acknowledges, he's had a tendency to "talk too much." But in the Soviet Union, with informers everywhere and circumspection in speech the wisest course, such a trait was inevitably a serious flaw. His minor complaints, which to him amounted to nothing more than constructive criticism, quickly became material for someone's report to superiors. There were spies everywhere;

even your best friend might be an informant. In fact, one day Yelin had been asked by the military intelligence officer at the school "to be vigilant." But the request was so oblique that Yelin did not realize until years later that the officer had been trying to recruit him. Perhaps *that* oversight, too, had been forwarded to the KGB and duly entered into his file.

As Yelin explains it, in their domestic surveillance operations the KGB employed a simple code for monitoring Soviet citizens. He likens it to a stoplight: everyone was rated "green," "yellow," or "red." Whenever you applied for a job or a visa or party membership, a call went to the KGB, and your file was pulled. If you were a "green," then the KGB found you unobjectionable. If you were a "yellow," then your fate depended on the mood of the KGB officer, or on some extenuating circumstance that would allow the KGB to overlook your demerits—for the time being. If you were a "red," then you could forget it and just be thankful you weren't packing your bags for Siberia.

By the time Yelin left the military and rejoined his volleyball club, his yellow light was flashing in the KGB's nebulous files. Fortunately for him, his athletic skills kept him out of immediate trouble. In fact, he was so good that in 1970, at age twenty, he was chosen for the all-republic team of Uzbekistan, one of the fifteen teams representing the fifteen Soviet republics in competitions for the championship of the USSR.

Being a star athlete meant that, "yellow" or not, Yelin merited privileges that were not available to the common Soviet citizen. He was immediately provided with an apartment instead of being placed on a yearslong waiting list. He had a car, a luxury item in the USSR. And he had shopping privileges at one of the "certificate stores," closed to ordinary citizens, where he could buy scarce commodities such as choice meats, fresh fruits and vegetables in winter, American cigarettes, and imported electronics.

In exchange for such privileges, the Soviet elite were held to a strict political orthodoxy. Everything they did was under close scrutiny. This was a bad arrangement for Yelin: he never did manage to control his loose tongue, and with every offhanded criticism his file grew a little thicker.

One of the benefits Soviet athletes enjoyed was the opportunity to travel. Yelin's team played matches and tournaments all over the Soviet Union and he greatly enjoyed the trips. But when the team had the chance to play abroad, Yelin was prevented from going. In order to participate in such trips, every player was required to fill out an application for permission to leave the country. Each time, Yelin's applications were turned down. The only explanation he received was that he had filled out the form wrong. Finally, he filled out the form with a friend, each doing exactly the same thing. His friend was approved, but once again Yelin was rejected. By this time, he had guessed that these rejections were political not bureaucratic, and he had to ask himself what he had done wrong.

By this time, too, Yelin was asking himself what and whom he believed. He had grown up accepting what he read about the West in his schoolbooks and in *Pravda*, the state newspaper: the excessive crime, the rampant poverty, the greed of the capitalist barons destroying society and the environment, the cruel and unusual punishment inflicted on political prisoners like Angela Davis. And he had likewise believed the official portrayal of the Soviet Union as a virtuous nation struggling for peace and worldwide prosperity. Yelin did not doubt that Soviet citizens lived more comfortably than those elsewhere and with greater blessings from their government.

It was, therefore, "a big shock" to Yelin when his teammates would come back from tournaments in Europe saying they had seen a West vastly different from the one depicted in Soviet publications and on Soviet television. It was now evident to him that someone was lying, either the government or the people he had known and played with for several years.

He didn't decide overnight that the government was untruthful, but he certainly found it hard to doubt the word of the people closest to him. He'd also been mulling over some other puzzling things. The defections, for example. Everyone knew that some high-profile people—scientists, artists, athletes—had defected. According to the government, these defectors were selfish egoists interested only in material wealth and personal fame. To the Soviet media, defectors were unpatriotic, and that was the worst crime possible. Yelin couldn't help but notice that while many people defected from the Soviet Union to the West, nobody defected from the West to the Soviet Union. If the USSR had the highest living standards in the world—a workers' paradise, as the schoolbooks said—and if the poverty, unemployment, and oppression were so bad in the West, why didn't suffering Westerners come to the Soviet Union? Yelin especially wondered why American Blacks didn't defect. He continued to talk about these things with his teammates and friends, and some of them listened carefully, noting instances of his dangerous talk. The former believer had transformed if not into an open dissident, at least into a malcontent. And his yellow light was now flashing a little more hotly.

Yelin now realizes that, in a way, the regime created fertile ground for defectors—and for the eventual downfall of the entire Soviet system—by treating athletes differently from ordinary citizens. The government expected orthodoxy in exchange for elite privileges, but orthodoxy proved difficult when those very privileges, such as international travel, led athletes to perceive the duplicity of the government's propaganda. Ironically, the sports program, which the Soviets touted as the pinnacle of communist achievement—had helped plant the seeds of the USSR's eventual dissolution. While Americans watched in dismay as Soviet athletes dominated Olympic gold medal counts, they didn't realize that this "proof" of communism's superiority was, in fact, contributing to the system's inevitable collapse. Yelin was a perfect example: a hard-core patriotic believer who had become disillusioned.

Yelin's growing dissatisfaction carried over to the volleyball court. Now twenty-four and playing for the Uzbek Republic team, Yelin found himself increasingly at odds with the team's coach, a martinet who scorned his players and treated them like mere automatons subject to his commands. Finally, Yelin could take no more, and—true to his character—did the unthinkable in Soviet sports: he spoke out, criticizing the coach's severity in front of the team. The team could not be good, Yelin said, if it didn't respect the coach. The team could not bring itself to play hard for him. For his insubordination, Yelin was benched. Realizing that he had no future with the Uzbek team, Yelin quit when he was offered a chance to play for a club in the Russian republic.

But then something happened that changed the course of his life. Before he departed Uzbekistan to join his new team, a friend asked him for a favor. Could Yelin run the Uzbek junior women's team practices for a week? He agreed. When the week was over, Yelin was offered the job as head coach. He was reluctant at first. He'd never thought much about coaching, especially teenage girls. But his friend pointed out that at twenty-four his playing days were numbered, and this was a chance to begin preparing for a future career. Yelin took the job.

Perhaps because he had experienced bad coaching when he was a player, Yelin had a natural feel for the job. He understood that a coach could not be as severe as his former coach had been. At the same time, a good coach could not be so friendly with his players that discipline was lax. He succeeded in finding a middle ground between friend and martinet. And he got results. Within three years, he took the team to a first-place finish in the national junior championship.

After that victory, Yelin was named head coach of Uzbekistan's women's team. It took him just one more year to win another championship, the USSR Women's World Cup in 1978.

The move into coaching changed Yelin's personal life as well. While he was in Moscow with the junior team for a tournament, he ran into a friend from his playing days with the Uzbek men's team. It turned out that other teams from Uzbekistan were also in the Soviet capital and they were having a party. Yelin went to the party with his friend and there he met Yelena, his future wife. Yelin already knew about her. A volleyball prodigy, she'd been practicing with the women's squad since she was fourteen. Now at eighteen she was a rising star. They had a good time at the party, and the next day Yelena came to see the junior team's practice. Leonid needed a watch during the practice and borrowed hers. But somehow he lost it and, embarrassed because a watch was a fairly precious commodity in the Soviet Union, he had to promise to find a replacement and deliver it to her when they returned to Tashkent. His irresponsibility proved fortuitous. Back in Uzbekistan, they began dating, and a year after Leonid became Yelena's coach on the women's team, he also became her husband.

It was 1978 and despite the successes on the court, life was getting more difficult. Even as a coach, Yelin wasn't allowed out of the country. When his teams went abroad for tournaments, an assistant coach had to take over while Yelin stayed home. Yelena went on trips to Portugal, France, and Japan without him (it was even less likely that couples would be allowed out together; if one stayed home, the other was more likely to return). Only once, finally, did Leonid get to join her: for a tournament in Bulgaria. The authorities didn't worry about that one because, as Yelin says, "No one could possibly dream of defecting to Bulgaria."

Their lives were strictly controlled in other ways as well. They had curfews and rigid schedules to follow, with as many as three practices a day. Their yearly bonus was a ten-day vacation, but "vacation" meant having only one practice a day instead of two or three. To do anything else, such as continue one's education, involved complications. Leonid and Yelena had to finish their university degrees through correspondence courses. The couple hardly had time alone together. They even had to obtain permission to have a baby. The lifestyle was physically and emotionally draining, and the Yelins were approaching burnout.

They reached the crisis point in early 1979. In its oblique way, the government had been publicly admitting to the need for greater individual freedoms. Rumor had it that this meant more people would be allowed to emigrate. Yelin had reached the point where he was fed up with the blatant hypocrisy of Soviet propaganda, the double standards, the lies, the excessive governmental control. Like many Soviet citizens, he grew increasingly cynical about the obvious chasm between the Communist Party's grandiose pretensions and the grim reality of Soviet life. Yelin decided that his own privileged life amounted to little if it were based on such lies. He was sick and tired of an arrogant Party line that belied stagnation and decline.

He and Yelena would have to give up a lot to leave the USSR. They knew that in the United States volleyball didn't have the prestige of other sports. They would have no status at all. But it wasn't status they sought, nor material wealth. Yelin was willing to drive a taxi in America; he just wanted out of the Soviet Union, whatever the consequences. The government was dead wrong, he now saw, in claiming that defectors were materialistic egoists. He and Yelena didn't look at things in that way at all. Instead, they thought about the future, the family they wanted to raise, the freedom their children could have only if they left the Soviet Union. They decided to emigrate. After months of collecting the paperwork, they submitted their application. And just like that, with that one imprudent move, their semaphores switched from yellow to red.

Looking back on it now, Yelin realizes that he was very naive to believe the rumors of a more open emigration policy. It was, he says, "a bad interpretation" on his part. His application was immediately denied. The director of the Uzbek volleyball program, a good friend of the Yelins, told Leonid that he had no choice but to dismiss him. Then the KGB called Leonid in.

The "interview" took place in a bare room with several KGB officials. They confronted Leonid with a thick file documenting his transgressions—several years' worth of his loose talk transformed into damning statements that made Yelin sound like a raging dissident. They accused him of betraying socialism. They grilled him on the minute details of his statements, twisting everything he had ever said into a pattern of sedition. Worse, they showed him sworn statements, written by fellow teammates and coaches, that denounced him as an enemy of socialism. To Yelin's surprise, the officials were willing to cut him some slack in exchange for a statement condemning the very teammate who had most vociferously denounced him. The KGB had reason to suspect this person of illegal trading on the black market. Surely Yelin knew something? Things would go easier on him if he could supply some information. But, Yelin explained, he really didn't know anything about it. He had nothing to tell them. They pressed him, raising their eyebrows and winking. Look, they said, this guy has said terrible things about you. What do you have to say about *him*? But Yelin remained adamant; he couldn't bring himself to lie. "Don't you know you're looking for more trouble?" his inquisitors shouted.

Then came a big shock. Just when the interview had reached its grimmest point, the door opened, and an old acquaintance walked in. Yelin looked up into the face of a former teammate from years past, an older player who had been at the end of his volleyball career when Yelin joined the team. The man was now with the KGB—nothing unusual since the KGB liked to recruit athletes (supposedly more loyal because of their privileges). Still, it surprised Yelin to meet up with this man after so many years and under these circumstances. Over the years, the ex-volleyball player had worked his way up the ranks and was now a high-level chief. They shook hands, exchanged pleasantries, as if they had just run into each other in a store or on a street corner and not in an interrogation room. But then the agent got down to business. "You have got yourself into some trouble," he said bluntly. He pressed Yelin to lie about the player suspected of trafficking. Things would be easier for him, the chief suggested, if he would denounce his teammate. But Yelin again insisted he knew nothing about the case.

The KGB's man shrugged his shoulders and dropped the matter. "It's just lucky for you we played on the same team," he told Yelin when they parted. "When your file crossed my desk, I recognized your name. That saved you."

Yelin's salvation was relative. His acquaintance with a high-level official kept the KGB from actively harassing him. He wasn't completely blacklisted, but Yelin and his wife fell into a limbo of sorts, deprived of privilege and status, forced to take jobs well beneath their talents. Yelena ended up teaching volleyball in a lowly technical school for troubled children. Fired from his elite position with the Uzbek women's team, Leonid began all over again with junior players.

These were the darkest years. Leonid Brezhnev, the stodgy leader of the Soviet state since Yelin was a boy, lingered in office, his geriatric dotage emblematic of the country's stagnation. Brezhnev finally died in 1982. But in response to Reagan's adamant Cold War policies, the Politburo selected KGB chief Yuri Andropov, himself old and ailing, to replace Brezhnev.

The new leader favored economic reform, but to achieve this end Andropov stuck to the harsh means that, as KGB chief, he knew best: cracking down on domestic dissent. To Andropov, economic reform meant enforcing discipline on a lax work force. Suddenly, the KGB was everywhere, hassling everyone. Yelin recalls sitting in a movie theater one Monday afternoon, when the projector was stopped mid-film and the lights came on. A pack of plainclothes agents rushed in and began an impromptu inquisition. Everyone in the theater was required to show documents and answer to the agents' scrutiny. Why was he in the theater on a Monday afternoon? an agent asked Yelin, the implication being that someone not at work at that time must be shiftless, or a malingerer, or worse yet a hooligan, the standard Soviet label for bad citizens. Under Andropov, such shakedowns could happen anywhere—in department stores, in subways, at sporting events. The fear of tattlers was greater than ever, and even the normally garrulous Yelin now kept his mouth shut.

Then in 1984 Andropov died and was replaced with a doddering Brezhnev crony, Konstantin Chernenko. Already senile, Chernenko lasted barely a year. With Reagan still in the White House and the Soviet populace deeply dissatisfied, the Politburo conceded that a totally new direction was needed. Eventually, Mikhail Gorbachev, a young reformer, brokered his way to the Kremlin's top spot. Yelin watched these developments take place, at first with despair as the Brezhnev-era despots clung to power and then with mild hope when Gorbachev instituted the economic reforms known as *perestroika*.

Yelin held out hope that Gorbachev's reforms would lead to serious change, but he remained cautious. He'd been too rash before, and he wasn't about to rush into anything this time. For two years he waited and watched as Gorbachev instituted unprecedented changes. Central to the reform movement was a new policy of "openness" that lifted censorship and ensured for the first time in Soviet history basic freedom of speech.

This openness, called *glasnost* in Russian, led to a sea change. The media abandoned its role as Party propagandist and began publishing critiques and exposés of the government. Banned books and films became available. Opinion polls and elections mattered for a change. Encouraging as all this was, Yelin still wanted to leave the Soviet Union. A joke making the rounds best explained his resolve: a reporter asks a dog at the Kremlin kennel how things have changed since Brezhnev died and Gorbachev took over. Well, says the dog, the chain is still too short and the food dish is still too far away but now I can bark as loud as I want. With his daughter now seven years old and another child on the way, Yelin wanted more than anything some hope for his children's future. The chance to bark was a welcome change, but it didn't release them from the chain. Deciding that this new openness might prove his best chance for that opportunity, he once again applied to emigrate.

Despite the fervor for reform in public discourse, the actual pace of change, especially in the government bureaucracies, was hardly discernible. Yelin found this out during his second time around with the emigration bureau. The whole procedure took months and months, a full-time paper chase. He had to file what seemed like hundreds of forms and documents, some of them making no sense at all. For example, he had to reproduce his grandfather's death certificate, even though he had never even seen his grandfather, not even in a photograph. If he asked why he needed these documents, he got a bureaucratic shrug or a glare that said, "put up and shut up." Perhaps it was just a cumbersome and obstructive bureaucracy keeping itself in business, but to Yelin all the paperwork seemed like a deliberate attempt to hassle people desiring to emigrate.

After a while the nightmare became a Kafkaesque exercise in the absurd. He had to appear in court with witnesses who could testify when and where his various relatives had died. Of course, he had no real witnesses so he was forced to hire people who would swear to this or that in court. In fact, bribes were necessary every step of the way.

Finally, the day came when everything was in order. The family went down to the emigration bureau to receive their visas. They had to turn in their passports and the keys to their apartment. Yelin didn't want to surrender his passport, but the official told him that all émigrés automatically had their citizenship revoked. Yelin handed over the passports, and the official ripped them up in front of the family. He was now a man without a country. All he had for identification was a badly typed visa on flimsy paper that easily tore when it was folded. With this paper he would have to confront the immigration authorities of the West.

Early in 1989, the Yelins left the Soviet Union on a flight for Vienna. They then traveled to Italy where they met for the first time with US immigration officials, who scrutinized with mild amusement the cheap visa Yelin carried. The Yelins ultimate goal was Florida, where Leonid had relatives. In July 1989, they received permission to enter the United States and flew to Miami, knowing nothing about the city except that it was warm and in America.

From the beginning of his new life in Miami, Yelin was willing to do whatever it took to support his family. He knew life would be hard. He couldn't even complete a sentence in English. But within days of his arrival, he got his first job. A German contractor hired him to lay tile in a hospital. He knew nothing about tiling, but that didn't matter. It was money to support his family. Later on, he realized that the job was not exactly legitimate. He'd found his way into the standard entry-level job for newly arrived immigrants: subcontracting with a contractor to complete a job for a fraction of the original contract. The German was like many contractors in Miami: an established immigrant looking for new arrivals to employ for well below the minimum wage. But the legality of the arrangement didn't matter to Yelin. He was just happy to work.

Next came a more stable job: delivering pizzas. Yelin thought it great work because he was forced to speak English and learn his way around the city. He considered it a lesson in street survival and felt lucky to have a job in which he could learn so much. For one thing, he picked up a lot more English on the job than he could in a classroom.

Then one day he caught a break. A Russian friend who was working at a department store arranged for Yelin to interview for a sales job. The interview with the store's personnel manager lasted thirty confusing minutes, during which Yelin understood maybe a tenth of what she said. He just kept nodding his head and saying "Yes, ma'am." When he left the office, Yelin had no idea what had happened, so his friend went in to ask the personnel manager. When he came back out, he told a surprised Yelin, "Congratulations, Leonid, you got the job!"

But Yelin's surprise gave way to panic when he was taken to his assignment: the women's perfume counter. He stared in disbelief. He didn't know enough about perfume to sell it. To tell the truth, he didn't even know enough English to sell *anything*. His first impulse was to flee as fast as he could. He managed to stammer out a few words to the assistant manager indicating that he was sorry, he just couldn't do the work. The assistant manager, a Cuban immigrant, understood Yelin's nervousness. "But Leonid," she encouraged him, "don't you have a family? You have to stay for them. At least get the first check."

Yelin stayed, though still scared to death. It was all so foreign to him, the number and variety of products so overwhelming. He had come from a place where stores sold only one brand of a product, the government brand. All too often the product wasn't even available. Now he was confronted with a glittering array of bottles, names, shiny boxes, scents, colors. And he had to keep them all straight in his head, ready to answer a customer's questions politely. That was another thing he had to learn: how to sell something, how to wait on a customer. It was a completely alien concept to a person raised in the Soviet Union. He had to learn that in American stores "the customer is always right." In Soviet stores, the customer didn't even merit an opinion. In the USSR, salesclerks controlled the counter, wielding power like petty tyrants; their typical response to a customer's question or complaint was a shrug. In the United States, Yelin had to adapt to the culture of commission, scrambling to assist a customer, practicing "service with a smile."

It was hard work, but not as horrible as Yelin had feared. For one thing, he soon discovered that in Miami's immigrant community a certain camaraderie prevailed, a spirit of helping one another out to pursue the immigrant dream of the promised land. Even though they worked on commission at the perfume counter, the salespeople did not compete with one another. They especially looked out for Yelin. A retired schoolteacher drilled him in English on breaks. The Cuban employees, themselves newcomers to capitalism, taught him the technical complexities of the cash register and credit card transactions. They helped him make sales, shared commissions with him, covered for his mistakes. "I never met a bad person in Miami," he says. "Everyone was such big help."

In many respects, the department store was Yelin's American school, his education in the languages and the cultures of his new home. Looking around the store at the excess of products and the crush of shoppers, he would feel a rush of pride in his success at making it this far. Sometimes he missed coaching volleyball, but when he reflected on his newfound freedom and the bright future his children would have, the sacrifice seemed worth it. If he lived out his days as a salesclerk, he could tolerate it.

Eventually he moved from perfume to men's clothing, an even better position. He liked the challenge of approaching customers and asking if they needed assistance. It forced him to be creative in conversation, extend his vocabulary. One day, it was just such a conversation that changed Yelin's fortune yet again. During the afternoon lull, when few shoppers were in the store, he fell into conversation with a customer who, perhaps curious about his accent, asked Yelin where he was from. By the end of the conversation, Yelin had told the customer his life's history, as best as he could. The man seemed especially interested in Yelin's coaching background. He scrawled out a telephone number on a scrap of paper and told Yelin to give him a call.

He didn't think much about it until weeks later when he told a co-worker about the encounter. "Let me see the number," the co-worker said. Yelin had to rifle through his wallet, finally producing the scrap. His friend read the name, and said "Leonid, you have to call this guy right away. He's a wellknown lawyer, he will help you." But Yelin was still too nervous about talking on the phone in English, so his friend grabbed the phone, dialed, and shoved the phone in Yelin's hand. Yelin found himself stammering through an introduction. No introduction was necessary. "Hey, what happened?" the lawyer said. "I've been expecting your call. Listen, there are some people I want you to call, they're waiting to hear from you."

The lawyer gave Yelin the number of Jim and Roberta Stokes, driving forces in Miami's volleyball scene. Yelin called and talked to them. They asked him if he wanted to coach volleyball again. "Are you serious?" he asked, flabbergasted. They invited him to a meeting of the South Florida Junior Volleyball Club, and by the end of the meeting, Yelin was offered the chance to coach the club's Elite squad.

Yelin coached the squad part-time, a frustration since he was used to the Soviet system, in which coaching was a full-time job and then some. He still had to work at the department store to make a living, but at least he was coaching. And in his first year, his new team qualified for nationals. It wasn't smooth sailing, however; Yelin's faulty English caused some problems. At the national tournament, he called a time out at a crucial juncture to set up a play. With only thirty seconds allotted for a time out in volleyball, he had to talk fast. But this time, the stress of the moment caused him to panic, and his mind went blank. He couldn't think of the words, so he hurriedly sketched a play on paper, grunting and pointing at his players. The befuddled girls went back onto the court with no idea what to do; before Coach Yelin could think of what to say the team was eliminated from the tournament.

Despite the language problems, Yelin's team was winning, and the success of the junior club soon caught the attention of the athletic director at Barry University, a Catholic college in Miami. She was looking for a new volleyball coach to rescue Barry's stagnant program and went to watch Yelin. She recognized right away that Yelin was an exceptional coach—a good communicator (language barrier or no) and teacher who had his players believing in themselves and his system. She had seen enough coaches to know that one didn't find people with Leonid's qualities every day. After a couple of interviews, she hired Yelin as a full-time coach.

Barry's program was a severe test of Yelin's coaching skills. In the Soviet Union and with the South Florida juniors he'd always had the best players to work with. Now he had nothing. In his first year the team went 8–17. He learned that in America he would have to do more than just run practices and coach during games. In fact, the most important part of his job would not take place on the court at all. He would have to play the recruiting game. The whole idea seemed strange and confusing to him. He had to wade through four huge notebooks of NCAA regulations. His slightest move, it seemed to him, was regulated. He had to learn when a prospective player could visit the university, how long she could visit, when and how often his team could practice. On and on the rules went. When it came to regulation and surveillance, the KGB had nothing on the NCAA. Long gone were the simple days in the Soviet Union when all he had to do was run three practices a day.

Despite the difficulties of adapting to this different cultural approach to sport, Yelin soon had the Barry squad winning. In his fourth year at the school, the Buccaneers went undefeated in the conference and made it to the quarterfinals of the national tournament. The next year, he brought his team back to nationals with the number one ranking. The local media, normally obsessed with football, latched on to the story, and Yelin found himself in the middle of some typical American hype and hoopla. But he had been through far too much in his life to get caught up with the excitement. For one thing, he knew he had the best-prepared team and that his women were going to win. For another, the tournament wasn't even the biggest event of the week for him.

Just days before the tournament, Yelin finally turned in his flimsy Soviet visa at the federal courthouse in Miami and was sworn in as a US citizen. There was a symbolic significance for him in officially becoming an American as he pursued his first US volleyball title. What he had wanted most in life was to become an American citizen. More than he wanted the championship.

When the final match was over and the national championship title was his, along with the honor of being named national coach of the year by the American Volleyball Coaches' Association, Yelin wept. At the courtside press conference, he couldn't speak through his tears. The reporters assumed that the thrill of victory had overwhelmed him, but that wasn't it. Later, he explained his feelings at that moment.

"I have been national champion before," he said. "Many times. But this was different, you know, because now I am national champion in my new nation."

Soviet Bloc Rock

1. Hooligans

For three days we shuttled around Moscow on the tour bus, a group of visiting students shepherded en masse to the show sites of Soviet achievement. The Intourist guide's amplified voice called attention to war memorials and Bolshevik monuments, model apartment buildings and heroic factories, halls of sport and culture. Young, pretty, and well indoctrinated, Svetlana said, "Here is Economic Exposition Hall. You will like it. Please, this way." We were invited to marvel at displays of assorted machinery, appliances, farm equipment. Then the gift shop. Smiling, brushing blond wisps from her eyes, Svetlana pointed out a selection of postcards: grainy photos of brutalist hotels, high-rise construction, milk production, and state farm harvests in progress.

One evening, I escaped from the hotel and walked alone to Red Square, a fantastical and disorienting place at night. Mesmerized, I stared at the glowing Byzantine geometries of St. Basil's Cathedral, the ornamental facade of the GUM department store outlined in lights, the dour watchtowers of the Kremlin. Buried in the necropolis at the base of the Kremlin wall, John Reed brooded on the ironies of the historical moment; nearby, Lenin's embalmed corpse slept furiously in the shadows of his mausoleum.

I crossed the square and came to the massive doorway of the History Museum. It was there I encountered the gang of hooligans. That was the word Svetlana had used to describe the scruffy young men who loitered near tourist sites and hotels hoping to barter for blue jeans or any article Western tourists might be willing to offer. Hooligan, my teacher explained, was the Soviet designation for nonconformists, misguided miscreants, and disaffected youth who had succumbed to a fascination for bourgeois trappings.

They came out of the darkness, drunk, blocking my path. Not threateningly—they were too emaciated to pose a threat. In the square's eerie glow I saw yellow eyes, gulag faces. Hollow and tubercular figures reminiscent of Dostoyevsky characters. They asked for cigarettes, one of the few Russian words I knew, an easy cognate. No cigarettes, I said, and then they perceived my foreignness, stepped closer, surrounded me, breathing furtive sentences beyond my abilities in the language and showing disappointment when I couldn't answer.

Americanski?

Yes, American.

Horrorshow, horrorshow, they said—a word I had learned, the Russian for "good" sounding just like an apt description of an Alice Cooper concert.

There followed a kind of charade in which they asked me questions, and I repeated a word or two I recognized to their encouragement, before finally admitting with a shrug that I didn't understand. We had reached a stalemate, no broaching the linguistic divide. They spoke among themselves, discussing some strategy for communicating with the stranger, then tried again, slowly repeating two tortured words that I at last came to recognize as English.

Rolling Stones? I said.

Da, da, Rullang Estonies. Horrorshow?

Yes, I said, yes, horrorshow.

Ping Flood, horrorshow?

Pink Floyd, yes, horrrorshow.

And so we proceeded through the late-night playlist of Radio Free Europe, the favored soundtrack of Soviet hooliganism, as I verified for them the hard rock tastes of American youth: Led Zeppelin: horrorshow; Jimi Hendrix: horrorshow; Cream: horrorshow; Allman Brothers, Grateful Dead, Jefferson Airplane: horrorshow, horrorshow, horrorshow.

2. A Bazaar in Tiraspol

Twenty-five years later, a visiting professor, I toured a bazaar in the post-Soviet backwater of Transnistria, a strange breakaway territory mired in a "frozen conflict" with newly independent Moldova. In Transnistria, a bastion of the defunct Red Army had entrenched itself, still clinging to the communist past and refusing to recognize the Soviet Union's disbanding.

A colleague led me around the place. We had walked a mile from the university, passing along the way first a small park with a display of antiquated Soviet military remnants, then a prison, where women stood on the sidewalk shouting messages to their incarcerated men.

The bazaar was situated in a muddy lot. A cold March wind blew. My colleague—a philology professor—said, "They call this place, in Russian, *tolchock*, meaning toilet, like a slang." The fringes of the bazaar were lined with people hopeful of selling off the litters of their pets: puppies tied together with rope, kittens mewling in crates. We traveled the rows, looking over scores of caged birds, perusing tarps spread in the mud for the display of scavenged auto parts and used tools. We had come to the bazaar to browse the selection of Soviet mementos—military medals, Lenin pins, Young Pioneer badges. The philologist spied something he thought I would like, an old army holster stamped with the Red Star. The vendor—as leathery and faded as the holster—wanted five dollars. The philologist, indignant, argued him down to two.

One section of the bazaar was devoted to compact discs.

Computer programs, music, video games. Thousands of CDs, all pirated copies of Western copyrights, knockoffs made in factories out on the Asian steppes, where shadowy ultra-capitalists operated beyond capitalism's regulated pale. The copies were faithful to the last detail: even the puritanical "Explicit Lyrics" warning label, meaningless in Tiraspol, had been carefully reproduced. The prices were too good to pass up: five dollars a disc. Impassive, the philologist waited while I flipped through the crates. I remarked on the music selection—pop, rock, jazz, classical, country, folk, international—a collector's paradise right there in a muddy lot in remote Transnistria. The most popular category seemed to be classic rock.

Oh, man, look at these, I said, pulling out copies of albums I hadn't seen in ages: The Zombies, Deep Purple, Badfinger, Captain Beefheart. Captain Beefheart!

I can't believe they're so cheap, I said.

A callous, thoughtless comment: five dollars was one-tenth a professor's monthly wage.

Walking back to the university, the philologist said, "What was once forbidden is now merely impossible, you see."

When we passed the prison, a woman with a red scarf tied around her head was shouting up to a grated window. "Nikolai, your son was caught stealing again. What is to be done? What is to be done?"

3. Back in the USSR

In far-off Kishinev, Pushkin endured a bitter and relentless exile. Decades later, Kishinev was the scene of slaughter—a sanguinary pogrom in which hundreds of Jews died. Its name changed to Chisinau, the city is now part of Moldova, a former republic of the USSR that, as an independent state, is fast slipping into economic perdition. The latest numbers put Moldova behind even Albania and Belarus.

On a wide and nearly empty boulevard—a desolation row of crumbling high rises and deteriorating storefronts—you find the Beatles Bar, a dim place devoted to the Fab Four, where bare bulbs cast feeble light on rustic, rickety tables. Every inch of wall space is covered with posters, photos, and drawings of the West's most iconic pop group.

There's a still from *Hard Day's Night* of the lads running down a London alley.

There's a poster depicting a scene from *Help!*—the boys being detained by bobbies.

There's a shot of the foursome clowning on a putting green.

There's the pen-and-ink drawing from the cover of *Revolver*.

And the poignant downward gaze that graced *Rubber Soul*.

And a cartoon still from *Yellow Submarine*.

And the photo of backward Paul from *Sergeant Pepper's*.

And the rooftop performance of "Get Back."

The Beatles with Ed Sullivan. The Beatles with the Maharishi. The Beatles with the Queen.

Familiar images, now strangely transformed, recontextualized—icons bordered by words, much like the holy images edged with Slavonic scripture that adorn Orthodox churches.

In this new context, the all-too-familiar words seem blatantly ironic. Yesterday. Tomorrow never knows. You never give me your money. You say you want a revolution. Helter skelter. Happiness is a warm gun. Let it be. Get back to where you once belonged. It's all too much. Slogans for a new world order, Lennon replacing Lenin, something no one could have imagined.

Just down the boulevard, there's an abandoned shopping center, built in the Soviet heyday, its collapsed stairways and eroded facades giving it the appearance of a war ruin. And throughout the city you see the skeletons of structures that were still under construction when Moscow's largesse vanished with the collapse of the Soviet Union. Long abandoned, they shed flurries of concrete in the winter wind.

Now, government workers receive sacks of sugar for their wages.

Only foreign aid keeps the place afloat.

Lenin's toppled statue lies buried in mud and snow.

Ask the man tending bar where the Beatles memorabilia came from, and he shrugs you off.

Ask who owns the place and he shrugs again, turns his back. He doesn't like the line of questioning.

An officer of the US Embassy explains: the only functioning businesses in the country are under control of the Russian Mafia. The Moldovan government can't do anything about it. Or won't. The Mafia and the government are entwined. A local journalist calls it Official Hooliganism.

The bartender is putting in a disc, cranking the volume to drown out your questions.

You see what it is: *The White Album*, side one—and before it even begins, you know what song comes next.

The Partisan

I was at Vasily's house and very drunk when I met the Partisan. There are times when I wonder if I didn't dream the whole encounter. It had been, after all, a hallucinatory month in Moldova, a former Soviet Republic now, according to the latest statistics, Europe's poorest country. Four hundred miles west, NATO bombs fell on Belgrade, sparking daily demonstrations at the US embassy in Moldova's capital, Chisinau, a block from my apartment. At the same time, spring had awoken traditional sentiment in the citizens of the capital. They tied red ribbons to trees and pinned little flowerets made from thread to each other's coats. Good luck, renewal, fertility, happiness—the explanations varied, but the springtime ritual was followed with steadfast earnest.

Electricity came and went. Penniless pensioners haunted street corners, stretching skeletal hands out to passers-by. Dog packs roamed the city rummaging through trash bins already picked clean by the legions of post-Soviet unemployed. Day after day, I found myself drawn into drinking bouts with my Moldovan colleagues, who were eager to numb themselves to the throes of what was being called the "New World Order."

It was in this context that I heard the Partisan's story.

I had already been at the house for hours when Vasily suddenly pulled me from my chair and said, "Come, there's someone I want you to meet." I set an unsteady course in Vasily's wake, my legs wavering as I left the room, suddenly very much aware of how much I had consumed during the previous hours.

The drinking had begun at ten in the morning. "What shall we start with, brandy or champagne?" Vasily asked when we arrived.

Previously, my wife and I had become very sick on Moldova's powerful, sickly-sweet brandy, and we had sworn off it. "Champagne," I said.

"But we always start with brandy!" Vasily declared, pouring out the shots that must be downed in one hearty gulp. Two more shots quickly followed, with cold herring and sour pickles as mid-morning hors d'oeuvres.

After that, the day became a blur, a marathon in excessive consumption that belied the country's poverty. Homemade wine. Vodka. Salami. Spaghetti. Lamb. More wine. More vodka. Cake. Some sort of whiskey that tasted like wood alcohol. We discussed the NATO bombings. We analyzed the renewed popularity of Stalinism in Moldova. We denounced the environmental crimes of communism. We looked at pictures of Disneyland. We quoted Dostoyevsky then recited Beatles lyrics. We caviled Lenin and extoled Lennon. Vasily toasted and I reciprocated. Night fell. Our wives looked through photo albums. Our sons watched a strange Romanian television program that featured disco music and striptease. The lights failed. Vasily proposed a toast. The lights came on. Vasily proposed another toast.

That was when Vasily led me from the dining room through the kitchen and onto an unlit porch where I lost track of him and banged into something. Overhead, I heard the tapping of Morse code—rain on the tin roof.

"Here, this way please." I followed the voice into a cold darkness and felt rain on my face. I misstepped into mud. Icy ooze covered my shoe. Vasily appeared at my side. I was aware of a frail light flickering just ahead. Raindrops drummed down. Vasily struck at something. A door materialized. He knocked again and called out, "Daniel! Daniel!"

At last, the door opened, and there in flickering candlelight stood Anthony Quinn's doppelgänger—leathery face, hard stare, black beret. Vasily greeted him in Romanian then spoke at length while squeezing my arm. The only word I understood clearly was "American." Quinn's double regarded me and nodded thoughtfully. I was pushed into the room, Vasily following, telling me in English, "This is Daniel, my neighbor behind." Daniel embraced me and smacked each side of my wet face with a kiss. He muttered something to Vasily, who laughed in response. "Daniel says, he always heard the American army was on its way, now at last here it is, much too late and only one measly soldier."

We sat down at a table. Daniel lit a kerosene lamp. "Can you imagine," Vasily said. "Here he lives with no electricity, no water. He can have them, you understand, but he chooses no. He says a man must work with his hands for daily bread, not push buttons. He is like Moldovan Thoreau."

Daniel produced glasses of wine—poured from what looked like a plastic petrol can. Homemade wine. Pungent and sharp. My mouth puckered. The conversation proceeded in a combination of Romanian and Russian, with occasional interpretation in English from Vasily. I tried to focus on the story Daniel was telling, not an easy task given the combination of languages and the alcohol storm in my head. And there were distractions and interruptions as well—the constant replenishment of the wine and the inevitable toast; a multitude of cats leaping onto the table, scratching at my legs, mewling; Daniel's stentorian belches. It all made concentration difficult. But over the course of an hour I pieced together the gist of the story (at one point, dimly aware that I should be taking notes—given my pretensions to journalism—I asked for a pencil and scribbled a nearly illegible jumble of words onto a square of butcher paper).

Daniel told me he had lived his whole life—more than eighty years now—in this same village. During that time, the village had been incorporated into four different nations. When he was born, the village belonged to Czarist Russia. A few years later, during the Bolshevik Revolution, Romania reasserted its hegemony over the village. The Soviet Union claimed the village at the end of the Second World War. And when the USSR fell apart in the early 1990s, the village became a part of the newly independent Republic of Moldova.

As a consequence of these events Daniel, a simple goatherd, had been forced to take up arms. First, he fought against the Soviets when they occupied the territory in an attempt to recover those regions that had once belonged to Czarist Russia. Daniel gave up goat herding and joined the resistance. For months his band pestered the Soviet posts and sabotaged the infrastructure used by the Red Army. They were never caught. Subsequently, Romania—trying to win back lost territory—turned fascist and joined forces with Nazi Germany. Daniel and the other partisans did not fight communists just to be taken over by fascists. So, they stayed underground, now fighting the Nazis with the same guerrilla tactics they had used against the Soviets. For three years they kept up the fight. Then the Red Army returned, driving the Germans back toward the Rhine. Daniel and the partisans joined forces with their former adversaries—Soviets being the lesser evil—and helped prepare the way for the Red Army's offensive by sabotaging the Nazi retreat.

When it was all over, Daniel's village ended up inside the boundaries of the Soviet Union. The very thing he had originally taken up arms to oppose had now come to pass. Worse, he was considered a dangerous element. For six years, he had fought in the resistance and avoided capture. Now, in peacetime, he was arrested, taken from his goats, and sent to a concentration camp in Siberia. He did hard labor in a mine. He endured the brutal cold. He nearly starved to death. Eventually, after a few years, he was released and made his way back to his village—a four-thousand-mile journey, most of it accomplished on foot. His prison-issue boots, made of wood, disintegrated as he walked.

His story finished, Daniel poured some wine and cut a chunk of bread from a black loaf. Then he slid the plastic jug and the loaf in my direction. Out of politeness, I took some, though I really had no intention of consuming any more of the sour wine or stale bread. Daniel dipped the bread in the wine and put it in his mouth. He chewed slowly, staring at the loaf as though meditating on it. Vasily did the same, and I saw that tears had filled his eyes.

It was then that I came to a somewhat sobering realization: this was an invitation to communion. Bread. Wine. Fellowship. I tore off some bread, dipped, and ate. We sat in silence.

When it was time to leave, Daniel embraced me, then kissed me—cheek, cheek, mouth. Despite my culture's apprehension over such gestures, I wasn't embarrassed or even surprised. It seemed the appropriate way to take leave, an acknowledgement of a bond.

Vasily and I stepped outside, paused on the stoop to gauge the rain's strength, then dashed across the dark gulf to his glowing house.

Incidents of Train Travel

I.

The others left the compartment in the small hours at a town whose name I didn't catch.

All four departed: the old soldier who during daylight had pointed out the battle sites we passed; the art school student with a sketchbook and wonderful auburn curls whose eyes I had tried to catch; the sad young couple who tightly held hands and looked frightened.

They slipped away, and I was left alone listening to the clacking wheels and muffled conversations in the passageway, a regional dialect I could not understand.

Dawn revealed that the train was passing through a birch forest. I left the compartment in search of coffee and bread, repeating to myself the proper shape of vowels for the necessary words. *Excuse me. How much. One small bun please.*

Of late, I had yearned to engage in more intelligent conversation, to present myself as something more than a simpleton. Even my thoughts had turned simplistic. In my dreams, I was fully mute.

Later in the day, with the train stalled on the industrial outskirts of a postwar boomtown, the compartment door opened, and the conductor entered. He nodded, angled his head to see the cover of my book, made a brief statement, then stood at the window peering out at the slag heaps, the factory smoke, the snowfall. Several times he sighed heavily, shaking his head.

And then he sat. Sat and spoke. Softly, steadily in a flat grim voice, staring at his feet, only occasionally glancing up at me. The lines around his eyes deepened when he frowned or grimaced. He took off his conductor's hat and ran a hand through thinning hair.

It was a long monologue that ended abruptly with a gesture of—what? Apathy? Despair? Resignation? Taking leave, he nodded somberly, formally, and the door clicked shut.

What had he been confessing to a stranger? A love affair? Fraternal envy? Parental neglect? Fear of failure? War crimes? Was it even a confession? I had understood only a handful of words: *mountain, old, listen, moon, bad, never, sleep.*

What is there for any of us but to lurch fitfully along from disillusion to regret, a series of poor choices, misguided notions, plans gone awry, sorrowful episodes? Brought to a standstill in a wasteland, what can one do or say to atone, to make amends, to account for oneself, to articulate the reasons when there truly are no reasons? To rationalize the irrational: a persistent urge. I felt deep pangs, a sudden, profound sense of loss. I was thinking of the people I had shunned, cut off from my life.

At a suburban stop, boisterous youths crowded into the compartment and filled the passageway. Waving scarves and banners with the name of a football club, they appeared to be on their way to a match. They sang songs that sounded belligerent, perhaps full of bile for the evening's opponent.

Meanwhile, the train eased through miles of slums toward the terminus, wailing at the roadway crossings where children gaped and buses spewed exhaust. Now and then rocks hit the train.

In the station I sat on a bench and watched an old woman sweep the floor with a twig broom. City names and departure times spun around on the destination board. Above the patriotic mural, full of brutalist symbolism, grime-coated windows let in the scarcest of light. The destination board indicated that my connecting train had been canceled. I put my pack on the bench for a pillow and stretched out in anticipation of yet another night in a cold, ill-lit station, stranded in a strange city, a country of broken dreams.

2.

A dubious train makes the slow slog from Palenque to Mérida in the Yucatán—eleven hours according to the deluded chalkboard sign in the Palenque station; twenty hours, in reality, if the train doesn't break down or derail and leave you stranded in some derelict town, lost on a dead-end sidetrack. With luck on your side, you'll make it in twenty.

That's twenty nightmare hours of lurching and skirling. And at each hot stop, the insects invade the cramped second-class carriage, along with hawkers bearing baskets of beer and banana-leaf tamales and pork rind and fried grubs. Rainforest gives way first to scrublands and then to unbroken swamps; a slow, feverish progress through Mexico's lowlands to the burning-oil twilight of Campeche, the Spanish city huddled behind walls thrown up to fight off the vast thorn and nettle wasteland that the Maya called "the place of the snake and tick."

But even nightmares can have a peculiar allure; when you wake, safe from dreamt dangers, the bizarre and unexpected phantas-magoria still lurking in your mind takes on a certain fascination. What an intriguing dream, you think. So it is with difficult travel; once the dread has passed, once the ordeal is done, you realize, with some surprise, just how stimulating, just how quickening it has been to cut so close to the unknown edge, to push the envelope—even if only the envelope of discomfort and tedium.

And on the long train trip up the Yucatán peninsula, there are moments when the discomfort and tedium yield to something pure and enchanting, something that inspires. For two hours, as the train crosses the forbidding region known as Sal Si Puedes, a campesino family (and some of their farm animals) have you pinned against the window, your buttocks numb on the wooden seat, your legs cramped. Then the train stalls in the middle of nowhere and vendors suddenly appear, invading the already jammed aisles with their bulky baskets and shrill voices and reeking foods. The family buys some pulque, sacred drink of the Aztecs, the sappy brew scooped from a stone urn by the vendor. The old man of the group unexpectedly passes the cup to you with two gnarled hands, and the little girl offers tortillas. There in the dark, stuffy carriage, stalled in the dead of night in some all but uninhabitable place, you come to understand the meaning of communion.

Near dawn, you push open the rear door of the carriage and stand on the platform in the fresh air. The train slowly sways and rocks along through the branches and fronds slapping up against the carriages. The sun rises, a great glowing orange fireball that suffuses everything—landscape, train, your hands—with vivid, vital color. And when the train comes lurching at last into the outskirts of just-waking Mérida, you think, "What a ride that was, what a wild and wonderful ride."

3.

I left Havana on the night train to Camaguey, Cuba's third largest city, some three hundred miles east of the capital. Cuba is the only Caribbean country that still operates passenger trains. Leftover from a long-gone era, the engines and coaches are old but reasonably well kept. Riding the train, like so much else in Cuba, feels like a venture in suspended time.

Two hours after the scheduled departure there was still no indication—other than a huge crowd waiting—that the train was ready for a journey. It sat idle on the tracks, no crew in sight.

Suddenly, the crowd murmured and stirred. About a dozen ladies were parading through the throng, single file. They wore pinstriped blouses, short blue skirts, and fishnet stockings. These were the *ferromozas*, or rail stewardesses, and their appearance touched off a flurry of activity. The engine abruptly roared to life. People grabbed their bags and surged forward in a madcap rush to funnel through a single gate where a detached official conducted a slow scrutiny of tickets and identification. For several minutes, I remained pinned against an iron fence while the main current shouted and shoved past me.

Beyond the gate, the scrutiny intensified: the *ferromozas*, two to a coach, checked tickets and identification on the platform outside the train. Then they passed down the aisle checking tickets again and entering information on clipboards. Armed guards patrolled the train. A conductor entered the coach to double-check the paperwork. But once the train got rolling, once the industrial sprawl of Havana's outskirts was behind us, things loosened up—considerably. An old man in a boat captain's cap wheeled a cart down the aisle, selling pork sandwiches, peanuts, rum, and beer. Soon blue cigar smoke filled the coach, several cassette players were turned on full volume, and a group of Cuban passengers gathered up front to talk to the four foreigners on board—two Englishmen, a Spaniard, and me.

The sun set behind the eastbound train, gilding the panorama of cane fields and palm groves. The train rocked languidly along, but inside the pace of conversation was much more energetic. Fortified by rum, cigars, and *Bucaneros*, a strong socialist beer, we touched on a range of subjects—sex, religion, international politics, sports, music, history—in rapid fire, high volume chatter. Was it true that the CIA was responsible for killing Kennedy, Martin Luther King and the singer Selena? Why did Americans call it the World Series when only American teams competed? The guards and *ferromozas* lost their stern demeanors and joined both the drinking and the conversation.

Night came on. The music, blaring from competing cassette players, reached distorted levels. Several people started dancing in the aisles, their sinuous arms swirling in the blue smoke. The *ferromozas* played matchmaker, pulling the foreigners to their feet and handing them over to dancing girls. One of the Englishmen, giddy with the sensuality of the moment, tumbled mid-merengue into the arms of an olive-eyed *Cubana*, while the passengers cheered and clapped.

At Camaguey, well past midnight, I stumbled from the train into the humid tropical night, an unfamiliar station spinning around me. Horn blasting, the train went on its merry way, rocking and rolling down the line, leaving me empty and dizzy and feeling like I had been booted from the party. The other departing passengers quickly vanished in the night, and I was left alone.

Well, not quite alone. A fleet of pedicabs—rickshaws affixed to bicycles—waited curbside. A dozen taxi-cyclists offered their services. "Is it possible I could find a pension this late?" I asked one. He wore a Nike swoosh ballcap and a T-shirt depicting Che Guevara's "heroic guerrilla" gaze.

"*Todo es posible*," he said, waving me onto the wooden bench seat of the makeshift but neatly maintained rickshaw. "Everything is possible." Over his shoulder he added, "So says Fidel."

While in Cuba, I had heard many people quote Fidel, and on this occasion, like the others, I couldn't determine the speaker's intention. Was the quotation ironic? Sincere? A reflexive product of indoctrination? Or were Fidel's words ubiquitous and hence readily repeatable earworms, like an inane commercial jingle in the United States?

The bicycle frame rattled and squeaked as we cruised the quiet streets of Camaguey. We passed the Workers' Plaza then the flickering fluorescent storefront of the Vietnam Bookstore, where a collection of Fidel's speeches was on display in the window next to a Spanish translation of *The Teachings of Don Juan*.

The pension, like every other residence, was completely dark. The cyclist knocked several times. I was ready to give up and head to a hotel when the door opened and a middle-aged woman in her nightgown peered out at us. The cyclist explained my situation to the *señora*. To my surprise, she greeted me like an old friend or lost relative. Without hesitation she invited me in and showed me to an available room. Breakfast, she said, would be waiting when I woke.

The next morning, her hospitality was still keen. The promised breakfast consisted of a ham sandwich on a crusty roll with a plate of tomatoes and cucumbers. I washed it down with a large glass of freshly squeezed orange juice. Caridad—the *señora*'s name meant "charity"—informed me that she was headed to the market to see what she could find. She wanted to make me a traditional Cuban meal, she said.

Caridad left me in the company of her son, Eduardo. Trained as a veterinarian, he now worked in construction because the hours were better and the pay was the same—fifteen dollars a month. He was all too willing to skip work if something interesting came up—a common phenomenon in Cuba, apparently—and on this day I was a sufficient diversion. Eduardo volunteered to show me the sights of Camaguey, including a couple of provincial museums and the houses of Camaguey's famous native sons: General Ignacio Agramonte, a hero of the War for Independence, and the internationally renowned poet Nicolas Guillen.

When Eduardo and I returned to the house, Caridad and Eduardo's wife Lidia were busy preparing dinner, evidently pleased—excited even—that they had been able to find most of the ingredients for a proper traditional meal.

Eduardo and I retired to the living room to watch the news on a flickering Soviet black and white. Several reports concerned Castro's decrees of the day. Several more highlighted the latest heinous acts of the US government. Finally came a lengthy report on the national baseball team. The team's victories, the newscaster said, signaled the inevitable triumph of socialism.

When Caridad called me to the table, I was presented with a smorgasbord of Cuban food. She identified each dish—*boniato, tostones, frijoles*—and then the entire family left me to eat by myself. They would wait for the leftovers. I urged them as strongly as I could to join me at the table, but they wouldn't hear of it.

Embarrassed to be left alone at the feast, I ate gratefully but mindful that the others could not eat until I had finished. I tried to gauge how much I should eat—enough to show that I enjoyed the food, but not so much as to deprive the family. I ate my fill then went to shower while the family took their turn at the table. After showering, I rifled through my bags looking for items I could give away, items that ordinary Cubans had a difficult time accessing. Eduardo had mentioned several necessities that were in constant short supply, toiletries topping the list. I decided to leave behind sunglasses, allergy medicine, aspirin, and extra socks. Eduardo really needed a belt—he had hitched his pants constantly while we walked around town—so I also set aside my spare for him.

A knock came at the door to my room. Eduardo and Lidia entered with the coffee service. We sat around a well-worn table. Lidia poured the coffee from a small metal pot into chipped demitasses. I gathered that this was a special treat for all, as I had been told that quality coffee was in short supply, difficult to obtain. For me, it was extra special: a cup of real *café Cubano* in the land of its origin.

Caridad entered the room, along with her husband and brother-in-law. As usual in Cuba I was immediately thrust in the midst of an intense, almost frenzied conversation. We touched on everything from the comic frustrations of learning another language to the beauty of a perfectly executed squeeze bunt to the death of those who tried to escape by raft to Florida. They had scores of questions—What about the racial violence in the United States? Did Americans really hate Cubans and Mexicans?

How much would a veterinarian (Eduardo's profession) make in America? Were there Cuban baseball players in the major leagues? Like most Cubans I met, they were inquisitive, loquacious, often argumentative. Good talk excited them.

Eventually, Eduardo repeated to everyone what he and I had discussed earlier in the day. He had been particularly interested to learn about things like credit cards and home computers and internet shopping.

"You see what is kept from us," Eduardo said, more sad than indignant, and they all nodded. My question was, who kept it from them? In all my conversations to date, I had been uncertain whether Cubans were blaming the decades-old American embargo or the socialist system for their problems. Now I asked the family directly. The discussion exploded. They all spoke at once, gesturing, raising their voices, arguing with one another until eventually they reached a consensus and shared it with me.

The revolution, they said, had provided many good things, especially education and health care. But socialism had turned into an unwieldy bureaucracy and, worse, a class system where the few at the top got everything and the masses nothing. As for the United States, it was a great nation with wonderful, creative people. But the actions of the US government baffled them: couldn't they see that the embargo did nothing to Cuba's leaders while the ordinary people suffered tremendously? The answer to my question, then, was that both sides were to blame. The majority of Cubans felt trapped between the incompetence of socialist bureaucrats who used, even relied on, the embargo as an excuse, and the intransigence of an American policy that insisted on punishing them out of fear of something that no longer existed, namely communist expansionism.

Throughout the evening, the conversation moved rapidly from topic to topic, from light to serious, from humorous to tragic. We laughed. We argued. We shook our heads at the strange, ludicrous world we shared. Above all, we reveled in the most important thing of all: the fellowship, the camaraderie of a shared moment.

Ecotourism

I.

Costa Rica. On the day of the "Jungle River Cruise," I joined my fellow daytrippers and ecotourists in the hotel lobby to await departure. A huge Mercedes Benz tour coach arrived with our guide, Johnny, a jovial and energetic man who, while evidently a good student of English, had mastered the lessons on tag questions a little too enthusiastically.

"Ok, everybody, we got a big day, don't we?" he said over the microphone as we boarded the bus. "We gonna have good time, aren't we?"

The bus took us through the city, and out into the surrounding valley. The road climbed past cattle pasture, coffee farms, and large, tarp-covered plantations where exotic flowers were grown for export. All the while, the guide chattered into the microphone, his amplified voice directing our attention from one side of the bus to the other.

"You see how the coffee plants need shade, don't they? So the farmer he plants the shade trees first, and it's maybe five years before he gets the first crop. Really amazing, isn't it?

"Ok, everybody, look here to the left, we see the farm for the flowers under the big plastic. That's a lot of flowers, aren't they?

"Ok, somebody ask me about the roads. Our roads are pretty bad, yes? But you know, the new president he's really doing something. He holds a news conference, you know, to say to Costa Rica people there used to be ten thousand potholes in Costa Rica. Now only five thousand. So, he's doing pretty good job. Then we find out the potholes they get so big, the ten thousand little holes go together to make five thousand big holes. Pretty good joke, is it?"

We arrived at our first stop. According to the itinerary, we were about to have "a delicious buffet lunch at one of the most beautiful jungle lodges in Costa Rica." The lodge proved to be one of those places that had proliferated since the advent of ecotourism—a place run by foreigners for foreigners who wanted to find themselves "surrounded by jungles and colorful gardens" without having to give up familiar conveniences. The slick brochures available in my hotel lobby promised air-conditioned transportation, haute cuisine, wine lists, nature-viewing from a balcony. A typical eco-paradise featured a twenty-four-hour bar, all-you-can-eat buffets, and "pleasant walks along prepared rainforest trails." The selling point was nature, but the majority of the lodges took pains to assure clients that nature could be had without sacrificing comfort or luxury.

Luncheon over, we followed the guide along a gravel trail to a stream for an opportunity to photograph some frogs. Frogs were one of the main emblems of Costa Rican ecotourism. They appeared on promotional brochures, T-shirts, postcards, and gift mugs. But, as in the rest of the world, Costa Rica's amphibians were endangered. Several harlequin frog species had disappeared. The golden toad was gone. The prospects for other frogs and toads were not good, even in the new, ecologically aware Costa Rica.

Photographing rare and vanishing species is one of the biggest thrills for ecotourists, and much of ecotourism's popularity is due to the popular desire to see forests, animals, and tribal cultures before they disappear for good. Johnny, our guide, knew this, and when he captured a small green frog, he had a little trick in store.

"Ok, everybody, get your cameras ready. Focus on this spot over here with the nice ferns."

He held his cupped hands up to his mouth and said, "Very sorry, Mr. Frog." Then he shook his hands hard. When the frog had had enough, Johnny placed him on the spot with the ferns as a backdrop. "Ok, everybody, now you take nice pictures."

The semi-circled tourists leaned forward, cameras clicking, video cameras whirring. "Wild frog, Costa Rica," one cameraman said into the microphone as he shot a few seconds of film. Meanwhile, the dazed frog sat inertly at our feet, as apathetic as any zoo animal. Its translucent lime green skin glistened as the cameras flashed, its limbs so thin you could see through the skin to the bones, as though the frog were made from jelly.

Eventually, the frog regained its bearings and hopped first one way then another—the ecotourists backing up as though it might attack—before finally finding the ferns and disappearing from view.

We reboarded the bus to travel to a landing on the Sarapiquí River, where the itinerary called for "a cruise through the tropical rainforest" on a "comfortable modern jungle river boat." From the embankment above the river, we looked down at the dock and a row of "modern jungle river boats": fiberglass longboats fitted with plastic seats and a canopy. Four of them, loaded with tourists like us, already plied the river, their engines coughing clouds of gray and blue smoke. Our group descended the embankment and climbed aboard one of the boats.

Over the loudspeaker, Johnny introduced Captain Pedro. The captain, he said, had lived all his life in the region and knew the jungle river "like his back or his hand." He would show us many interesting things, many animals. Captain Pedro, wearing a white captain's hat, turned and grinned at us. He had maybe five teeth.

The boat drifted in the current while Captain Pedro fooled with the starter. The engine growled once, twice, then came on full force, and a wave of exhaust passed over the passengers. "Ok, here we go!" shouted Johnny. "Look for animals, everybody!"

It didn't take long. Just ahead, up on the embankment, we made our first sighting: a cow tied to a tree. Down in the river, three young humans splashed water on one another. The tourists aimed their cameras at the children, who obliged by waving and laughing.

Then Captain Pedro was vigorously pointing up at a tree. "Look everybody," our guide said over the loudspeaker. "Captain Pedro sees something. What is it, Captain Pedro? An iguana, everybody! Two, three ... *five* iguanas!"

The boat rocked as the tour group shifted weight, everyone leaning out to see, then frantically unzipping bags, grabbing cameras, and fiddling with fancy video equipment. While the humans fumbled about in a tizzy, the iguanas lolled, sunning themselves, blending in with the leaves and fading from sight. About half the group saw them and tried to point them out to the more myopic members of the party.

"Right there, see? Follow the branch out to the cluster of leaves. See him?"

The flurry of excitement over the iguanas proved unnecessary, for soon iguanas were everywhere in the trees above us as we chugged past. For twenty minutes, in fact, they were the only wild animals we saw, and Johnny's amplified call of "Iguanas!" prompted little enthusiasm from the now-jaded ecotourists.

Were we ecotourists? The section of the Sarapiquí River we were seeing could hardly be called wild. Up above, on the steep banks, shacks and bungalows stood in the clearings. There were corrals and fences and gardens, pigs and cows and horses. For a good part of the river trip, we passed through a banana plantation—row after row of monoculture. Blue bags covered the fruit, protecting it from insects. Discarded bags were everywhere, turning like jellyfish in the river current, snagged in overhanging branches, stuck in the muddy banks.

Just when it looked as though we would have to be content with iguanas and the odd heron, Captain Pedro came through.

Or rather his fellow captains came through, and Pedro was sharp enough to get in on the action. What Pedro had spotted, some fifty meters downriver, were the maneuvers of his comrades as they converged near the riverbank. A growing cloud of exhaust indicated that at least one boat was trying to hold steady against the current—the evident sign of an animal sighting.

Immediately, we were roaring at full throttle to join the flotilla and catch a glimpse of whatever creature had deigned to show itself. With our arrival, four boats bearing some one hundred ecotourists idled in the current, bows pointed to the bank, while the guides' amplified voices broadcast facts about the creature—a modest-sized caiman.

It rested on the riverbank, perfectly motionless in confronting the humans' gaze and the commotion of clicking cameras. The caiman bore it all with such reptilian aplomb that a few tourists wondered if it were still alive. Even though we were within ten meters of the caiman, we didn't have a good view. The breeze carried the engines' exhaust over the passengers and the riverbank, obscuring the caiman in a gasoline haze. The tourists muttered complaints—first that they couldn't get clear pictures, then that they couldn't breathe.

Eventually, Captain Pedro backed us away from the shore, and the current swung the boat out of the exhaust cloud. We continued downriver in search of more curiosities. Whenever Pedro thought he saw something, he threw the engine into reverse, holding the boat steady while the vapors once again enveloped us. Pedro was seeing phantoms, however; no other animals materialized, and after an hour on the river the ecotourists no longer cared. The fumes were too much, and the complaints were getting stronger.

But just as we started back upriver, we scored big. A terrible roar shook the air and startled everyone, including Pedro, whose captain's hat came tumbling from his head when he jumped in his seat.

Another roar, and the guide made the sighting up in the trees ahead: a family of howler monkeys. Our boat churned straight for them, the other tour boats in close pursuit. There was a bustle in the boats; monkeys of any kind are the golden fleece of ecotourism, the prize animal everyone hopes to sight and photograph. Even Johnny seemed fairly surprised that we had actually encountered a family of them. "Oh my god, look everybody," he exclaimed, "one, two, three, four howler monkeys!"

The monkeys seemed less pleased. They peered down through the leaves at the posse of boats circled beneath them. The male let loose with a tremendous throaty roar then broke off some twigs and threw them toward the boats. Undeterred, the boats maneuvered to give the tourists a better shot at the monkeys. Johnny used his loudspeaker to coax them with kissing sounds into plainer view, but the howlers stayed coyly behind their branches until they had seen quite enough of the humans and headed for denser canopy.

On the bus ride back to San José, I had to wonder about the value of the jungle river cruise. "Nature," as experienced on this tour—and I presumed it was typical of what was being offered by many of the so-called ecotours in Costa Rica—had been kept at a distance, safe, tame, packaged for viewing. We'd looked at it from platforms, from prepared paths, from boat decks. It had stayed alien and removed from us. By the time we came to the boundary of Braulio Carrillo National Park, the nature experience had been reduced to absurdity. Although the park had been touted as part of the ecotour, we weren't going to see it up close. In fact, we weren't even leaving our seats. We gazed at the Carrillo—an expanse of territory as wild and unknown as any place in Costa Rica—from the air-conditioned bus as we sped along the new motorway that had recently been gouged across the national park to facilitate motor traffic from the capital to the Atlantic coast.

The guide entertained us with stories about the wilderness we were bypassing—stories of adventurers disappearing, of animal attacks, of a terrain so rugged it had never been mapped. But all we saw was dense vegetation clinging to the cloud-forested slopes. Most of the ecotourists had fallen asleep. The rest of us had to wipe mist off the windows to see anything: the air conditioning was so strong that it had obscured the panes as we passed through the cool, rain-soaked mountains on the way back to San José and the comforts of our hotel.

2.

Tikal, the Maya ruin in Guatemala. I woke before dawn and joined a group of fellow tourists in the lobby of the Jungle Lodge. About twenty of us had signed up for a guided hike into the ruins to climb Temple IV and view sunrise from the tallest of Tikal's pyramids—a spiritual experience, we hoped. I recognized most of the group members from communal meals in the lodge's restaurant. About half came from a German tour group, another handful were American teachers, and the rest were teenagers from a Baptist church in Arizona. A diminutive, machete-bearing man named Jorge was responsible for leading us by flashlight along the dark jungle trail to the ancient temple.

We descended the driveway of the lodge and turned onto the path that led into the ruins. Like most of the paths at Tikal, this had once been a Maya road, a causeway of plastered limestone laid through the rainforest. The ancient plaster still existed, a hard shell that turned slick when wet and made walking somewhat treacherous, especially on slopes. By the time we reached the Great Plaza, three tourists had slipped and fallen, notwithstanding their state-of-the-art hiking boots.

It was still pitch black when we passed beneath the temples of the Great Plaza—the Temple of the Giant Jaguar and the Temple of the Masks—and made out their imposing dark outlines against the night sky. Already, birds were warbling and chirping, their loud chorus anticipating daylight. The wet air was heavy with the pungent aroma of the *ramón* trees, a smell reminiscent of cooked beans. On the far side of the Great Plaza, we plunged into forest again, marching to the steady knocking of a woodpecker. The causeway took us around Temple III then along the Bat Palace and past two small mounds, formerly Maya buildings, now stone heaps. In the shadows to our right stood two carved stones, darkness concealing the images engraved on them. One, I knew, a round altar, depicted two elaborately dressed men conferring over an altar upon which were laid bones and a skull.

Eventually, we came to the base of Temple IV, the Temple of the Two-headed Serpent. Unlike the renowned temples on the Great Plaza, the pyramid's stairway was too ruined for climbing, and ladders laid against the slope led up through the trees and the snake-like roots that entangled the temple's terraces. Jorge scrambled over and around the roots to climb alongside the embedded ladders, stabilizing some of the shakier tourists as we made the ascent.

The last ladder brought us to the top platform, above the tree line, where already a good-sized crowd had assembled to celebrate the sunrise. A long-haired young man sat cross-legged, playing an out-of-tune guitar, while a group of people seated in a circle around him chanted in a language I couldn't identify. Nearby, a man and a woman wearing chic adventure gear had assumed meditative positions; they sucked in deep breaths then loudly exhaled. Their breathing exercises continued unabated even when the *ramón*-pungent smell of Tikal was periodically replaced by clouds of repellent as one or another of the tourists doused themselves with DEET. The whine of the mosquito horde challenged the chanting of the guitar player's entourage and the Pentecostal murmuring of the Baptist youths holding hands in prayer. To one side, Jorge and a park guard stood watch and shared a cigarette.

The sudden roar of a howler monkey, eerie in the gray predawn light, cut off all the tourist racket. We listened to the slow, disturbed cry coming from the tree canopy somewhere beneath us. We strained to see into the dense vegetation, but the roars were diminishing, moving away from us.

Then, abruptly, day broke without sunrise, the enigmatic horizon gray and misted. Here in the tropics, daylight happened quickly, undramatically, darkness surrendering all at once to a milky light. The anticlimactic sunrise caught the would-be worshippers off guard. The music, chanting, and prayers had ceased; the spiritual moment we had been seeking was summarily denied to us. We stared eastward toward the murky dawn, finally realizing that nothing spectacular or mystical would happen.

We retraced our steps to the Great Plaza and turned down the long causeway leading to the hotel area. An enchanting green light filtered through the dripping canopy, and the loud songs of the birds and tree frogs silenced our sporadic conversations. Just then, a branch above us cracked. We heard the rustle of leaves, the crashing of branches, followed by a sudden thud right in our midst. Several people gasped. Someone yelped. Someone brayed. We turned, startled, then hurriedly scrambled back: a snake had fallen from the branches overhead. Before we could move, the guide dashed forward, waving his machete, and brought down the blade on the stunned creature, cutting its body in two.

For several seconds, everyone stood motionless, too stupefied to react. Then, slowly, we came back to life—nervous giggles, cautious approaches, exclamations of amazement. The guide was congratulated, photos were taken—each tourist wanting a picture of themselves crouching over the dead snake and another of the guide poking it with the machete. It was, everyone agreed, an incredible occurrence, the highlight of the morning. Back at the lodge, the snake was the talk of breakfast, and excited descriptions and pantomimes were provided for those unlucky to have missed it. No one mentioned, if anyone even knew, that the snake was a tree boa—quite harmless to humans.

3.

Honduras, the Mosquito Coast. We landed just shy of the *barra*, a gap that allowed choppy passage from the lagoon to the Caribbean. A short walk on a sand trail brought the three of us— the missionary pastor, Old Jim Goff, and I—through some palms to the beach and a wide vista of the sea. We sat down in palm tree shade and drank in the scene. The waves rushed toward the shore in a series of breakers. A flock of pelicans in file skimmed the surface of the sea. In either direction, the beach was completely devoid of human activity, the empty littoral matched by an unbroken horizon with no ships in sight. It was probably the most remote place I had been in my life.

Once we started our hike, however, it didn't take long to find evidence that ships did occasionally pass nearby. We came upon scattered pieces of trash washed up on the sand: a plastic cola bottle; a chunk of Styrofoam; an orange life jacket; a sheet of cellophane turning in the surf. It was all rather strange jetsam to find among the sand dollars and crab shells and dried starfish and turtle tracks of the Mosquito Coast. None of this debris escaped Old Jim's eyes. To him, it was all treasure. He picked up whatever glass, plastic, and metal objects were of interest to him and secreted them in a satchel slung over his shoulder. His biggest find was the pink torso of a plastic doll. Old Jim washed it carefully in the surf then added it to his eccentric collection.

It was a three-mile walk from the *barra* to the Río Plátano, a couple of hours of trudging along the shoreline, sandflies biting us as we went. Tourist posters of tropical beaches show a paradise of palms, sand, and surf; but the lovely photos don't depict sandflies, the nearly invisible—and ubiquitous—blight on any paradisal beach scene. We each kept to our own pace, each plodding along as best he could in the soft sand. The pastor, with his greater girth, soon fell behind. Every so often, I turned to see him huffing along, his face bright red with strain and sunburn. I fared a little better but could not keep up with Old Jim. The spry old man fairly scooted ahead of us, his bare feet slapping the surf, eyes scouting sea and shore for treasure as he went. From afar, I watched his slight frame dart back and forth—into the waves, up to the tree line—as he spotted some piece of jetsam and hurried to retrieve it. When he got too far ahead, he paused in the shade until I caught up. We looked over his sundry discoveries while we waited for the sweat-soaked pastor to arrive.

We reached the tiny settlement at the mouth of the Río Plátano late in the afternoon. A cluster of palapas stood just upstream from the sea, and we headed directly for the largest one, a stilted structure near the river that Old Jim called the *depósito*. Old Jim's cousin worked there, and while my companions went in to speak to him, I sat on the steps and contemplated the river.

Here it was, the object of my quest, the Río Plátano. It took a few moments for the realization to sink in. Ever since I had heard of the newly created Río Plátano Biosphere Reserve, I had drifted my way toward it, first studying maps and plotting the journey, then riding buses from Tegucigalpa to La Ceiba, then taking a flight on an old DC-3 from La Ceiba to the tiny village of Brus Laguna on the Mosquito Coast. It was in Brus Laguna that I had met the pastor. Interested in extending his ministry, the pastor volunteered to accompany me and suggested Old Jim as guide. The idea was to trek to the mouth of the Plátano and make inquiries as to the viability of a journey upriver into the heart of the biosphere.

Having arrived at the object of my quest, I should have felt exhilarated, but in fact I felt vaguely disappointed. I had no idea why. Maybe it was just exhaustion. Or maybe the biosphere had become in my mind something so fantastic, a place supposedly so sublime, that the reality was bound to seem anticlimactic: a collection of ramshackle huts; a brown, opaque river; a muddy bank on which a pig rooted and squealed; a cloying hothouse stink. Was this really the "pristine rainforest" that UNESCO had designated for protection?

I joined the others inside the *depósito*, where the fate of my intended journey upriver was under discussion. The building was some kind of storehouse or depot, a musty place filled with large large sacks of rice and beans. Huge stems of green plantains lay on the floor. In the corner I saw a stack of something that looked like army helmets; when my eyes adjusted to the dim light, I saw that they were turtle carapaces.

Old Jim's cousin looked just like him—small, dark, and wiry. A perfect double. When we were introduced, the cousin stared up at me, wide-eyed, as if to say, *So, this is the crazy gringo.*

"What's the verdict?" I asked.

"He says it's not a good idea," the pastor told me. "Maybe not even possible. The river's already high, and more rain is on the way. Anyway, they don't have any working motors available."

Old Jim's cousin said something in Miskito and the pastor translated. "He says there are many things in the river. Branches. Logs. It's dangerous."

I couldn't admit it, but in a way I was glad to be relieved of the obligation of going upriver. I had reached the Río Plátano, the edge of the biosphere. I had tried. At that moment, it seemed enough.

With the plans for a river trip scotched, we set about preparing a place to pass the night. Since the stilted *depósito* was the highest, driest structure around, the pastor and I were given the honor of spending the night on the floorboards among the sacks and plantains. We rigged up the mosquito netting with some twine around a beam. It looked like feeble protection, but it would have to do. The pastor didn't care about the mosquitoes so much. It was, he said, the tarantulas he wanted to keep out.

When we finished arranging our quarters, we sat out on the steps to await the return of Old Jim, who had gone to visit his cousin's hut. The sun had almost set, and redolent fragrances drifted from unseen night-bloomers. In the last light of day and with the air freshened, the Río Plátano seemed every bit the sublime place I had imagined. Muddy in daylight, the river now took on a dark sheen and whispered past. Frogs croaked. Birds whistled and cawed. Crickets chirruped. Fireflies filled the purple air.

Even the mosquitoes, besieging us in hordes, added a certain perverse charm to the setting. After all, it wouldn't be the Mosquito Coast without them; the place's isolation depended on their hostile presence. The pastor and I slapped and waved in a futile attempt to fend off their needling. The best we could do was don long-sleeved shirts and denim pants and accept the plague with stoic disregard, accept it as the sting inevitably associated with the sublime in nature.

With nightfall, the locals came to call on us. Only a handful of families lived in the vicinity. The area around the mouth of the river served primarily as a temporary fishing and hunting camp and as a sort of transit zone. Sometimes men came from the interior, dropping off crops and fruit at the *depósito* and taking back staples and other supplies (including bags of cement powder and cases of Coca-Cola). Cargo boats arrived by sea to exchange rice for plantains, beans, and fruit. Miskitos sold hawksbill turtle shells to the boats, a prized commodity that eventually made its way to Japan as *bekko*—ornamentation for furniture.

Three men visited us. They shook our hands and solemnly asked the pastor for a prayer. Towering over them, the pastor mumbled a few words as he laid his hand for a few seconds on each of their bowed heads. We stood a moment longer in silence. The nearly full moon had climbed above the tree line and gilded the edges of some clouds—the billowy, innocuous kind rather than the thunderheads that usually appeared in the evening. I realized that we had been lucky to avoid thunderstorms during our trek.

It turned out the men wanted more than prayer from us: they wanted to do some business as well. One of them reached into a sack and pulled out something long and shiny for our scrutiny. The pastor switched on his flashlight and played the beam over the object. It was a snakeskin.

"A fer-de-lance," the pastor said. "Pretty deadly. Around here they call it a *masagua*."

"*Masagua*," the men nodded. I looked closely at the splayed skin in the electric light. It was maybe six feet long, an olive-gray color crossed by dark bands.

"They want to sell it to us," the pastor said.

Even after we declined the offer, the men remained before us, holding out the skin as though the temptation to possess it would soon overwhelm us and lead us to change our minds. After a longish silence, the men restored the snakeskin to the sack then asked if we wanted to see the *tigrillo*.

We followed them into the darkness on a path that took us along the river to a collection of palapas. The pastor's flashlight beam revealed mandala-like spider webs and a trail of leaf-cutter ants in the gleaming mud. One of the men stooped and caught something—a tiny yellow frog. He showed it to me, pinching it between his fingers, its bulging eyes fighting the light that shone down on it. I nodded and then the man flicked it toward the river, where it plopped and vanished.

Behind one of the palapas, we came upon a makeshift cage made of wooden slats and odd strands of barbed wire. "*Tigrillo*," the men announced. The pastor lit up the animal, an ocelot. It lay curled in a corner, like a large house cat, breathing heavily. We pressed closer. It tensed, tried to stand, and it was then I saw that its leg was broken. The injury had allowed its capture, and now, frightened and in pain, the wretched creature trembled and hissed at us.

"What will happen to it?" I asked.

The pastor spoke with the men.

"They say they will kill it for you if you want the pelt."

"They seem pretty convinced we want animal skins," I said.

The pastor shrugged. "They make some money that way. It's one of the few commodities they can sell to the outside world. Animal skins. Turtle shells."

Such a waste, I said.

The pastor shrugged again. "Somebody somewhere is buying."

Just then Old Jim turned up to lead us through the trees to the beach, where about a dozen men had a fire going and a pot simmering atop the flames. We sat down on the trunk of a fallen coconut palm and were given plastic bowls steaming with turtle soup.

I looked up at a sky sequined with stars and listened to the singsong voices of the Miskito men blend with the sounds of the rushing waves and the crackling fire. Most of these men lived upriver in small villages and settlements within what was now the biosphere reserve. For a few weeks at a time, they came to the coast to fish and hunt turtles. One of the men spoke Spanish, and I asked him about turtling. He told me how they caught the turtles in nets, hauled them aboard their boats, and clubbed them—not an easy task given that the turtles weighed over a hundred pounds. Sometimes they would catch a nesting female coming ashore at night to lay her eggs. The eggs were very good to eat, the man told me. They would find maybe a hundred eggs buried in the sand beneath the bushes. But nowadays it was difficult, for few turtles returned to this part of the coast. The hunting was better to the south, on the islands off the coast of Nicaragua. The men hunted two kinds of turtle: green turtle (which we were having for dinner) and hawksbill, very valuable because it had a beautiful shell. The man's father had caught many, many hawksbills in these waters, but now there were very few. They stayed away and didn't come to nest anymore, he said sadly. This year the catch was very small.

Old Jim came over to ask me if I had liked the turtle soup. "Very good," I lied. In truth, I couldn't bring myself to taste it and had spilled my bowl onto the sand behind me. In the course of a year's travel, I had, in circumstances such as this, been offered guinea pig, piranha, stork, and iguana. I had sampled them all, but I balked at eating turtle. In college, I had read the naturalist Archie Carr's book *So Excellent a Fishe*, in which he described the brutal procedure for extracting calipee—the essential ingredient of turtle soup. Calipee was cut from the bones of the bottom shell, often while the turtle was still alive. Once the calipee cartilage had been extracted, the turtles were abandoned, left for scavengers. I didn't know if that had been the case with this turtle—probably not—but the recollection of Carr's account had quelled my appetite.

"Yes," I told Old Jim, "very good soup."

He then presented me with the turtle's green and yellow carapace, a good-sized one at about a foot long, and squatted in the sand next to me in the dying firelight to point out the shell's qualities. "Look," he said, tracing a finger over the smooth, marbled scute. "Good, good shell," he said, rapping his knuckles on it.

At some point in the evening, clouds had moved in to blot out the stars. Out over the sea, the massing cumulonimbi trembled with heat lightning, evanescent flashes touching the beach, the sea, and the circle of men with a ghostly blue light. Thunder began to rumble, and the temperature dropped suddenly as the wind picked up. We hurried back along the trail toward the *depósito*, the first drops of rain splattering in the foliage above us. The pastor held the flashlight as he jogged ahead, the beam jumping over the path, the ferns, the thick snake-like tree roots, the river. We passed the palapas to the sharp crack of lightning—the jungle suddenly seared white with electricity—and there was a deep rattling explosion as we passed the cage where the ocelot was dragging itself painfully in a nervous circle, droplets of rain glinting on the strands of barbed wire.

We reached the *depósito* just as the torrent was unleashed, and for the better part of an hour the heavy downpour battered the tin roof, and thunder shook the roof timbers. I was exhausted but couldn't sleep. I lay on the floor under the mosquito netting trying to find the least uncomfortable position. A damp, noisome smell rose from beneath the floor, and I imagined the swollen river rising to carry us out to sea. I was especially glad, just then, that the trip upriver was not going to happen.

The storm finally passed, and frogs emerged to serenade the night. Eventually, I dozed off, but a scraping sound woke me. It stopped when I stirred and reached for the pastor's flashlight. I played the beam over the room and saw the turtle shell Old Jim had given me rocking back and forth: a rat was inside, gnawing at the residue that lined the shell.

Down to the Banana Republics

In the early 1980s, the place for foreigners to hang out in Tegucigalpa, the capital of Honduras, was O. Henry's, a wild expat bar whose atmosphere somehow combined nervous energy and fecklessness. Because of civil wars in neighboring Nicaragua and El Salvador, there were plenty of war correspondents and would-be mercenaries alongside drug dealers, hookers, and an odd assortment of ambiguously sourced expats who seemed to have no purpose. The major activities in the bar were excessive drinking and bullshitting. Over bottles of bland Nacional Beer, you could always listen in on someone's tall tale; dubious accounts of gunrunning, rebel encounters, and jungle treks predominated. Almost anyone in O. Henry's could be heard subconsciously humming that Warren Zevon song about desperately hiding in Honduras as the shit hits the fan.

At some point, I wondered why the place was called O. Henry's. After asking around and mostly encountering "who-cares" shrugs, I found someone who knew, one of the war correspondents doing a story on the Nicaraguan contras for a "men's magazine." As it turned out, Honduras had once been a hideout of sorts for O. Henry, the renowned American writer of short stories that always seemed to end with an ironic twist. O. Henry was, in fact, a nineteenth-century precursor to the latter-day expats hanging out in his namesake bar. I had had no idea, when reading "Gift of the Magi" long ago in seventh grade, that one day I'd follow in the writer's footsteps to a country that, at the time, I would have been hard put to locate on a map.

Curious about the backstory, I sought more information at the library of a bilingual school where I sometimes gave lessons. There it was, in an outdated set of the *Encyclopedia Americana*: O. Henry (real name: William Sydney Porter) had fled embezzlement charges in Texas, winding up in Honduras, which had no extradition treaty with the United States. A fugitive, O. Henry was thus the forerunner of Zevon's "desperate man" hiding out in Honduras for unclear but probably illicit reasons. I also learned that O. Henry had written *Cabbages and Kings,* a book of interconnected short stories about Honduras and his exile in the coastal town of Trujillo. All very interesting, a backstory worth pursuing, I decided. I turned it into an assignment of sorts: first tracking down a copy of *Cabbages and Kings* to read, then heading out to Trujillo in pursuit of O. Henry's ghost.

In those days, getting to Trujillo required some effort—a four-day trip by bus and boat. On the map it didn't appear to be such a long trip, but back then Honduras played bigger than it looked on the map. I had to go in stages, first on a bus from the capital Tegucigalpa to San Pedro Sula, a hot commercial city "of little charm," as the guidebooks liked to put it. After a sweaty night in San Pedro, it was another long bus trip past miles and miles of banana plantations to La Ceiba on the Caribbean coast. Then two nights in La Ceiba waiting for a boat that could take me on to Trujillo (the road from La Ceiba to Trujillo in those days was only theoretically passable). In retrospect, I should have flown. By air, Trujillo is only 150 miles from Tegucigalpa, but then as now I generally preferred to take the overland route whenever possible, the better to see the land and life as it is lived in places I've never heard of before and may never see again. Furthermore, the prospect of flying around Honduras at the time was none too appealing. Two airlines serviced the country, SAHSA and LANSA. Expats said the acronyms stood for "Stay at Home, Stay Alive" and "Lost and Never Seen Again."

I certainly never imagined myself making a journey to Trujillo, Honduras. Will Porter (he hadn't yet become O. Henry) probably didn't either, and may very well, like me, have known nothing about the place before he landed there in 1896—nothing except that it possessed the qualities he required: remoteness, lack of contact with the outside world, and a laissez-faire vibe that would allow him to guard his secrets.

Presumably, Porter had done some research and learned that Honduras was the closest country to the United States without an extradition treaty. Escaping Texas and the charges against him, he went to New Orleans and eventually hopped a ship, probably a fruit steamer returning to the banana plantations. How Trujillo became his specific destination in Honduras is not known, though the town's isolation would have been enticing to the fugitive. Or it may have been mere chance: the banana boat made a call at Trujillo, and Porter abruptly decided it was as good a place as any for his exile.

Porter spent approximately five months in Trujillo. There is little hard evidence of what he did during that time. He apparently made acquaintances with the Jennings brothers, Al and Frank, fugitive outlaws who had arrived in Trujillo fresh from robbing banks in the States. The only account of their encounter, however, comes from Al Jennings's memoir, an unreliable source, since much of what Jennings wrote is obvious fabrication. Otherwise, an inkling of Porter's life in Honduras can be inferred from the stories in *Cabbages and Kings*, in which Honduras becomes "Anchuria" and Trujillo becomes "Coralio." Writing as O. Henry, Porter romanticized the setting for these stories, describing Coralio as a languid and enchanted town. In one story, he listed some of the main reasons his protagonist found satisfaction with the place: "The climate as balmy as that of distant Avalon; the fetterless, idyllic round of enchanted days; the life among this indolent, romantic people—a life full of music, flowers, and low laughter; the influence of the imminent sea and mountains, and the many shapes of love and magic and beauty that bloomed in the white tropic nights—with all this he was more than content." For this O. Henry character, an exiled American like Porter, "those old days of life in the States seemed like an irritating dream." Porter probably felt something similar; he apparently was eager to stay in Honduras and hoped to bring his wife and daughter down to join him. But his wife was too ill to travel (she died within the year), and eventually he decided to return to the States to face the charges against him (the upshot: he was convicted and spent time in prison, where he gathered still more inspiration and material for future stories).

Although he never returned to Honduras, he spoke fondly of the place throughout his life and sometimes expressed a wish to return to "the fetterless, idyllic round of enchanted days" that he knew while in Central America. Despite his predilection for Trujillo's apparent tranquility, O. Henry realized that more invidious forces were at work behind the scenes. He saw that Honduras was the playing field for what we now would call neocolonial exploitation, though his language tended to make light of what he calls "the game" (a term that Mark Twain similarly used to criticize America's imperialistic designs on the Philippines). O. Henry spoke of "brigands," "fakirs," and "hucksters" who sought concessions from Central America's nominal rulers. At times, this game of neocolonial exploitation seemed comic: "The little *opéra-bouffe* nations play at government and intrigue until some day a big, silent gunboat glides into the offing and warns them not to break their toys." *Cabbages and Kings* was published in 1904, just as the United States was starting to exert economic, political, and military hegemony throughout Central America and the Caribbean. Already the banana companies were dominating regional politics, and the US military was demonstrating a willingness to intervene or invade the countries of Latin America as it deemed necessary (1904 was also the year that Theodore Roosevelt issued his corollary to the Monroe Doctrine, justifying America's exercising of "international police power" in Latin America).

O. Henry saw the process unfolding. It may have seemed comic to him at the time, but the consequences—as more and more gunboats patrolled the coasts to enforce neocolonial dictates—would become deadlier with time. O. Henry wasn't exactly prescient or deeply insightful about the situation, but he did see a glimmer of the region's near future: in *Cabbages and Kings* he coined a term that would soon become pertinent and catch on, quickly gaining favor as an epithet for the whole region. Anchuria was, O. Henry said, a "banana republic."

The Trujillo I saw decades after O. Henry's sojourn still looked very much like the place he had described. Or perhaps a better way to put it is that I let O. Henry guide my perceptions, and what I saw in Trujillo confirmed the expectations I had, expectations derived from O. Henry's writing. I didn't really realize it at the time, but my prior reading about Central America and Mexico—particularly books by Graham Greene, Joan Didion, Robert Stone, Paul Theroux, and Malcolm Lowry—had decidedly shaped my interpretation of the region when I subsequently visited for myself. There was nothing unusual in this; throughout life we confront the problem of anticipating what an experience will be like based on what others have said it will be like. These expectations become a screen or a filtered lens that highlights what we expect to experience while obscuring what falls outside our expectations. In Central America, one banana-laden donkey on the streets will capture a visitor's attention and (this is the crucial part) become indicative of the norm even as hundreds of late-model automobiles rush past. Why? Because one has expected to see that donkey cart, while the cars don't fit the preconceived picture. I have even caught myself working hard to frame a photo of a fruit-vendor's donkey cart so as to exclude the motorcycles and trucks—any sign of modernity—that lingered nearby.

Suffice it to say that in Trujillo I saw what O. Henry described, namely "side streets covered by a growth of thick, rank grass;" "mean and monotonous adobe houses;" "palm-thatched huts;" "shabby cabins;" and "a ruined cathedral"—all images straight out of *Cabbages and Kings*. "On the principal street running along the beach," O. Henry wrote, "were the larger stores, the government bodega and post-office, the cuartel, the rum shops, and the market place." I walked along what I took to be this same street, and it seemed to match. Anyway, it was close enough for me—uncritically following in O. Henry's footsteps—to believe that O. Henry had got it right and that not much had changed. I found the old post office and the market and dutifully snapped some photos, imagining that someday I would show friends and relatives the picturesque town that O. Henry had written about in *Cabbages and Kings* and that I had adventurously traveled off the beaten path to find.

In truth, there wasn't much to do in Trujillo except walk around and imagine the place through O. Henry's eyes. It didn't take long to cover the entire town, so I had time on my hands and three days to kill before a boat would be leaving for the return trip to La Ceiba. Trujillo did have some attractions: fine sandy beaches, a steady supply of seafood and lukewarm beer, and the ruins of some fortresses the Spanish had built long ago to defend the fledgling town—at that time Honduras's only port—from English pirates. With little else to do, I lazed on the beach or splashed in the surf until midday when the fishermen returned with their fresh catch and fires were stoked in the seaside shacks and the daily fish fry got underway. After lunch, lightheaded from beer or rum, I strolled the town, dodged rainstorms, made small talk with shopkeepers, contemplated the fortress ruins ten times over, and snapped scores of photos in the washed-out tropical light.

On one of my walks, I visited the local cemetery. As I wandered among the mossy headstones, a man bearing a machete approached me. This was the caretaker. He peered at me from beneath his broad-brimmed hat. "You come to see the grave of the gringo," he said, a statement not a question.

I didn't know what he was talking about, but I agreed with him: Yes, I had come to see the grave of the gringo. He waved for me to follow him. The caretaker led me to an old grave isolated inside a waist-high fence of rusted iron. The gravestone, chipped and scored, reclined in a bed of moss and mud. *William Walker,* read a bronze plaque set in the stone, *Fusilado. 12 de Septiembre 1860.*

I looked at the caretaker. "*Fusilado?*"

He nodded and repeated the word, then pantomimed the firing of a rifle. "Bap," he barked to imitate the sound of gunfire. "Bap, bap!" Then he cackled as if he had told a good joke.

Why? I asked. Why was he shot?

The caretaker shook his head and sputtered. "*Un hombre malo. Muy malo.*" A very bad man.

So here lay one William Walker, mysteriously shot to death on September 12, 1860. I snapped a few pictures and figured I had a good anecdote for future telling. At the time, knowing nothing of Walker's backstory, I didn't have the slightest clue as to the historical importance of the site.

Later, I happened across a passage in the "Historical Background" section of a guidebook that outlined the story. William Walker, I learned, had been an "American adventurer," a filibuster who in the mid-nineteenth century had attempted a quixotic takeover of Nicaragua. Believing he had a grandiose destiny to rule Central America, Walker had landed in Nicaragua with a band of mercenaries and immediately began waging an improbable war on the country. He even succeeded in claiming the presidency of Nicaragua for a brief period, before the combined forces of the Central American republics drove him out. Back in the States, he stewed about his defeat and plotted a return to what he considered his rightful fiefdom. A few years later, he attempted a new invasion. When he landed on the coast of Honduras, he was promptly captured and executed. Hence his grave in Trujillo. Hence the epitaph "*fusilado.*" Hence the caretaker's summation of Walker's character: *un hombre muy malo.*

As I continued my travels in Central America, I came across Walker's name again and again, primarily in Nicaragua and Costa Rica. I soon came to understand that he was considered one of the greatest villains—maybe the greatest—of Central American history. Central Americans saw Walker as synonymous with Yankee imperialism. I was, quite frankly, baffled: if Walker was so significant, why had I never heard of him before? Why didn't American history books mention him? To me, he sounded like a crackpot engaged in a fatuous adventure, meriting a footnote to history at best.

I was set right on this score as I learned more about the complexities of the region and its history. Above all, I came to recognize the manifold ways that the United States had thwarted, manipulated, exploited, and even invaded countries that I—like many of my compatriots—had a difficult time identifying on a map. Rather little—if any—of that history had made it into the textbooks I had been assigned in school. In Central America, however, evidence of the intrusions was all too apparent. It was there in the omnipresence of American pop culture, in the poverty of the banana and coffee workers employed by US companies, in the military hardware wielded by CIA-propped dictators.

I met up with Walker just about everywhere. In Costa Rica, I saw numerous memorials in parks commemorating Costa Rica's triumph over Walker. For Costa Ricans, the defeat of Walker was a defining national moment. They had consecrated the battlefield where Walker was thwarted. They had dedicated a museum to the events. They had engraved their money with depictions of the glorious triumph and named their national airport for the general who defeated the filibuster.

In Nicaragua, too, Walker's specter turned up at historical sites, monuments, and museums. In Guatemala and El Salvador—two countries Walker never entered—textbooks told the story in detail, a narrative repeated at all grade levels. Anyone with a modest education in Central America knew all about Walker and his exploits. Back in the States, however, I discovered that almost no one, even those with an advanced education, knew anything about him.

After traveling extensively in Central America and living in Guatemala for two years, I came to understand the importance that Central Americans assigned to the Walker story, and I could appreciate their pride in defeating the megalomaniac invader, but I still felt that Walker was a historical aberration, a delusional charlatan who wasn't truly representative of official US policy (which was certainly bad enough when it came to Central America).

Then one day I encountered Walker again, this time in the United States. Walking around Nashville, I came upon a historical marker that summarized his career:

William Walker
"Grey-eyed Man of Destiny
Born May 8, 1824, Walker moved to this site from 6ᵗʰ Ave. N.
in 1840. In early life he was a doctor, lawyer, & journalist. He
invaded Mexico in 1853 with 46 men & proclaimed himself
Pres., Republic of Lower Calif. Led force into Nicaragua in
1855; he was elected its Pres. in 1856. In attempt to wage war
on Honduras was captured & executed Sept. 12, 1860.

This marker was typical of so many that I had seen in my travels across America: blithe and oblique in its summary of sanguinary events, content with half-truths, evasive in overlooking key parts of the story, and essentially wrong in other matters. But the marker did rekindle my curiosity in Walker. I decided I needed to learn more about him and the events of the 1850s in Nicaragua. I knew that Walker had written a book about his adventures in Nicaragua. That seemed to be a good place to start, so I tracked down a copy and read Walker's side of the story.

The book was published in 1860, a few months before Walker's death in Honduras. Walker wrote *The War in Nicaragua* upon returning to the United States after his two-year engagement in Nicaragua, first as leader of a mercenary force, then as commander-in-chief of the Nicaraguan national army, and finally as president of the country. Very few books on Central America had appeared in the United States before Walker's. The most significant were Maya explorer John Lloyd Stephens's hefty *Incidents of Travel* (1841) and the several works by Ephraim Squier, an amateur ethnologist and diplomat stationed in Nicaragua in the late 1840s. Despite growing interest in a canal across the isthmus and in US territorial expansion into Central America, the American public had only limited information about the region. Walker's book was among the first to offer an interpretation of Central America and its peoples as seen through Anglo eyes.

The War in Nicaragua recounts the events of Walker's first invasion and takeover of Nicaragua. But the text looks to the future as well. Having been defeated and driven from Central America, Walker was eager to return to the country to reclaim what he considered his rightful position as president. One motive for writing the text, then, was the recruitment of mercenaries who could assist Walker in his quest to return to power in Nicaragua.

To excite interest and win support for his cause, Walker argues that Nicaragua is ripe for and in need of colonization. The argument is presented roughly as a syllogism. First, Walker points out that the land is extraordinarily rich with boundless potential for development. Second, he contends that Nicaraguans, given their natural indolence and backwardness, have done little to exploit this potential. In fact, he claims, the country is in a state of perpetual corruption. Central America suffers from "a radically bad social organization," he says, and Central Americans themselves evince "serious defects." With these as his premises, Walker concludes that Nicaragua is in need of regeneration—a key trope for Walker, and indeed in much of the discourse surrounding Manifest Destiny at the time. Walker and other apologists for Manifest Destiny used the term "regeneration" in much the way that "regime change" is used today—as a seemingly positive, progressive-sounding term that calls for the elimination of corruption and degradation. To Walker, this need for regeneration means that North Americans—even those acting on their own initiative—are justified in taking over (or, in Walker's terms, "civilizing") a foreign country so that the land can be used as God intended.

The War in Nicaragua functions on one level as a travel account, albeit a highly unusual travel account given that the traveler in this case ended up taking over the government of the country. Still, one of the aims of the text is to do what travel accounts, particularly those of the nineteenth century (as written by Americans and Europeans), commonly do: excite interest in a new and unfamiliar part of the world, especially one that might be ripe for colonization.

The underlying goal of Walker's text—its subtext—is to expound for his Anglo-American readers the necessity of the Americanization of Nicaragua, or as he terms it, "the introduction of an American element in Nicaraguan society." Once this element is introduced, Walker argues, Central America will be "regenerated." Walker believes that change, the kind of change he brings, is inevitable, provident, and foreordained; this is a crucial aspect of his thinking. Walker has an almost Cortez-like faith in the ability of his paltry troops to overcome much larger armies. And, indeed, there are occasions during the war when he scores lucky victories or benefits from some natural occurrence such as the outbreak of cholera. This faith in predestination is rooted in Walker's belief that North Americans, "the robust children of the north," are superior and must perforce dominate the weaker "mixed race which is the bane of the country." In keeping with his habit of elevating his own prejudices into universal truths, Walker summarizes the connection between Manifest Destiny and his own actions in Nicaragua: "The Americans, with that faith in themselves which has carried them in a wonderfully short period from one ocean to another, regarded their establishment in Nicaragua as fixed beyond the control of casualties."

Not surprisingly, Walker's argument appeals to racist tendencies (at least some of his support in the United States was predicated on the hope that Nicaragua would eventually become an additional slave state). This appeal makes it easy in our time to dismiss Walker as an eccentric or fringe thinker. In fact, Walker was in the mainstream for his time, and *The War in Nicaragua* delineates attitudes and assumptions typical among Americans of his generation, especially as those attitudes were applied to US intervention in Latin America. Although Walker acted privately, his actions had at least some tacit support from the US government and more explicit support from the populace and the press.

To the extent that Walker receives any attention at all in American history, he is regarded as an aberration, but in fact a staunch belief in Anglo America's racial superiority and expansionist destiny had been the norm since the founding of the United States. For example, Thomas Jefferson preceded Walker in assuming that American hegemony should extend to Cuba and beyond. Even Emerson and Whitman, though more intellectual about the issue, sounded Walkeresque on occasion, as when Emerson stated that "it is very certain that the strong British race, which have now overrun so much of the continent, must also overrun [Texas], and Mexico and Oregon also, and it will in the course of the ages be of small import by what particular occasions and methods it was done." Or consider this line of thinking from Whitman, written during the War with Mexico: "What has miserable, inefficient Mexico . . . to do with the great mission of peopling the New World?" That Walker was in the mainstream of his time is evidenced by an obituary that appeared in *Harper's Weekly*, which soberly contended that Walker had died pursuing "America's historic mission."

Few expressions of Manifest Destiny match Walker's zeal for undertaking the mission of "civilizing" foreign lands. "The war in Nicaragua," he writes "was the first clear and distinct issue made between the races inhabiting the northern and the central portions of the continent." The tone of the passage, which appears in the concluding paragraph of *The War in Nicaragua*, is distinctly ominous. Walker suggests, in essence, that the continent is not big enough for two radically distinct cultures and that "the struggle . . . was not passing or accidental, but natural and inevitable." At this climactic moment in the text— the culmination of his argument—Walker radicalizes the issue: "whenever barbarism and civilization, or two distinct forms of civilization, meet face to face, the result must be war."

In Walker's mind, any possibility of peaceful coexistence must be adamantly rejected: the superior race must, through violent means, suppress the inferior races. Warfare of this type, he concludes, is necessary and legitimate in the service of a just cause.

Walker's quixotic adventures in Central America are considered a mere footnote to American history, a somewhat bizarre story of delusion and excess produced by the national enthusiasm for Manifest Destiny. Mainstream accounts of US history characterize Walker as an outlier, an aberration. And yes, he was a strange, obsessive man who acted on his megalomania and ended up dying obscurely in an outpost of the nascent American empire. There are, however, good reasons for not dismissing Walker so readily; Walker's text is significant in part because it is an exceptional exposition of the prevalent attitudes toward "inferior" peoples at the time when the United States was beginning to expand into the territories of these peoples. Walker articulated the philosophical and moral underpinnings of subsequent US adventurism as that adventurism shifted from private activity (such as Walker's and the examples alluded to in O. Henry's *Cabbages and Kings*) to officially sanctioned interventions undertaken by the US government and military. Walker's rhetoric anticipates the argumentation used to justify US foreign policy in the decades following his bizarre invasion of Nicaragua.

Many years later, I make a return visit to Trujillo. This time around, the bus I take from San Pedro Sula is sleek and new. It makes the journey in a matter of hours, and there are onboard movies to fill the time. The roads are more or less decent. The big tour bus swerves smartly around scores of ancient buses identical to the rattletraps I rode on years before.

In Trujillo, there are changes, big changes. Most noticeably, there's now infrastructure—solid infrastructure—down at the port. Cruise ships regularly stop, and tourists trundle all over town. Big hotels. Resorts. Fancy restaurants. Souvenir shops. Air conditioning. Signs in English. Agencies touting ecotours into the rainforest, out to islands. Ziplines, kayaking, snorkeling. Trujillo is now a little tourist paradise.

I sit in a swank restaurant-bar and dig into a seafood meal: cushy surroundings, for sure, but the food can't compare to the meals I had long ago in an open-air shack with planks and sand for a floor, plastic for the table setting, ants crawling over the sugar bowl. Out on the main streets, tour buses and upscale cars create actual traffic, nonexistent years ago in what seems the dim past.

I study the facades trying to find any sign of "Coralio" and the backwards, indolent village that O. Henry recreated in his stories. The O. Henry atmosphere has seemingly gone missing. It's not immediately obvious, anyway. The place he wrote about, the place I was sure I had found perfectly preserved decades ago, is at best a ghostly presence identifiable only in bits and pieces—a balcony here, a coral rock wall over there, remnants of the old Spanish fortress (now heavily trafficked by tourists), a barefoot coconut vendor wielding his machete.

I fall in with a walking tour, the guide reciting tidbits of Trujillo's history. His patter is mostly about the colonial era, but at one point he mentions O. Henry, though the name doesn't seem to register with the tourists (the pronunciation "Oh-ahnree" probably doesn't help).

A few turns down side streets and I see where we're headed. We pass through the gateway into the cemetery, and here I am standing once again at the rectangular iron fence, staring at the mossy grave of William Walker. Nearby, a groundskeeper is whacking branches with a machete, looking very much like the groundskeeper who spoke with me years ago.

The tour guide is giving a brief summary of Walker's story, and the tourists are squinting, shading their eyes. They snap a few pictures and repeat the name as a question. William Walker? An American, you say? Never heard of him. Crazy, was he?

Attention wanders. Someone spots a parrot. Everyone takes a picture of the squawking bird. They turn their cameras toward some of the more "picturesque" tombs. And then the tour guide shepherds the group toward the exit. I linger—no need to keep up with the tour. For a few minutes more, alone now, I hover over the grave, pondering those things that have changed over the years and those that have not.

Overlooking Guantánamo

One day, our dispatch-boat found the shores of Guantanamo Bay flowing past on either side. It was at nightfall, and on the eastward point a small village was burning, and it happened that a fiery light was thrown upon some palm-trees so that it made them into enormous crimson feathers. The water was the colour of blue steel; the Cuban woods were sombre; high shivered the gory feathers. The last boatloads of the marine battalion were pulling for the beach.

—Stephen Crane, "War Memories"

In 1998, I went to Santiago de Cuba to gather material for a magazine article on the centennial of the Spanish–American War. Over the course of several days, I visited Daiquirí, Siboney, Las Guásimas, El Caney, and, of course, San Juan Hill—all the main sites associated with the war. All, that is, except one: Guantánamo Bay. But visiting Guantánamo was practically impossible, even then, five years before it became a detention camp for prisoners of the "War on Terror." The sites related to the Spanish–American War were located inside the perimeter of the US Naval Base—"Gitmo," to use the military's shorthand designation—and there was no access to the base from Cuba proper. The only way to enter Gitmo was to fly in on a navy transport airplane from Virginia Beach, Virginia. And to do that, I would have to obtain permission—rarely granted—from naval authorities. So, much as I would have liked to visit the scene of the war's first clash between Spanish and American troops, I had to accept the impracticality of such a visit.

Forgoing Guantánamo was especially disappointing because of Stephen Crane's connection to the place. Crane's writing about the war and his various adventures in Cuba had long intrigued me. He was one of the few reporters to witness both the landing of the marines at Guantánamo and their subsequent skirmish with Spanish troops. He wrote several accounts of the event, a couple of which are counted among his best work. In fact, a significant portion of Crane's writing concerns Cuba, including a book of short stories (*Wounds in the Rain*), a long semiautobiographical essay ("War Memories"), and some of his best journalism. The time he spent on the island—a little over five months all told—holds outsized significance in his biography and his oeuvre. It was in Cuba that Crane—already famous for writing a war novel—finally witnessed warfare firsthand and up close. Shortly after hostilities ended, Crane came down with a severe bout of either yellow fever or malaria and had to be evacuated in a state of delirium. The "Cuban fever," as he called it, exacerbated his latent tuberculosis; nevertheless, while he was still recovering Crane mysteriously returned to Cuba—well after the other correspondents had left—and spent the better part of four months living a kind of underground existence in Havana. Though he filed an occasional report for Hearst's *Journal*, he was for the most part incommunicado; even his closest companions and his common-law wife had no idea where he was or what he was doing. The Havana sojourn remains something of an enigma in Crane's biography.

As it turned out, though I had all but given up on the possibility of visiting Gitmo, while I was in Santiago I fortuitously learned of an opportunity to see the base—or at least to see *into* it. I was told that a Cuban travel agency, Gaviota, offered tours to a Cuban military facility, an observation post called Mirador de Malones, located on a hillside just outside the American-occupied site. From there, one could look through a telescope and spy on the naval base. It sounded too bizarre to be true—as so many things in Cuba do; but when I inquired at the Gaviota office in Santiago, the bizarre turned out to be true—as it so often does in Cuba. The agent told me that a German tour group was going to the military lookout the next day. I could join the group if I wished. Moreover, the Germans were going to pass the night in Caimanera, the small town closest to the naval base, a town normally off-limits to visitors. This, too, I could do if interested. I booked the tour.

The following day I joined the Germans on a sleek tour bus that raced along a highway all but devoid of motorized traffic. There were plenty of bicycles, horses, and pedestrians but few buses or trucks and even fewer private cars. After a couple of hours, we passed through Guantánamo City, once a favorite destination of American sailors on liberty call but now a sleepy provincial town "with little to recommend it," as guidebooks like to say. Beyond Guantánamo City, the road passed through sugarcane fields until, after twenty-five kilometers or so, it arrived at the northern edge of Guantánamo Bay. The bus left the main highway and came to a checkpoint, the entrance to Cuba's military zone. From there, the road led into the hills overlooking the wide southern portion of the bay where the US base was located. At the foot of one hill, we exited the bus, passed through a concrete bunker, and climbed steps to the lookout—which proved to be not much more than a ramada draped with camouflage netting.

A thousand feet below and several miles distant, the bay and the naval base rippled in the tropical haze. It looked unreal, like some mythic realm. But once I got my turn at the military telescope, what I saw through the viewfinder was not mythic in the least. It was, in fact, all too familiar and mundane: cars on a boulevard, a shopping center, a church, a golf course, the American flag flapping. What made it strange, of course, was that this All-American scenery was on Cuban soil, situated behind concertina-wire fencing and bordered by a minefield.

The guide, speaking in German, drew attention to various features of the base, first on a detailed map and then in reality, pointing to one hazy sector or another while the German tourists craned necks, snapped photos, and tried to clarify for one another what the guide was pointing at. Unable to follow the German conversation, I moved a little way off and tried to correlate the panorama before me with what I knew from reading Stephen Crane's account of the Guantánamo episode, the first battle of the Spanish–American War.

On June 6, 1898, Crane arrived at Guantánamo Bay just after the marines had landed and secured the location. With night falling, Cuba appeared "sombre" to Crane. Come daylight, he would note that it was a craggy country cut with ravines. Sandy paths disappeared into thickets of tropical vegetation. Along the coastline, chalky cliffs and cactus-covered ridges overlooked the sea. "The droning of insects" competed with the sound of waves lapping the shore. Crane watched as the marines—a force of over six hundred—set up camp and dug trenches. Encamped on the beach beneath ridges, they were in a vulnerable position. But the marines had met no resistance upon landing and for a day and a half all was tranquil: "There was no firing," Crane reported. "We thought it rather comic."

The tranquility did not last. The next night, Spanish snipers opened fire, and the Americans scrambled for cover. "We lay on our bellies," Crane wrote. "It was no longer comic." Crane, who had written a famous novel about war without any personal knowledge of warfare, was finally experiencing what he had only guessed at beforehand. For the first time, he felt "the hot hiss of bullets trying to cut [his] hair."

But whatever satisfaction or thrill he felt in finally experiencing battle conditions was soon undercut: on the third night, the sniper fire intensified. The company's surgeon, struck by a Spanish bullet, lay suffering a few yards from Crane. "I heard someone dying near me," Crane wrote.

> He was dying hard. Hard. It took him a long time to die. He breathed as all noble machinery breathes when it is making its gallant strife against breaking, breaking. But he was going to break. He was going to break. It seemed to me, this breathing, the noise of a heroic pump which strives to subdue a mud which comes upon it in tons. The darkness was impenetrable. The man was lying in some depression within seven feet of me. Every wave, vibration, of his anguish beat upon my senses. He was long past groaning. There was only the bitter strife for air which pulsed out into the night in a clear penetrating whistle with intervals of terrible silence in which I held my own breath in the common unconscious aspiration to help. I thought this man would never die. I wanted him to die. Ultimately he died.

Crane did not know the man's identity until a voice in the darkness announced that the doctor had died. He then realized that the dead man was John Gibbs, whom Crane had befriended during the previous two days. War was suddenly very real to the previously inexperienced war correspondent: "I was no longer a cynic," he wrote. These first nights under fire proved to be trying in the extreme: "With a thousand rifles rattling; with the field-guns booming in your ears; with the diabolical Colt automatics clacking; with the roar of the [USS] *Marblehead* coming from the bay, and, last, with Mauser bullets sneering always in the air a few inches over one's head, and with this enduring from dusk to dawn, it is extremely doubtful if any one who was there will be able to forget it easily."

The next day, there were services for Gibbs even as the Spanish resumed their sniping. Crane retreated to the beach and sat on a rickety pier with a bottle of whiskey that he had procured from a fellow journalist. He stared into "the shallow water where crabs were meandering among the weeds, and little fishes moved slowly in the shoals."

Though he confessed to feeling somewhat unnerved from "the weariness of the body, and the more terrible weariness of the mind" that came with being under fire, Crane accepted an invitation to tag along with a detachment of marines on an expedition to flush Spanish guerrillas from the surrounding hills. Some two hundred marines left camp at dawn, guided by a contingent of fifty Cuban insurgents. American correspondents covering the war generally expressed a negative view of Cuban soldiers such as these. Crane's impression of them was more ambivalent: "They were a hard-bitten, undersized lot," he wrote in a dispatch for Pulitzer's *World*, "most of them negroes, and with the stoop and curious gait of men who had at one time labored at the soil. They were, in short, peasants—hardy, tireless, uncomplaining peasants—and they viewed in utter calm these early morning preparations for battle." In Crane's view, they demonstrated a similar stolidity and nonchalance in response to their officers' orders.

Crane thought he detected greater determination in the American soldiers: "Contrary to the Cubans, the bronze faces of the Americans were not stolid at all. One could note the prevalence of a curious expression—something dreamy, the symbol of minds striving to tear aside the screen of the future and perhaps expose the ambush of death. It was not fear in the least. It was simply a moment in the lives of men who have staked themselves and come to wonder which wins—red or black?"

The Cuban terrain impressed Crane as he followed the American soldiers. A narrow path wound around the bases of some high bare spurs then ascended a chalky cliff and passed through dense thickets. Insects hummed all around. Reaching a clearing, Crane and the soldiers could look down the chaparral-covered ridges to the sea. Next came a steep climb through cactus patches and then a hike along a ridge to where the troops—exhausted and thirsty but also, according to Crane, "contented, almost happy"—encountered the Spanish guerrillas who were hidden in a thicket, waiting to open fire on the Americans and Cubans.

"The fight banged away with a roar like a forest fire," Crane observed. During the ensuing combat, this intense noise proved overwhelming. "The whole thing was an infernal din. One wanted to clap one's hand to one's ears and cry out in God's name for the noise to cease; it was past bearing." Amid this din, Crane detected a variety of sounds, the nuanced noise of war: "And still crashed the Lees and the Mausers, punctuated by the roar of the [USS] *Dolphin*'s guns. Along our line the rifle locks were clicking incessantly, as if some giant loom was running wildly, and on the ground among the stones and weeds came dropping, dropping a rain of rolling brass shells."

Crane's propensity for eliciting such precise details from a scene amazed—and exasperated—his fellow correspondents. They readily perceived his obvious disdain for the grind of daily journalism; Crane often said his real aim was not to produce dispatches but to collect material for a new novel. According to his colleague Ernest McCready, Crane was "contemptuous of mere news getting or news reporting." In composing his dispatches, Crane was, according to another colleague, "an artist, deliberating over this phrase or that, finicky about a word, insisting upon frequent changes and erasures." Reportedly, he went through many cigarettes as he wrote (despite being tubercular). McCready, a journalist with long experience, urged Crane "to forget scenery and the 'effects'" and stick to the fundamentals: "This has to be news," the veteran correspondent told him, "sent at cable rates. You can save your flubdub and shoot it to New York by mail. What I want is the straight story of the fight."

But Crane could not easily settle for the straight story, even if months had to pass before his personal impressions yielded up the deeper story that he sought. In the case of Guantánamo, half a year went by before Crane turned those impressions into what his colleague and rival Richard Harding Davis called "one of the finest examples of descriptive writing of the war." The story, published in *McClure's Magazine* (February 1899) and later in Crane's collection *Wounds in the Rain*, was "Marines Signalling Under Fire at Guantánamo." The narrative concerns "four Guantanamo marines, officially known for the time as signalmen, [whose duty it was] to lie in the trenches of Camp McCall, that faced the water, and, by day, signal the *Marblehead* with a flag and, by night, signal the *Marblehead* with lanterns." No other journalist mentions these signalmen; Crane, however, devoted an entire story to them, closely observing them and detailing their extraordinary courage—a trait that always fascinated Crane—as they were called upon "to coolly take and send messages." Crane described how, without hesitation, a signalman would stand on a cracker box to send messages to the ships offshore, exposing himself to sniper fire. "Then the bullets began to snap, snap, snap at his head, while all the woods began to crackle like burning straw." Watching the signalman's face "illumed as it was by the yellow shine of lantern light," Crane noted "the absence of excitement, fright, or any emotion at all in his countenance" as the signalman performed his duty. In contrast, watching from the relative safety of the trench, Crane felt "utterly torn to rags," his nerves "standing on end like so many bristles."

Later, during the hilltop skirmish with Spanish guerrillas, another signalman stood exposed on a ridge to send the requisite message. "I watched his face," Crane wrote, "and it was as grave and serene as that of a man writing in his own library. He was the very embodiment of tranquility in occupation. ... There was not a single trace of nervousness or haste." Crane's admiring account of this "very great feat" emphasizes the stoic, masculine qualities that he saw in the regulars, the foot soldiers who did the arduous fighting. Elsewhere, he would criticize the press corps for ignoring these paragons of courage in favor of heaping praise on volunteers such as Teddy Roosevelt and the Rough Riders. Crane refused to overlook the regulars, making them the focus of his dispatches and stories, lauding their stoicism and grace under pressure, and holding them up as exemplars of what Crane perceived as American ideals.

Crane tried to live up to those ideals himself, according to those who observed his activities during the fight. A letter from a marine commander recalled Crane's bravery at Guantánamo. An official navy report recognized Crane's "material aid during the action" in delivering messages between platoons. The report does not say whether Crane did more than carry messages, but a biographer (Paul Sorrentino) says that "he quietly carried supplies, built entrenchments, dragged artillery up hills, and helped to fire guns." In "War Memories," which is taken to be semiautobiographical, Crane's stand-in narrator (named Vernall) is asked by a Marine captain to undertake a brief scouting mission. Vernall does so: "All the time my heart was in my boots," he says, contrasting his fear with the stoic regulars "who did not seem to be afraid at all, men with quiet composed faces who went about this business as if they proceeded from a sense of habit."

Shortly after the hilltop battle, an exhausted and somewhat unnerved Crane left Guantánamo on the dispatch boat with his fellow journalists. Ahead of him were the events at Daiquirí, Siboney, Las Guásimas, and San Juan Hill, followed by a breakdown (perhaps malaria or yellow fever), which further eroded his already precarious health. Just shy of two years after the events at Guantánamo, Stephen Crane was dead at twenty-eight.

Standing at the Malones Lookout, gazing across the hills at the approximate location of these events, I recalled Crane's description of this same landscape. He wrote two versions—one version in a news dispatch and a second version in "War Memories." Both passages involve a panoramic survey from atop the mountain where the skirmish took place. In the dispatch, Crane noticed the view in the heat of combat: "The sky was speckless, the sun blazed out of it as if it would melt the earth. Far away on one side were the waters of Guantanamo Bay; on the other a vast expanse of blue sea was rippling in millions of wee waves. The surrounding country was nothing but miles upon miles of gaunt, brown ridges. It would have been a fine view if one had had time."

In the second version, Crane (through his fictional narrator Vernall) takes in the view during the relative calm after the fight is over: "I discovered to my amazement that we were on the summit of a hill so high that our released eyes seemed to sweep over half the world. The vast stretch of sea, shimmering like fragile blue silk in the breeze, lost itself ultimately in an indefinite pink haze, while in the other direction, ridge after ridge, ridge after ridge, rolled brown and arid into the north."

This was essentially the same panoramic view that I now had at Malones Lookout, although my view—if I had the geography right—was a little farther inland and little higher up. And, of course, later in time by a century. Because of the time that had passed, I could see what Crane could not: the upshot, the end result of the marine action at Guantánamo in June 1898—namely, the naval base spread out before me. As Crane sailed out of view, off to report on the coming battles of the war, I turned my attention to Gitmo, one of the principal prizes of that war.

What a convoluted history had gone into the making of the base and the odd little township that had developed along with the naval facility. Following Spain's surrender in the Spanish–American War, Cuba became a protectorate of the United States. Overt American administrative control of the country lasted a little over three years while US officials and Cuban representatives negotiated the conditions of Cuba's independence. That any terms at all should be imposed was outrageous to Cubans; even worse, the United States insisted on particularly onerous terms. These were outlined in the notorious Platt Amendment of 1901, which the United States insisted on inserting into the new Cuban constitution. The Platt Amendment (so called because, as introduced by Senator Orville Platt, it had amended an army appropriations bill in the US Congress) gave the United States the right to intervene in Cuban affairs whenever American interests were threatened. It also stipulated that Cuba would lease territory to the United States for the purpose of establishing a coaling station and port facilities. The territory in question was Guantánamo Bay.

The war had demonstrated to the navy the bay's strategic value: a protected body of water from which the navy could monitor approaches to New Orleans and the Panama Canal (then in the planning stages). Although Cubans were loath to accept the base of a foreign power within Cuban territory, the United States insisted: no base, no independence. By 1903, it was a done deal; the United States had secured the right to operate, essentially in perpetuity, a naval base of forty-five square miles on Guantánamo Bay. Remuneration was to be around two thousand dollars a year. "Naval Station Guantánamo Bay" became one of America's first overseas naval bases (it remains the oldest overseas American base still in operation).

Despite the navy's insistence on Guantánamo's importance, development of the facilities occurred fitfully. Congress did not provide sufficient funding for many years. Early photos show that the naval station was not much more than a camp with rows of tents for marines and sailors. Early on, however, the base proved useful as a staging area for American interventions in Cuba and the Caribbean region, and eventually the facilities were improved. By 1920, the base could accommodate visits from the naval fleet; periodically, training exercises involving twenty thousand sailors were conducted there. A *National Geographic* correspondent accompanied the fleet in 1921 and reported that Guantánamo, a "plant of extraordinary value," featured rifle ranges, a landing strip, a balloon school (at the time, hot-air balloons were considered to have military utility), hospitals, clubhouses, canteens, and a sports complex with baseball fields and tennis courts. There was also a pigpen, which the *National Geographic* writer called a "principal attraction" for sailors from the Midwest "with fond recollections of the old farm."

The correspondent marveled at the base's natural setting: "Now and then the sharp fin of a shark is seen. Pelicans drift overhead with their air of aldermanic dignity. Fish hawks are forever circling against a sky of almost incandescent blue." Summarizing the near-pristine quality of the place, the writer called it a "sanctuary" for "the wild animals of the hills."

In years to come, the base continued to expand with more permanent facilities and housing for military personnel. A community developed, a small American town in the tropics, as families of officers arrived. By 1927, according to a visiting journalist, there were "low green bungalows" nestled "in a tangle of palms and trumpet vines, a flowery oasis in a desert of scrub and thorn." The wives of naval officers rode "lazy ponies over the hill to call on the ladies of the Marine Corps at Deer Point." It was, when the fleet was not in port, a place of "vast, placid stillness"—a languid and somewhat dull outpost of the expanding American Empire. "Old Civil Service clerks thankfully close their desks as the shadows start to lengthen," the journalist observed, "and scramble into motor boats to go home and loll on their breezy porches on the bare yellow crest of Hospital Key. A shout or a loud, hearty laugh would be as noteworthy in Guantanamo as it would be in a church. There was just enough tennis to keep in condition, just enough swimming to keep moderately cool, just enough bridge of an evening to exhaust the conversation of your neighbors."

Such were the appearances. Beneath the placid surface, Gitmo could be stultifying and dismal. This was the impression conveyed in an anonymously written "tell-all" magazine article published in 1930. Under the byline of "Navy Wife," the writer described what she called the "Guantanamo Blues." The article's subtitle coyly promised "A Taste of Tropical Fruits of Prohibition." For the most part, the writer agreed with previous observers that life on the base was merely dull: "no daily papers, no real news except a few items that sifted in by radio." During the Prohibition years, not even alcohol was available on the base—at least not officially. According to the "Navy Wife," American women living on the base spent the bulk of their time playing bridge, holding teas and dinner parties, and gossiping, sometimes ruthlessly, about one another ("the usual post-mortems," she called such gossip). It was a life of "coffee cups, long ribald conversations about nothing." One lived with "an inescapable smell of stale paint ... the buzz and thud of tropical insects against the screens."

But when the fleet returned, so did the excitement—sometimes more than was welcome. With men outnumbering women forty to one, every woman, even those who were married, received plenty of unwanted attention, especially at fleet dances. These were "a nightmare," the Navy Wife recalled. She was sweet-talked, pulled onto the dance floor, propositioned, and groped.

She was "protected only by the thin shred of circumstance which lies in the proximity of others." Her "woman's instinct" told her she "must not dare get outside the circle of light and moving white figures," lest she become subject to "a violent seizure as if I were to be the victim of a rape."

This undercurrent of lust, potential violence, and vicious gossip hidden below the superficial boredom made Guantánamo seem like a tropical Peyton Place. Over the decades, other residents and visitors noticed this undercurrent as well, even as the base was growing and taking on the appearance of a typical All-American town with outdoor movie theaters, hamburger joints (including, eventually, a McDonald's), Little Leagues, Scout troops, bowling alleys, golf courses, skating rinks, playgrounds, and skateboard parks. But this surface placidity concealed—barely—drug and alcohol addiction, racism, classism, and sexism. Crime was minimal, but visiting journalists noted that violence did occur now and then, particularly alcohol- and jealousy-fueled spousal abuse.

In publications provided to newly arrived families, however, the navy continued to project the image of Guantánamo as an idyllic community. "One of the nice luxuries of Guantanamo Bay," one such publication noted, was "the fact that domestic help is available." Besides the cheap labor of Cuban maids, residents on the base could enjoy a variety of recreational activities, hobby shops, libraries, and theaters, along with "dances, special parties, bingo and the like." There were religious services, Bible studies, choirs, and Sunday school. Residents could join any number of clubs, from the PTA to Toastmasters. Touting these perks, the navy publications presented life on the base as pleasant, even blissful. And indeed, former residents typically have fond memories of their time at Gitmo.

After 1960 and the success of Fidel Castro's revolution, however, life on the base became even more insular. As tensions between the United States and the new Cuban government mounted, the gates to Guantánamo closed. US personnel were no longer allowed to venture beyond the perimeter to explore and enjoy Cuba proper. Both sides mined the area around the perimeter—making it the largest minefield in the Western hemisphere—and cacti were planted to make the barrier even more difficult to penetrate. This so-called "cactus curtain" featured sandbagged outposts, watchtowers, and perimeter patrols. The base was turned into a sealed-off garrison. Guantánamo became what a *National Geographic* reporter in 1961 called "an idyllic prison camp." One military wife told the reporter that life at Gitmo could be described as "comfortable claustrophobia." The base had everything families needed, she said, "but in fifteen minutes you can drive from one end of it to the other. ... It's the same old thing day after day."

In such circumstances, the "Guantanamo Blues" that the anonymous writer struggled with in the 1930s became all the more acute. Visiting journalists in the 1960s and 1970s reported on racial tensions, drug and alcohol problems, and occasional violence. According to a 1973 article in *Esquire*, "Guantanamo is a good place to become an alcoholic. During the last twelve months gin has been the leading seller at the base Mini-Mart, with vodka a close second."

A strange place to begin with, Gitmo became even stranger during the Cold War period, given that it was a US military facility on the sovereign territory of a country aligned with the Soviet bloc. By the time I stood at the Malones Lookout in 1998, with the Cold War supposedly a thing of the past, Gitmo seemed like a weird anachronism of neocolonialism and the Cold War. My opinion at the time was that Guantánamo was outdated and unnecessary; keeping it seemed counterproductive and returning it to Cuba seemed like the right thing to do. I had said as much in some of my conversations with Cubans. In fact, I had told many of my interlocutors that I had a gut feeling President Clinton was going to normalize relations with Cuba and begin the process for returning Guantánamo before he left office in two years' time. What I didn't understand then—even though I lived in Miami—was that both political parties were already anticipating that Florida would be the decisive state in the 2000 presidential election, so Clinton could not possibly consider jeopardizing the Florida electoral vote by making amends with Cuba.

As I studied Gitmo from the overlook, I thought the base was an absurdity, a ludicrous embodiment of America's imperial ambitions (past and present); but I did not regard the base as particularly invidious or inimical or evil—a characterization of the place that shortly would become more accurate. Moreover, on that day in 1998, I had forgotten that just a few years before my visit Guantánamo had already been deployed as a prison camp of sorts. In the early 1990s, Haitian refugees captured on the open seas had been diverted to Guantánamo and held there in what were reported to be deplorable conditions; the practice, which included isolating HIV-positive people, ended in 1995 after the camp was declared illegal by a US district court judge. At the time, US government officials were already claiming that Gitmo was not subject to laws of the mainland because Guantánamo was not technically US territory. In retrospect, dealing with the Haitian refugees turned out to be a logistical trial run for what was to come later, after 9/11.

The tour guide had finished with his overview of Guantánamo's topography. The German tourists had taken their photographs and wandered away from the lookout platform to the outpost's other attraction, a diner that served up chicken and drinks. In fact, the price of the tour included a complimentary drink from the bar, your choice of rum mixed with fruit juice or cola. The Germans were jovially imbibing. I went over to the bar for my drink. It was very strong, more rum than juice, and I said as much in Spanish to the bartender. He beamed. This was the highest quality rum, he asserted, the best in Cuba. In the whole world. Of course, it was strong. Cuban rum was the strongest and the best. He asked me how to say "best" in German.

Not German, I told him. American.

His response was typical of what I had encountered in Cuba—surprise and keen interest.

"A Yanqui!" He called over to the waiter to tell him the news: a Yanqui in their midst. The waiter came over to have a look. "A Yanqui, eh? Don't you know you're supposed to be down there"—he waved toward the base—"not up here? Did you get lost? Or maybe you are a defector!" He smiled broadly. He was getting a kick out of teasing me.

No, just a tourist, I said.

"So, you want to see what your imperialist government is up to, eh?"

Yes, I agreed, that pretty much summarized it.

He nodded. "Tell me, amigo, are you a baseball fanatic? Yes? Then tell me—I need inside information—who is strong this year? Who will win the championship of American baseball? I have bets with my *compañeros*."

"Hard to say," I said, "but definitely not Miami."

"No? But they are last year's champions, the defenders."

"Yes, but they sold their best players."

"Sold?"

"Yes, or traded them."

"Sold. Traded. I see, like slaves."

"Something like that."

"This," he asserted, "is why Cuban baseball is better than American baseball. In America, the players must perform as slaves for the owners. No matter how much money the players get, they are still property. In Cuba, they play for love of the sport. They play with their hearts. Now, then, tell me, who will win this year's championship?"

"Good question," I said. "Probably the Yankees. The Yankees always win."

"Always? Well, we will see. We will see. Perhaps one day the Yankees will prove not so powerful as they think." He smiled and shook my hand.

Having basked in the warm sun and indulged in the strong drinks, we tourists tipsily boarded the bus for the short ride down to Caimanera, a fishing village situated just outside the perimeter of the naval base. There were more checkpoints, then a causeway lined with salt dehydration ponds. On the other side of the causeway, Caimanera was perched on an extension of Guantánamo Bay. The hotel occupied a small hill looking onto the waterfront. The hotel grounds included a pool and a watchtower, the latter built to give hotel guests a better view of the perimeter of the base.

After getting settled in my room, I went out to ascend the tower. Meanwhile, the Germans, lolling around the pool, were drinking again—mojitos and daiquiris. Music played over the loudspeakers, including, inevitably, the popular song, "Guantanamera."

The observation tower offered a partial view of the inner bay and the base, not nearly as good as the view from the overlook where I had just been. So, I turned my attention to the little town. It appeared to be as sleepy and slow as you would imagine a waterfront town in the tropics to be. A few people strolled the streets, kids played in the dirt, dogs sniffed puddles and trash cans. Here and there people stood in clusters or sat on doorsteps engaged in casual and sometimes spirited chatter. As usual in Cuba, the conversations were not hushed; voices carried, and I could almost eavesdrop on the gossip, the friendly arguments, the earnest conversations taking place several blocks away. Three men peered into the open hood of a car, deep in deliberation over the vehicle's malfunction and possible solutions. Two women laughed heartily at a joke. A boy whistled as he rode a bicycle.

During Gitmo's heyday, in the years before Castro came to power, Caimanera was quite a lively town, with several bars and brothels attending to the desires of American servicemen. During Prohibition, when drinking was not allowed on the base, Caimanera was especially active—and atmospheric. According to *National Geographic*'s reporter in 1921, "one thousand associated smells assail the nostrils when one climb[ed] on [Caimanera's] rickety boat wharf" to visit the town with its "sordid streets of one-story shanties." Dogs and "naked gourd-shaped babies" predominated while a two-goat cart hauled water to the plaza for domestic use. There were "dark-skinned women dressed in flowing white, languidly fanning themselves as the ship's barge put in." The bars were "Sis's Place," "The Two Sisters," and "The American Bar." These were open-air saloons, and the action was frenetic. The bartenders would "rain perspiration from their dark brows" as they prepared "the seductive daiquiri." On Sundays, the town featured day-long cockfights. Beyond the bars, "down the dingy, dusty, sometimes flagrantly muddy street, with its weird multitude of vicious odors," the *National Geographic* writer detected the symbolic aura of another continent: "All the way up the Guantanamo River the atmosphere has suggested Joseph Conrad's African backgrounds. The dark currents, the violent green of the contorted mangroves that curtain the banks, the 'Red Mill' at which a sugar schooner bakes lazily in the sun and near which a solitary saloon is thrust invitingly forward over water—all have a remote and exotic air." In such a setting, American soldiers could well imagine that they had truly taken up "the white man's burden," as Kipling had exhorted them to do in his well-known poem written on the occasion of America's defeat of Spain in 1898—the victory that had delivered Guantánamo to the United States. In the poem, Kipling spoke of America's "new-caught, sullen peoples/ Half-devil and half-child." The American view of Cubans echoed Kipling's attitude toward colonial peoples.

The pre-1959 literature on Guantánamo Naval Base—primarily magazine and newspaper articles—usually gave Caimanera a lot of attention. For example, a 1927 article published in H. L. Mencken's magazine, *American Mercury,* described Caimanera as a "queer little village" where American officers drank daiquiris in "a rickety wooden building like a squat barn built on piles over whispering, greenish water." At "a long, battered mahogany bar," the sailors sang songs about life on the base with lines like, "We're sitting here so free swallowing Bacardi" and "Put your troubles on the bum, here we come full of rum." Dogs scavenged the floor and a character named Peanut Mary stood in the doorway hawking peanuts and lottery tickets. (In *American Mercury*'s rendition, Peanut Mary is made to speak with some sort of Southern black or perhaps Jamaican dialect.) Meanwhile, the residents of Caimanera were on the outside looking in: "A hundred grinning black faces at the wide glassless windows on the street side." The "Navy Wife," too, in her 1930 article "Guantanamo Blues," ventured into Caimanera to describe Pepe's Bar, "a small picturesque but smelly shed which might have been put together in a movie studio for a Mexican melodrama."

In 1958, when civic unrest during Castro's rebellion put Americans in danger, Caimanera and the rest of Cuba became off limits for Gitmo's personnel. But in the years leading up to the closing of the gates, Caimanera was a riotous—and repugnant—place. Sailors who had been stationed at the base later recalled Caimanera's muddy streets and wretched poverty. Shacks wobbled on stilts over the bay. Garbage and human waste drifted in putrid water. Atrocious smells predominated, venereal diseases were prevalent, typhoid a constant concern. Caimanera was "a large-scale brothel," according to one sailor who visited in the 1940s, with girls available for the going rate of two dollars and fifty cents. The navy operated an off-base first-aid station right in Caimanera, dispensing condoms and penicillin.

Cuban discontent over the US presence at Guantánamo began the moment the 1903 treaty granting occupancy to the United States was signed. It continued through the decades and fed the ire of revolutionaries. Cuba had been prostituted to the United States metaphorically—billions in profits from sugar production, casinos, and tourism left the country for the United States—and literally in places like Caimanera. The United States was always quick to point out that American investment had brought major improvements to Cuba, especially in terms of infrastructure. The base at Guantánamo, the argument went, was the economic engine for the region (a similar argument was also made about the US Naval base at Subic Bay in the Philippines). Many locals had jobs on the base—good jobs—and without those jobs the region would be mired in economic depression. Such arguments did not account for the huge social costs that Caimanera and nearby Guantánamo City were forced to pay. The sailors' and journalists' descriptions of the towns at the time suggest that seediness prevailed, that the wealth supposedly generated by the American presence never really trickled down.

Certainly the vast majority of Cubans have seen little to no good in the US occupation of Guantánamo. Like the Filipinos who objected to the US naval base at Subic Bay, Cubans have longed desperately for an end to the imperial occupation. Fidel Castro called the base "a dagger in the heart of Cuba," and there is every reason to believe that he spoke from the deep anguish of a patriot and not as a posturing propagandist (as many American officials were keen to characterize him).

The wounds have been very real. Consider "Guantanamera," the irresistible song that celebrates the charms of a young woman from Guantánamo province. It is probably the most famous, the most world-renowned piece of music to come out of Cuba (and that is saying something given how musically prolific the island has been), a universally recognized manifestation of Cuban culture. Americans never think of this, but many Cubans do: during the years when the song was gaining in popularity and earning international renown, there was a very good chance that any given Guantanamera was a prostitute entertaining American servicemen for two dollars and fifty cents.

My view of Caimanera from the observation tower suggested that the little town was much better off now that it had no traffic with the base. It was relatively clean, and sanitation was adequate. People were not rich, but they were able to get by with dignity. Prostitution was a thing of the past. Life was tranquil and, by all appearances, pleasant enough. I doubted that anyone wanted to go back to prior arrangements.

The sun was now setting and the people ambling the streets of Caimanera were receding into shadows. The bay waters flashed with silver. At that moment, I felt fortunate to have had the chance to visit this part of Cuba, fortunate to have had a glimpse of the base, fortunate to have seen this once notorious little town now so much changed from what it had been when the sailors and marines hooted and howled and puked on its streets. Most of all, I felt fortunate to have had the chance to see, however distantly, a place of importance to Stephen Crane's personal history and to the ongoing story of US–Cuban relations.

In retrospect, my casual and pleasant visit with its complimentary rum drink has taken on a more sobering quality. The tropical haze hovering over the place has become thicker, darker. Imagine someone in 1950 recalling a 1925 visit to the once tranquil

German village of Dachau: that is how I now feel about my brief glimpse of Guantánamo. Years after that glimpse, Gitmo, having been repurposed as a Kafkaesque penal colony, can no longer be dismissed as the odd neocolonial outpost that I thought I saw from the Malones Lookout. What had seemed merely ludicrous and anachronistic in 1998 has become, in hindsight, something much more insidious.

By 2004, nearly eight hundred prisoners in the War on Terror had been brought to Guantánamo and incarcerated in an isolated sector of the base known as Camp Delta (giving an odd retrospective irony to *National Geographic*'s 1961 description of Guantánamo as an "idyllic prison camp"). Over the years, reports of mistreatment and torture have surfaced, leading to international condemnation. Though the number of prisoners has steadily been reduced, to this day the prison camp remains operational and, by presidential executive order in 2017, will remain operational indefinitely. Meanwhile, the United States has no plans to turn the naval base over to Cuba.

By coincidence, the place where Stephen Crane and the marines landed in 1898 is located just four miles from Camp Delta. As Crane reported, he and the marines came ashore at nightfall. Nearby, a small village was burning—the result of American bombardment. From this first beachhead, the Cuban interior appeared "sombre," a place of "mysterious hills" covered with "a thick, tangled mass." The marines did not know what awaited them in that interior, but they were, as Crane described them, confident that they could subdue whatever force they encountered.

In 1898, with one of the nation's major writers as witness, some of the defining attributes of American hubris were on display from San Juan Hill to the shores of Guantánamo Bay. They still are.

Coda:
Cottonwood Campground

It is hard to escape the sense of mastery as the stars move in the wide clear heavens to risings and settings unobscured. They look large and near and palpitant; as if they moved on some stately service not needful to declare. Wheeling to their stations in the sky, they make the poor world-fret of no account. Of no account you who lie out there watching....
—Mary Austin, *The Land of Little Rain*

Late in the day—the sixty-eighth day of my haphazard journey westward—a BLM sign directs me to follow a dirt track toward a small mountain range a few miles south, the Green Mountains according to the map. The range comprises three peaks: Crooks Mountain, Green Mountain, and Whiskey Peak. There's a remote BLM campground somewhere up there, little visited. And that is exactly what I'm looking for: remote and little visited.

The van rattles over a cattle grate and churns up dust as I set out across high desert toward the Greens. It's the same terrain that I've seen for hundreds of miles: sagebrush holding down powdery soil. Not a tree in sight. Stoic-eyed pronghorns observe my slow, unsteady advance over the washboard track, their muscles tense, ready to spring away should the intrusion become a threat. Prairie dogs pop up, scamper across the roadbed, then vanish down one or another of their innumerable tunnels. Off to the west, silhouetted by sundown, a more skittish herd is startled into flight: mustangs.

The foothills bring a change in the landscape: a trickling creek lined with trees, then thicker stands as the road ascends, a welcome contrast to the scrublands below. A sign announces the turnoff for Cottonwood Campground, and a wide, recently graded road climbs into the mountains. The explanation for this unexpected improvement in road conditions soon appears: a sign, warning drivers to watch for logging trucks. This overlap of conservation, recreation, and exploitation is all too typical on BLM land. Expensive to build, roads are seen as serving multiple purposes; the same road that brings campers in to see the trees allows logging trucks to take timber out. BLM: It's officially the Bureau of Land Management, but some detractors suggest that the acronym more accurately stands for "Bureau of Logging and Mining."

Despite its spotty conservation record, the BLM maintains the kind of campground I favor: isolated and undeveloped—"primitive," to use the Bureau's descriptor. There might be a water pump; maybe an outhouse, maybe not. A place where you won't find casual campers. Cottonwood fits the bill. A quick circuit reveals that the campground is empty. Excellent. Looks like I will have the place all to myself tonight. Pleased, I get out my gear and set up camp.

Everything seems perfect. The moment couldn't be better. I have this idea that I'm in the process of restoring my soul in the wilderness, just like Hemingway's Nick Adams. I relish the thought of passing the night alone in quiet contemplation, just enjoying the trickling stream, the aromatic pines, the clear night sky coming alight with stars.

But sometimes there's too much of a good thing.

Spend a night alone in the wilderness, and maybe you'll see what I mean. Sit for a while on top of a boulder as I did;

eat soup from a can; stare up at the Milky Way—stunning to see if you've lived too long with light pollution. Look for planets and constellations: Scorpio, with its huge, curling tail. Jupiter. Cygnus. Then think about the distances between you and those stars, the thousands of light years, the billions of miles. There's Deneb, for example, the alpha star in Cygnus—2,600 light years away. Think of all the history that has occurred since the light you are seeing began its cosmic journey. Think about that historical marker out on the main highway, the one that told you the rocks in these mountains are some of the oldest on Earth.

And if in total solitude you dwell on these things awhile, you might suddenly feel just a little overwhelmed. Perspective changes in an instant. The encompassing vastness—vast space, vast time—can seem terrifying. The tremendous age, the imponderable size of the universe: just what are you supposed to make of these facts? How do you measure your minuscule existence against such incomprehensible numbers? Billions of stars, billions of miles, billions of years. To what end is your life? Any sort of destiny or purpose seems improbable in the context of such vastness. No getting around it, no comprehending it. You feel a profound chill in your spine, the frisson of existential fright that hardens into dread, a pit in your stomach.

These thoughts vex you and keep you awake all through the night. The solitude you had sought now makes you nervous and agitated. All you can think to do is maintain the fire and watch the stellar dance above, trying to find some sign, some hint of meaning. You'd like to take some sort of comfort in the continuity of the heavens and the perfect flow of time. But there isn't any comfort. You're feeling spooked and distressed. The solitude is unexpectedly oppressive. Dawn can't come soon enough.

After a sleepless night, I come down off the mountain feeling dazed. The morning light is brilliant, and the sage plain is lit with gold. I stop the van and stare at the vista for a few moments. Something compels me to get out of the vehicle and walk into the sage, breathing in the pungent smell. A good hundred yards from the van, I squat and dig my hands into the powdery soil and sit for a moment clutching the earth, sifting handfuls of dust. I don't know why I am doing this, but it feels right just to touch the earth. And when I look up, there's a pronghorn watching me from maybe thirty yards off, an old buck. He holds perfectly still, gazing at me, gazing *through* me with piercing black eyes. I've read that pronghorns are curious creatures, that they will investigate when something strange appears in their world. Maybe this is what's happening here—my red shirt has caught his attention. To him, I am the oddity in this scene, the thing that doesn't belong. I've also read that old males are often solitary, wandering the sage plains by themselves, curious as ever, as if seeking to know the world in every detail. They undertake this wandering as if there is a purpose to it, some meaningful end.

The old pronghorn and I hold each other's gaze for a moment before he decides to move on in his investigations. I should take it as a hint: I must do the same. All along I've been drifting, just rambling from place to place, generally heading westward without aim or purpose. But sometimes aimless wandering can be a quest in disguise if you are willing to see things in a new light. "Over everything stands its daemon," says Emerson. Maybe this pronghorn standing watch over me is my daemon, my spirit animal urging me to discover the purpose of my quest. Why not? Is the notion too mystical for credence? But the universe is deeper and stranger than we can comprehend. Both science and religion suggest as much.

My pronghorn has reached the vanishing point. He has moved on. I will take it as a sign: it's time for me to move on, too. Time to continue with the journey. Time to learn what this quest is all about.

Works Cited

Adams, Ansel. *An Autobiography*. Boston: Little, Brown, 1985.

Adams, Ansel. *Born Free and Equal*. New York: U.S. Camera, 1944.

Adler, Stephen. *The Jury: Trial and Error in the American Courtroom*. New York: Times Books, 1994.

Alinder, Mary Street. *Ansel Adams: A Biography*. New York: Bloomsday USA, 2014.

Ambrose, Stephen. *Undaunted Courage*. New York: Simon & Schuster, 1996.

Austin, Mary. *The Land of Little Rain*. 1903. Reprinted with an introduction by Terry Tempest Williams. New York: Penguin, 1997.

Bateman, Paul C. *Deepest Valley: Guide to Owens Valley*. San Francisco: Sierra Club, 1962.

Bierce, Ambrose. *The Collected Writings of Ambrose Bierce*. New York: Citadel Press, 1946.

Bishop, Elizabeth. *One Art*. New York: Farrar, Straus and Giroux, 1994.

Crane, Stephen. *The Work of Stephen Crane*, vol. 9. New York: A. A. Knopf, 1925.

de Tocqueville, Alexis. *Democracy in America*. 1835. Translated by Henry Reeve. New York: Bantam Dell, 2002.

Dean, Sharon E. *Weaving a Legacy: Indian Baskets & the People of Owens Valley, California*. Salt Lake City: University of Utah Press, 2004.

Ewan, Rebecca Fish. *A Land Between: Owens Valley, California*. Baltimore: Johns Hopkins University Press, 2000.

Goodman, Susan and Carl Dawson. *Mary Austin and the American West*. Berkeley: University of California Press, 2008.

Gordon, Linda. *Dorothea Lange: A Life Beyond Limits*. New York: W. W. Norton & Co., 2010.

Hansen, Jonathan M. *Guantánamo: An American History*. New York, Hill and Wang, 2011.

Henry, O. *Cabbages and Kings*. New York: Doubleday, 1904.

Madley, Benjamin. *An American Genocide: The United States and the California Indian Catastrophe*. New Haven: Yale University Press, 2016.

Momaday, N. Scott. "The American West and the Burden of Belief." In *The West: An Illustrated History*, by Geoffrey C. Ward, 377–383. Boston: Little, Brown, 1996.

Okubo, Miné. *Citizen 13660*. New York: Columbia University Press, 1946.

Parkman, Francis. *The Oregon Trail*. 1849. Reprinted. New York: Library Classics of the United States, Inc., 1991.

Reisner, Marc. *Cadillac Desert*. New York: Viking Press, 1986.

Sanders, Scott Russell. *Earthworks*. Bloomington: Indiana University Press, 2012.

Sorrentino, Paul. *Stephen Crane: A Life of Fire*. Cambridge: Belknap Press of Harvard University Press, 2014.

Steward, Julian. *Myths of the Owens Valley Paiute*. Berkeley: University of California Press, 1936.

Stineman, Esther Lanigan. *Mary Austin: Song of a Maverick*. New Haven: Yale University Press, 1989.

Twain, Mark. *Roughing It*. Hartford: American Publishing Company, 1872.

Walker, William. *The War in Nicaragua*. Mobile: S. H. Goetzel, 1860.

Wehrey, Jane. *Voices from This Long Brown Land: Oral Recollections of Owens Valley Lives and Manzanar Pasts*. New York: Palgrave Macmillan, 2006.

About The Author

Along with two books of travel essays—*Guatemalan Journey* (University of Texas Press) and *Green Dreams: Travels in Central America* (Lonely Planet)—Stephen Benz has published essays in *Creative Nonfiction*, *River Teeth*, *TriQuarterly*, *New England Review*, and other journals. Three of his essays have been selected for *Best American Travel Writing* (2003, 2015, 2019). His poems have appeared in journals such as *Nimrod*, *Shenandoah*, and *Confrontation* as well as in a full-length collection, *Americana Motel*, published by Main Street Rag Publishing Co. *Topographies*, a collection of essays, appeared in 2019 from Etruscan Press. Formerly a writer for *Tropic*, the Sunday magazine of the *Miami Herald*, Benz now teaches professional writing at the University of New Mexico.

Books from Etruscan Press

Etruscan Press Is Proud of Support Received From

Wilkes University

Youngstown State University

Ohio Arts Council

The Stephen & Jeryl Oristaglio Foundation

Community of Literary Magazines and Presses

[clmp]

National Endowment for the Arts

Drs. Barbara Brothers & Gratia Murphy Endowment

The Thendara Foundation

Founded in 2001 with a generous grant from the Oristaglio Foundation, Etruscan Press is a nonprofit cooperative of poets and writers working to produce and promote books that nurture the dialogue among genres, achieve a distinctive voice, and reshape the literary and cultural histories of which we are a part.

etruscan press
www.etruscanpress.org
Etruscan Press books may be ordered from

Consortium Book Sales and Distribution
800.283.3572
www.cbsd.com

Etruscan Press is a 501(c)(3) nonprofit organization.
Contributions to Etruscan Press are tax deductible
as allowed under applicable law.
For more information, a prospectus,
or to order one of our titles,
contact us at books@etruscanpress.org.